D1522329

## CHILDREN'S UNDERSTANDING OF DEATH

In order to understand how adults deal with children's questions about death, we must examine how children understand death as well as the broader society's conceptions of death, the tensions between biological and supernatural views of death, and theories on how children should be taught about death. This collection of essays comprehensively examines children's ideas about death, both biological and religious. Written by specialists from developmental psychology, pediatrics, philosophy, anthropology, and legal studies, it offers a truly inter-disciplinary approach to the topic. The book examines different conceptions of death and their impact on children's cognitive and emotional development; it will be useful for courses in developmental psychology, clinical psychology, and certain education courses, as well as philosophy classes – especially in ethics and epistemology. This collection will be of particular interest to researchers and practitioners in psychology, medical workers, and educators – both parents and teachers.

Victoria Talwar is an Associate Professor in the Department of Educational and Counselling Psychology at McGill University. She is a graduate of the University of St. Andrews, Scotland, and Queen's University, Canada. She specializes in the social development of young children. She has published numerous papers in various journals including *Child Development, Developmental Psychology, Law and Human Behavior*, and *International Journal of Behavioral Development*.

Paul L. Harris is the Victor S. Thomas Professor of Education at Harvard University. He is a graduate of Sussex and Oxford universities and has previously taught at the University of Lancaster, the Free University of Amsterdam, the London School of Economics, and Oxford University. He is a Fellow of the British Academy and of the Norwegian Academy of Science and Letters. A developmental psychologist with interests in the development of cognition, emotion, and imagination, Harris is currently studying how young children learn about history, science, and religion on the basis of what trusted informants tell them, rather than from first-hand observation. He is the author of *The Work of the Imagination* (2000).

Michael Schleifer is a professor in the Faculty of Education at the University of Québec in Montreal. He is a graduate of Oxford University (Philosophy) and McGill University (Psychology). His past appointments include being Professor of Ethics at McGill University and Clinical Psychologist at the Montreal Children's Hospital Department of Psychiatry. He has published more than one hundred articles in philosophical, psychological, and educational journals and has edited works on identity, cooperation, the development of judgment, morality, and emotion. His latest books are *Talking about Feelings and Values with Children* (2006) and *How to Have a Dialogue of Mutual Respect with Your Teenager* (2007).

# Children's Understanding of Death

## FROM BIOLOGICAL TO RELIGIOUS CONCEPTIONS

Edited by

### Victoria Talwar
*McGill University*

### Paul L. Harris
*Harvard University*

### Michael Schleifer
*Université du Québec à Montréal*

CAMBRIDGE
UNIVERSITY PRESS

CAMBRIDGE UNIVERSITY PRESS
Cambridge, New York, Melbourne, Madrid, Cape Town,
Singapore, São Paulo, Delhi, Tokyo, Mexico City

Cambridge University Press
32 Avenue of the Americas, New York, NY 10013-2473, USA

www.cambridge.org
Information on this title: www.cambridge.org/9780521194594

First published 2011

Printed in the United States of America

*A catalog record for this publication is available from the British Library.*

*Library of Congress Cataloging in Publication data*
Children's understanding of death : from biological to religious conceptions /
[edited by] Victoria Talwar, Paul L. Harris, Michael Schleifer.
p.  cm.
Includes bibliographical references and index.
ISBN 978-0-521-19459-4 (hardback)
1. Children and death.   2. Children and death – Cross-cultural studies.   I. Talwar,
Victoria, 1974–   II. Harris, Paul L.   III. Schleifer, Michael.   IV. Title.
BF723.D3C57   2011
155.9′37083–dc22       2011000386

ISBN 978-0-521-19459-4 Hardback

# Contents

# Figures and Table

# Contributors

RITA ASTUTI
London School of Economics

BENJAMIN BEIT-HALLAHMI
University of Haifa

PAUL L. HARRIS
Harvard University

RAY MADOFF
Boston College Law School

MARGARET M. MAHON
George Mason University

MIRIAM MCCORMICK
University of Richmond

MICHAEL SCHLEIFER
Université du Québec à Montréal

VICTORIA TALWAR
McGill University

# Preface and Acknowledgments

This book examines different conceptions of death and their impact on children's cognitive and emotional development. It not only addresses practical and clinical issues related to children's developing understanding of death, but also focuses on theoretical and philosophical aspects linking children's concept of death to religion, morality, politics, and law. The material is drawn from a wide range of disciplines including psychology, anthropology, philosophy, medicine, education, and the law. This collection will be useful for courses in developmental psychology and clinical psychology, certain education courses, and philosophy classes – especially in ethics and epistemology. It will be of particular interest to researchers and practitioners in psychology, medical workers, and educators (parents and teachers).

The first three chapters of the book examine children's conceptions of death in different cultures. All three chapters focus on how children acquire a biological conception of death as well as how they acquire spiritual or religious ideas about an afterlife. Chapter 1, by Rita Astuti, provides an ethnographic account of how Vezo children living in a rural community on the western coast of Madagascar experience animal and human death. She describes how Vezo adults conceive of death and the life of the ancestors, how Vezo children are protected from ancestral threat, and how, as spectators to the rites and rituals that surround a death, Vezo children nevertheless construct an understanding of the ancestral afterlife. In Chapter 2, Paul L. Harris further examines how children develop two distinct conceptions of what happens when we die: a biological appreciation that living processes cease and a spiritual or religious expectation that some processes will continue. Both of these chapters suggest that children's initial conception

ix

of death has a strongly biological focus. Children come to understand how the end of the lifecycle implies the end of vital processes. On that biological foundation, children then construct a conception of the afterlife – a conception that involves God and Heaven in the case of Christian children, or the world of the ancestors in the case of Vezo children. Chapter 3, by Benjamin Beit-Hallahmi, examines the changing nature of the conflict between two psychological realities: the inevitable confrontation with the biological facts of death and the impulse to deny, hide, or transcend those facts. He emphasizes the fact that even if death cannot be abolished, medicine and the life sciences can, in many cases, help to postpone children's first encounters with death and all its implications. As a result, we face a dilemma. Do we capitalize on such advances to further protect children from an understanding of death? Alternatively, do we help them to understand its biological reality?

The next two chapters discuss conceptualizations of death from the perspective of those educating and caring for children. These chapters build on the previous chapters by examining exactly how adults can help children understand the biological reality of death and cope with loss. In Chapter 4, Margaret M. Mahon discusses the challenges of discussing death with children in palliative-care settings when either the child is dying or a loved one dies. She underlines the need for medical professionals to help alleviate children's suffering by addressing their fears about death. In Chapter 5, Victoria Talwar examines the attitudes of teachers and school psychologists toward discussing death. She describes different methods of discussing death within a classroom context that can help children understand the concept of death. In both chapters, the authors note the pervasive "taboo" regarding death and adults' (parents, medical and educational professionals) reluctance to discuss death and dying with children. Both authors emphasize the importance of discussions about death in helping children develop their conceptual understanding of death, answer questions about what happens after a death, and help promote children's healthy mourning and grieving when they suffer a loss.

Chapters 6 and 7 analyze, from a philosophical standpoint, the validity of beliefs about the afterlife. Miriam McCormick in Chapter 6 discusses "evidentialism" (the view that we should only believe what is warranted by evidence) and our warrant for holding nonevidentially based "supernatural" beliefs. She argues that children and adults can believe responsibly, even when some beliefs are not evidence based. She examines what norms ought to govern our belief formation and belief maintenance in general. McCormick points out that William James, the great psychologist-philosopher (1842–1910) supports her view. In Chapter 7, Michael Schleifer examines the perspective of children concerning thoughts and emotions. For children, these are different from, but as real as, physical objects; they reject "materialism." Schleifer also invokes the works of William James, showing how he defended the legitimacy of the nonmaterialist perspective that is displayed by children. James accepted beliefs about the afterlife and immortality for which the evidence may be lacking, as McCormick demonstrates. Schleifer further shows that James accepted that there *was* evidence for some of the contentions of religion or spiritualism that are beyond science.

Finally, in Chapter 8, Ray Madoff discusses how society views death from a legal perspective. She examines how the law has constructed and modified its understanding of when death has occurred, the rights of the dead, and the implications for children. She discusses how law provides a form of immortality by protecting the interests of people even after they have died, and more specifically how the law treats children, including the fact that under American law parents can freely disinherit their children whereas in other parts of the world they cannot. Among the many things we learn is that American parents can leave enforceable instructions for their children, including threat of disinheritance unless they marry someone of a particular religion and other such control devices (this is unique to the United States and is contrasted by Madoff with the law in other countries). Another intriguing topic concerns the legal definition of death, again very different among various cultures and legal jurisdictions. Is it the nonactivity of the brain or the heart? The answer, we find, is very different in Japan from the rest of the world. Many other nuggets of information important to our understanding of children and death will be found in this chapter.

We would like to thank Shanna Williams and Sarah-Jane Renaud for their assistance in preparing the manuscript. We would also like to give a special thank you to Andrea Salguero for her patient and diligent help in completing this book.

July 2010

# Death, Ancestors, and the Living Dead: Learning without Teaching in Madagascar

## RITA ASTUTI

At the time of my last period of fieldwork in Madagascar,[1] Brika was seventeen. I had invited him to my house to participate in the study I was conducting about death and the ancestors (cf. Harris, Chapter 2). As with all other participants, I introduced Brika to the task by telling him that I was going to narrate a short story followed by several questions. I reassured him that these questions did not have "right" or "wrong" answers, because people have different opinions about them. I told him that I just wanted to learn about his own way of thinking.

Brika carefully listened to the story and patiently answered all my questions. Once the formal interview was over, he engaged thoughtfully with a number of additional open-ended questions about the meaning of the word *angatse*, the reasons for offering food to the ancestors, the significance of dreams, and the existence of people who, having died, come back to life. He explained that when a person dies "the body rots and turns into bones," but the spirit (known as *fanahy* when the person is alive and as *angatse* once the person has died) "continues to be there." He knew that the enduring presence of the *angatse* is revealed through its apparition in people's dreams, and he was aware that such dreams are serious matters that call for ritual action:

It's like, for example, myself, if my father dies, if there is something that I do that is not OK, his spirit will approach me and will talk to me ... He

---

[1] Fieldwork was conducted in the coastal village of Betania in western Madagascar where I have undertaken anthropological research since 1987. The village has, at present, a population of about 1,000 people. It lies a few miles south of Morondava, the main town in the area, which hosts governmental offices, a market, a hospital, a post office, and an airport. The livelihood of the village depends on a variety of small-scale fishing activities and on the daily trading of fish at the Morondava market. For this reason, like other people who live on the coast and "struggle with the sea," Betania villagers call themselves Vezo (cf. Astuti, 1995).

comes, like when one has dreams, one has those dreams, it's like you are seeing him as he approaches you, and one is afraid, and this is what brings about … it's like he talks to you and says: "this and that is what you've done and I don't like it." And you are startled as you are afraid of that thing [the dead person], and you are all shaken because the dead is what you're afraid of, because you're alive. And so when it's morning, you talk to, for example, your mother or your elder sibling, and you say: "Mother, my father has revealed himself to me" – that is the *angatse* – "he has revealed himself and I'm scared." "Did he say anything?" "He said this and that and this and that." "All right then, let's have an offering." This is what causes people to do that [giving offerings to people who are dead].

As for the people who die and come back to life, known as *olo vokatsy* (literally, people who reemerge from the earth), Brika was careful to stress emphatically and repeatedly that he had heard stories about *olo vokatsy*, but that he had never seen them with his own eyes. It felt as though, despite asserting rather humbly that he was only a child, he was actually distancing himself from what had been related to him. Even so, he was able to imagine his reaction were he to encounter *olo vokatsy* one day: "If I were to see them, I would probably be scared, because these were dead people – they were dead but they came out of the ground." Brika was also aware of the relationship between *olo vokatsy* and *angatse*: "*Olo vokatsy* don't have *angatse*, for they are [living] people too; they don't have *angatse*, but when they are still dead under the ground, they have *angatse*." In other words, *angatse* is only a state of being of the dead.

Brika was exceptional. No other adolescent, boy or girl, was able to articulate as Brika did the various elements that make up the adult representation of what happens after death to the deceased and to the people that are left behind. Impressed by his knowledge and thoughtfulness, I asked him how he came to know all this, whether someone had explained it all to him:

How I came to know this? I came to know about it like this: when you are still little, when people chat – here's your mother, here's your father, and you are bound to be sitting near them – and they tell stories about the *angatse* … for example, there are also other people around, like when you go to a funeral, and they also say: "This is what happens to the *angatse*," "that thing came out of the ground," and so on and so on. You hear this, and you are still just learning. And so you just get it and you take it with you, you take it with you in your games when you are little. For example, you say: "There is a *biby* [animal] over there!" "There is an *angatse* over there!" And so, in the end, you hear about this thing. And even when one is big like me right now, one is staying with people, with big/old people, and they talk about these things, and so in the end one knows these things. This is how I've come to know about it. Since I'm not a person from the past, but a little person, but I've heard the stories of my "fathers-and-mothers" [elders] and this is how I came to know about it when I was little. But there was no teaching me this stuff, no there wasn't.

In what follows, I shall take Brika's observation, that learning about the afterlife does not involve any overt teaching, as my entry point into the learning environment in which Vezo children construct their understanding of death and of what lies beyond it. Although I agree with Brika that children gather bits and pieces of information as they overhear adults' conversations, I shall argue that the process of learning is more complicated than his account suggests. In particular, I shall explore whether children bring more than their alert ears to the task of learning, and whether, along the way, they construct representations of the afterlife that are rather different from those of their parents and elders.

## "THEY DON'T KNOW A THING" – AND IT'S BETTER THAT WAY

Vezo adults were generally bemused by the fact that I spent so much of my time asking children questions about what happens after death. It is not that they regarded my questions about the death of a made-up character as inappropriate or upsetting for the children; rather, they thought that I wasted my time asking questions of children who patently did not know any of the answers – for children, they insisted, do not know a thing.

More than once I asked adults whether they ever attempted to explain to children what happens to people after they die in the same way they explained things to me: what happens to the body, what happens to the *angatse*, where it dwells and how it behaves, how it reveals itself in dreams, and so on. They always replied that they do not, and they typically invoked two reasons, one general and one specific.

The first, general reason is that children lack wisdom and, consequently, understanding. It follows that it makes no sense to explain to them what they are unable to understand. Of course, there are things that adults expect even the youngest of children to learn. For example, as soon as children are able to hold objects in their hands, they are taught that if they are offered something, they should extend their right hand, palm up and slightly cupped, with the left hand holding the right one from below. Children quickly learn by having their left hand hit if it is presented first and, initially at least, having both hands placed in the correct position by an adult or an older child. In adulthood, this submissive posture will be incorporated in a wider pattern of bodily and verbal behaviors aimed at neutralizing, while also conceding, the hierarchical nature inherent in many acts of giving and receiving: Those who give will approach the recipients slowly and tentatively, will avert their gaze, will belittle what they are giving; those who receive will extend both hands like children, stressing the magnitude of what they are receiving and acknowledging the kinship-like bond that is being created with those who are giving. However, of course, no one expects young children to understand the deeper implications of the hand action – all they are expected to do is to perform it. Similarly, adults do not expect children to be able to understand the actions they witness and themselves perform during ancestral rituals. All that matters, as we shall see, is that they are present in large numbers, because the multiplication of life that they instantiate, the noise and laughter that they generate, are what the ancestors are imagined to long for and to want to enjoy for the duration of the ritual (cf. Astuti, 1994, 1995).

The second, specific reason why adults do not talk to children about what happens after death is that they wish to protect them from the ancestors' unwelcome intrusion into their already vulnerable lives. If children were told, for example, about the continuing existence of dead people's *angatse*, they would end up carrying in their heads thoughts that are far too "difficult" (meaning dangerous) for them. Such a state of mind would put them at a greater risk of being visited by the *angatse* of a disgruntled ancestor who might appear in the child's dream, offer her food, touch her, and perhaps even lead her away; as a result, the child would fall ill and even die. It is thus safer if children are told nothing, which is actually not so hard to do because, several adults remarked, children are only interested in eating, playing, and sleeping.

### "WHEN YOU ARE STILL LITTLE, WHEN PEOPLE CHAT . . ."

Vezo children enjoy a remarkable degree of freedom. Depending on their age, sex, and position in their sibling group, they may be expected to perform various chores, including fetching water and firewood, doing the dishes, washing clothes, or carrying fish to the market. Even so, they have control over much of their time (school provisions being extremely erratic), which they spend in large groups of full and classificatory siblings, the older looking after the younger ones. Within the village, there is no clear demarcation between adults' and children's spaces, nor are there public contexts from which children are banned. Whether adults are gathering for a casual chat after a day at sea, for a discussion about a serious ancestral matter or an important financial decision, for some gossip about a neighbor's infidelity, or for a conversation with the resident anthropologist, there are bound to be children around. Adults may become irritated by children's rowdiness, leading to some shouting and aggressive posturing; dutifully, the children run off to a safe distance, only to creep back into their original position. Whereas some are oblivious to the adults' conversations, others follow them intently. It is probably because they assume that children lack wisdom and understanding that adults do not bother to prevent them from listening in irrespective of the topic under discussion. Thus, although they are adamant that children are best kept ignorant of ancestral matters, children do get a fair exposure to them: They may hear, for example, about a dream in which the spirit of a deceased relative asked for food and complained of being cold; or about the fears that a baby's illness may not be due to a simple malaria attack, but rather to the intervention of a disgruntled grandmother whose tomb has lain unrepaired for far too long. Still, children are never more than passive (if noisy) listeners, never asking a question or requesting an explanation.

## "LIKE WHEN YOU GO TO A FUNERAL ..."

A couple of elderly villagers told me that in the past children were not taken to funerals, but because people die so often nowadays, it has become quite impractical to keep children away. Whether or not this is a correct depiction of what happened in the past, the prohibition against their attendance was motivated by a belief that it would be better if children did not have to think about things that are too difficult for them. As it is, children regularly attend two of the three main components of a funeral, the communal meals and the wakes, but they are usually not allowed to join the procession that takes the corpse to the cemetery for burial.

Funerals are centered around the house where the deceased is laid out on a bed, protected by a mosquito net and guarded by close relatives. Villagers typically approach the gathering around the house in small family groups, the men finding a place to sit in the male section of the crowd, the women and children in the female section. For the wake – which consists of uninterrupted singing from sunset to sunrise – people bring mats and blankets, and each family group colonizes a small patch of sand. For a few hours, children stay awake, playing hand games or just talking among themselves. The older ones might join in the singing, and, if the organizers have managed to rent a generator and are able to provide some light, they might be allowed to run around at a safe distance from their patch. Eventually, they all fall asleep, bundled up next to each other, apparently undisturbed by the loudness all around them.

Children have more freedom of movement during the communal meals, which happen twice a day for the duration of the funeral. The food – a large mountain of rice, topped with a few pieces of meat and wetted with broth – is served in large bowls and is shared by four or five people. Adults are eager to stress that because the food is cooked in the presence of death, it does not taste good (although every effort is made to cook it well), and that they only eat it out of respect for the bereaved family. Their body language[2] says it all. When the food is delivered, the four or five people who are to share from the same bowl move hesitantly: They shuffle on their bottoms to come closer to the food; somehow they always seem to purposefully end up in rather awkward positions, which makes reaching for the food just a little difficult. Once they are settled, they wait a while before, somewhat reluctantly, picking up a spoon with which they slowly scoop up a small quantity of rice and timidly dig down for some of the broth. The movements are exaggeratedly measured, with spoons traveling from bowl to mouth and back again at an unusually slow pace.

This is the adults' experience. The children's is markedly different: They eagerly circle around the food and dig into it with gusto. They eat plentifully, first the food that is designated for them, and then what is left by the grown-ups. I have never seen adults making any attempt to contain children's greediness and stop them from wolfing down whatever food they can get their hands on. The reason, I suggest, is that they find comfort in children's carefree behavior, because it confirms their view that children are only ever interested in having a full stomach. In other words, children's single-minded focus on the food confirms that they are safely unaware of their closeness to death. Yet is that really so? Sure, when they dig their spoons in the food they seem oblivious to the fact that a dead body is lying only a few meters away and to what that might mean. However, there are other moments when children confront the physical and emotional reality of death and seem to take notice.

In the heat of the summer, corpses decay fast. If people can afford it, they will inject the body with formalin, but they will also resort

---

[2] Because I never sat with men, the description that follows only refers to women.

to more traditional and less expensive methods to delay the onset of decomposition: Little openings are made in the walls of the house to create a gentle breeze around the body, and leaves with cooling properties are placed all around it. When the body starts to decompose, small piles of cow dung are burned near it to mask the stench. Unlike adults, who sit in the proximity of the house and politely endure the rotting smell, children relocate themselves and their games in order to avoid it – and in the process presumably learn something of the consequences of death.

If children move far from the house for one reason, they move closer to it for another. On approaching the gathering for the first time, people are expected to enter the house to view the corpse and give their condolences to the bereaved relatives. These visits provoke bouts of wailing, which erupt from the inside of the house and carry on for several minutes as more men and women join in the lament. These events typically attract small groups of children, who come close to the house and try to gain a view of the inside by climbing to a window, squatting next to the door, or peering between the cracks of the wall. Their demeanor is serious, curious, and somewhat frightened. They watch intently, no doubt taking in the distress of the living and the eerie stillness of the deceased.

Some of the children will get a much closer look at the corpse. Depending on the age of the deceased, either sons and daughters or grandsons and granddaughters will be called into the house just before the coffin is closed. In the instance I witnessed first hand, the deceased was a thirty-seven-year-old woman and the mother of a girl of about two and a boy just under five. The girl was to be raised by her father's sister, and she was deemed too little to miss her mother; by contrast, there was much concern about the boy, who was very attached to her. Still, for the duration of the funeral the boy had been playing around as usual, seemingly unaware of the fact that the wailing, singing, and cooking that had taken place over the course of two and half days had been caused by his mother's death. However, this was going to change. At a prearranged time, behind closed doors, the corpse was lifted off the bed and into the wooden coffin. Several items of clothing, some chewing tobacco, and a little bottle of perfume were neatly arranged around the body in the hope that the spirit of the deceased, on finding her favorite possessions, would refrain from coming back to bother the living by asking for more. After several sarongs and a few blankets were laid over her body, only her face remained visible – and she looked strangely beautiful. When the door was sprung open, several men walked in with the coffin's lid, a hammer, the nails. They stood to one side of the coffin while too many other people crowded around. Then the two children were ushered in. The girl looked confused and tried to run away; the boy looked terrified. Both of them were forced into position near the head of the coffin. The girl, too little to stand on her own, was held up to face her mother; the boy, strong enough to resist, had his head held down, almost touching his mother's face. An old woman shouted: "Do you see, that's your mother, she is dead. You shall never call her name again!" As soon as the statement was uttered, the children were rushed out of the house, leaving the men to close the coffin and hammer in the nails.

Both children were to see the coffin one last time. Having exited the house from the eastern door feet first, the coffin was placed on the ground. Standing on the north side was the woman's husband, with the two children clinging on either side, and on the south side, her sister and her brother's wife. They held two strings over the coffin, knotted loosely together. In a final act of separation, the strings were pulled on both sides and the knot was undone. At this point, in the midst of a frenzy of crying and wailing, the coffin was lifted and taken away. The husband collapsed and was dragged away; the children were swiftly picked up and taken to a relative's house. They were not allowed to join the procession that delivered the body to the cemetery because it was thought that their mother would not let them come back.

When I asked the deceased's sister if she thought that bereaved children understand what it means for a parent, a grandparent, or a sibling to have died, she responded that children are told that someone close to them has died, and that as a result, "they know, but don't know fully." As we have seen, children are unquestionably made aware that someone close to them has died – they are forced to stare into the face of the deceased and ordered never again to call his or her name. Perhaps the reason they are told with such forcefulness is that gentler, symbolic acts of separation, such as the loosening of a knot, are too subtle for them. Even so, adults seem comforted by the fact that children "know, but don't know fully." For example, a few weeks after the funeral, the little boy heard someone trying to get a cat's attention by calling out "*piso, piso, piso!*" – *piso* being the term for cat. The boy, whose mother's name was *Ka-piso*, complained loudly, saying that it is taboo to use the word *piso*. In recounting this episode, the adults who witnessed it were pleased that the boy had interiorized the prohibition of never calling out his mother's name, yet they were also amused by his naïveté and commented that he clearly understood nothing. The fact that the boy took the prohibition far too literally and overextended it demonstrated that he did not understand that the ban on his mother's name was meant to target his lingering attachment to her, which could cause her spirit to seek him out with ill consequences. As far as I could gather, the combination of zeal and naïveté was, for them, the best possible outcome: a boy who knows what he should not do, but does not understand why.

### "ALL RIGHT THEN, LET'S HAVE AN OFFERING"

As I mentioned earlier, it is desirable for children to be present whenever the living interact with the ancestors. This is because dead people are imagined to have an insatiable longing for life, which their living descendants try to appease by staging ritual events that momentarily bring the world of the dead into contact with the world of the living (cf. Astuti, 1995 for further details). At these moments, the ancestors delight in seeing the children, grandchildren, great-grandchildren, great-great-grandchildren, and so on (the Malagasy language names up to seven generations of descendants) that have been generated since their death. It is therefore essential for large numbers of noisy, exuberant, lively children to be present, because they *are* the life that the ancestors long for and want to enjoy.

By now it should come as no surprise that children's participation in such ritual activities is largely untutored. Children might be told factually that they should not stand to the east of the pot where the rice is being cooked for an offering, or they might be chased away if they step inside the tomb enclosure. However, these injunctions are not accompanied by an explanation as to the reasons for the cooking or the opening of the enclosure. In one instance I witnessed during my last period of fieldwork, an offering of rice was presented to an ancestor who had appeared in a dream to one of her descendants and had caused her a severe case of earache and swelling. In such cases, only five small balls of rice are offered to the ancestors – one thrown to each of the four cardinal points and one to the sky – and the rest is passed on to the children, who wait expectantly for the formal offering to be over. When the pot is handed to them, they crowd around it, digging their fingers into the scorching rice and devouring it in no time. On this particular occasion, I had my tape recorder on, and I tried to talk to the children about what had just happened. Why was the rice cooked outdoors? Why did their grandfather throw balls of rice in the air? Who was the rice for? All I got on my tape was the children's joyful laughter and a boy's high-pitched concluding statement: "Let's go home now that our tummies are full!"

And yet, children are not as clueless as adults think and no doubt hope. The following day, once the excitement had died down, I asked my questions again. True, none of the children knew the exact reasons why this particular ritual offering had taken place, but a few guessed that it might have something to do with one of their uncles, the relative that had died most recently, and that a dream must have been the trigger for what they were well aware was not their everyday cooking or eating. Their narratives were not as well informed or coherent as those of the adults, but they demonstrated some awareness that dead people can make demands on the living and scare them by appearing in dreams.

One plausible account of how children come to know this much is that, as described by Brika, they pick up bits and pieces of information as they overhear adults' conversations. Although this is certainly the case, in what follows I want to suggest that the process of learning about the existence and properties of the ancestors is less linear than this account suggests.

### COULD VEZO CHILDREN ESCAPE KNOWING ABOUT THE ANCESTORS?

In his book on Kwaio religion, Roger Keesing (1982) offers a rare description of how children are introduced to the world of the ancestors. In a way reminiscent of Kopytoff's argument (1971) that ancestors in Africa are not significantly different from elders – they simply require a slightly different mode of communication because they happen to be dead – Keesing brilliantly evokes the immediacy of Kwaio ancestors as full participants in and members of the community in which children grow up. From a very young age Kwaio children, especially girls, learn that there are things, places, and foods that are prohibited because the ancestors have made them so; and in the same way in which children learn to obey their parents, they learn to obey the ancestors. Children also hear that people are sick because they have displeased the ancestors, or that they are rich and healthy because they have pleased them. They hear of dreams in which the ancestors reveal themselves, asking for or complaining about something. By seeing their parents talking to the ancestors, offering food to them, and obeying their rules, Kwaio children "come to understand in a general sense that a realm of the invisible lies behind and parallel to the visible, material world" (Keesing, 1982, p. 35). Keesing concludes: "No child could escape constructing a cognitive world in which the spirits were ever-present participants in social life, on whom life and death, success or failure, depend" (1982, p. 38).

By contrast, Margaret Mead (1932) famously contended that Manus children grow up totally unaware of and immune from the animism that infuses the thought of their parents and elders: Whereas adults will attribute the unmooring of a canoe to supernatural forces, children will attribute it to human error and stupidity (1932, p. 185). Mead's explanation for the absence of animism in children's thinking is that Manus adults encourage the development of children's "physical adjustment" to the environment while holding back on instructions regarding the social and religious aspects of their lives (1932, p. 188). Thus, Mead reports that it is only around puberty that Manus youth learn to adopt the animistic stance that is characteristic of adult life.

Despite their apparent incompatibility, both Keesing's and Mead's accounts apply to the case of the Vezo. As with Kwaio children, it is hard to imagine how Vezo children could ever escape noticing the existence of the ancestors. Nonetheless, if instead of taking the learning outcome for granted we investigate the active process through which children engage in the construction of their ancestral knowledge, we discover that, as with their Manus counterparts, Vezo children's point of departure is the exploration of the natural world.

## "I CUT ITS HEAD OFF"

As reported by Harris (see Chapter 2 of this book, also Astuti & Harris, 2008), the results of the death studies, in which children of different ages were asked to judge which properties cease or continue to function after death, reveal that there is a moment in the life of Vezo children when they view death as causing the annihilation of every aspect of the person. Thus, whereas five-year-olds were as likely to predict continuity as discontinuity of functions after death (and they were as likely to attribute continuity to bodily as to cognitive, emotional, and perceptual properties), seven-year-olds were uncompromising in their judgment that all functions cease when a person dies. In other words, the first systematic understanding of the consequences of death is one that leaves no room for the ancestors, their desires, and interventions. Such a biological construal of death is likely to be rooted in Vezo children's very direct experiences of both human and animal death.

As discussed earlier, children have close encounters with human death when they observe the stillness of a corpse, avoid the stench of decomposition, or come face to face with a lifeless parent or grandparent. Granted the importance of these experiences, it is arguably their interactions with animals that are of greater and more immediate significance.

To an observer with modern, urban, Western sensibilities, Vezo children's treatment of animals might seem shocking. Gorgeous swallowtail butterflies and any small bird unlucky enough to fly by the village are chased by hordes of children, stoned to the ground, attached to strings, and made to fly as if they were kites; small beach crabs are dug out of the sand, have their pincers removed for safety reasons, and are made to run at the end of a string; lizards are ambushed and "fished" off the sand with the use of slip knots. In all of these instances, animals are used as toys, their entertainment value being provided by the fact that they move – just like the battery-operated toys of First World children. Unsurprisingly, the movement does not last for long. In one memorable instance, a three-year-old boy ran to his grandmother, holding a decapitated bird in his hand and crying desperately because the bird was no longer "going." His grandmother got him to sit in her lap, wiped his nose and face, and reassured him that everything was all right, paying no attention whatsoever to the bird. When the boy calmed down, still holding the bird tight, I asked him what he had done to it, and he replied: "I cut its head off." He threw it away, and ran off to play.

Aside from these playful, if cruel, interactions, children are always keen to take a close and investigative look at animals. When a sea turtle was brought back to the village, a small group of boys gathered around it, waiting for the moment when it was to be ritually killed by its hunter (cf. Astuti, 2000). The boys inspected it in great detail, poking its eyes, blocking its nostrils, forcing its mouth open, pulling at its neck, fingering its genitals, and touching its wound; as they did this, they shared interesting anatomical and physiological discoveries. Eager to get their share of tasty meat, the same boys were of course also present at the dramatic moment when the turtle was ripped open, revealing its heart, lungs, and other vital organs. Their eyes remained glued to the still-beating heart until its gradual and final arrest.

Crowds of children are present whenever any other large kill occurs. They are partly motivated by the hope that they might get some tasty shreds of meat, but they are also clearly fascinated by the process of dying. When a large bull was killed to provide meat for the funeral of a well-respected elder, the children surrounded the grounds where the slaughtering was to occur. They gasped at the raucous noise that erupted from the cut throat, shrieked at the last expulsion of excrements, marveled at the amount of grass contained in the stomach, and stared at the glassy eyes.

It is my contention that these very close encounters with death, especially that of animals, provide children with the raw material that enables them to construct a coherent understanding of the biological causes and consequences of death: that death is caused by the breakdown of the bodily machine and its various components, and that it causes the cessation of all the functions that make life possible.³ My further contention is that it is the emergence of this understanding that in turn enables children to construct the view that some functions remain viable after death.

Logically, there is no reason why young children, who do not yet have a coherent understanding of the biology of death and live in a world in which people talk to the ancestors, offer them food, and worry about their intentions and desires, could not just simply learn the facts: that dead people can hear, need food, and have intentions and desires. Indeed, children's ignorance of the biological consequences of death could facilitate the assimilation of the idea that cognitive, emotional, and perceptual capacities remain viable among the ancestors. Yet our studies suggest that children come to represent death as the end of everything before they learn that something can survive. In other words, they build their understanding of the properties of the ancestors on their knowledge – not on their ignorance – of the biological consequences of death. Thus, although it might well be the case that Vezo children cannot escape learning about the ancestors, they get to know them in their own nonobvious ways – not just by passively absorbing fragments of adults' conversations about dreams and spirits, but also by actively and inquisitively working out how the bodies of birds, turtles, and bulls work and die.

However, children's construction of their knowledge of the ancestors is even less linear than this. As we shall now see, when children start contemplating the possibility of an existence after death, they begin by entertaining ideas that are very different from – and not just immature versions of – those of their parents and elders.

## "THEY WERE DEAD BUT THEY CAME OUT OF THE GROUND"

As explained by Harris (Chapter 2), one of the death studies administered to children (aged eight to seventeen) and adults (aged nineteen to seventy-one) was designed so that half of the participants were told a "hospital" story (priming them to think of death as a biological phenomenon), while the other half were told a "tomb" story (priming them to think of death as a transition to an ancestral existence). Both adults and children were sensitive to the narrative manipulation: Whereas in both instances they

---

³ Given their predatory approach to animals, it is perhaps not surprising that, when asked about the causes of a bird's death, most children (68 percent) aged five to seven invoked human factors such as "people cut off its wings," "throwing stones at them," "sling-shots," "twisting its neck or cutting its neck with a knife," or just and simply "people."

differentiated between bodily and cognitive/emotional functions, they were more likely to judge that functions had ceased when they heard the hospital story than when they heard the tomb story.

A closer look at the way adults and children shifted their judgments, however, reveals that adults' judgments regarding the viability of the deceased's bodily functions were not significantly different in the two conditions, whereas children's were. In other words, the ancestral priming made children, but not adults, more likely to attribute a partially working body to the deceased. There was also a qualitative difference in the way adults and children presented their judgments that bodily functions would be viable after death. Whenever adults made such judgments, they spontaneously explained them by reference to the survival of the deceased's *angatse*. For example, a twenty-four-year-old man answered the question whether the deceased's stomach needs food by stating that "food will be needed, but it is not him that needs it but his thoughts will need it." Even more explicitly, a nineteen-year-old woman answered the question whether the ears work by asserting that "with regard to his being dead (i.e., to the corpse) the ears don't work, but with regard to his spirit that wanders around his ears work." Thus, in the case of adults, continuity judgments for bodily properties were not meant in any literal, physiological sense, because the eating or the hearing were not attributed to a physical body but to an immaterial spirit.

By contrast, there is no evidence that children who judged that the deceased maintain some viable bodily functions meant it in anything other than a literal sense. Of course, the fact that less articulate children failed to specify what their answers referred to – an immaterial spirit or a physical body – is not, in itself, evidence that they reasoned any differently from the adults. Nonetheless, several informal conversations I had with children individually or in small groups gave me reasons to believe that when they envisage a person's survival after death they attribute to it a palpable and visible body that craves food, looks old and decrepit, stinks, and walks about on its legs.

Children's attribution of a physical body to the dead is likely to originate in the very popular stories and eyewitness testimonials about *olo vokatsy*, the people who, after having been dead and buried, come back to life. The stories about *olo vokatsy* describe what happens to these unfortunate people: They die and they are buried as usual under the sand; after people have left the cemetery, a swirling wind removes the sand on top of their coffin, an explosion rips the coffin apart, and the *olo vokatsy* stand up and walk away. Such people are typically rejected by their families and are destined to conduct a miserable life in hiding, roaming the forest in search of wild fruits, or entering the village at night to steal leftover rice intended for the pigs. If sighted, they are easily recognizable because they smell bad and they are draped in white cloth.

Predictably, there are endless variations to the basic story, which children recount enthusiastically, mixing fear and excitement and adding tales of their own sightings and nearly missed encounters. It should be noted that Vezo adults are equally fascinated by *olo vokatsy*, and that they mostly endorse their existence either by stating that they have themselves seen them "with their own eyes," or by deferring to other people's first-hand experience with such ill-fated and scary people. Either way, it is obvious to adults that *olo vokatsy*, with their visible, material bodies are *not* the same as the immaterial spirit of the dead, the *angatse*, which they dream of, talk to, cook for, and seek protection from.

My suggestion is that, by contrast, this distinction remains elusive for most children. Thus, whenever I asked them to explain what the word *angatse* refers to, I either received firm "don't know" answers or lively descriptions of people who wander around the forest searching for wild fruits, steal pigs' food from the village troughs, stink, wear white, and so on – the telling signs of *olo vokatsy*. Children's characterizations of what happens when food is offered to the ancestors points in the same direction. Admittedly, children are not inclined to reflect on the exact nature of the offerings' intended recipients, probably because, as we saw, they themselves are their primary and most voracious consumers. Nonetheless, when they were asked to do so by my probing questions, most children ended up giving me recognizable descriptions of *olo vokatsy*. For example, I asked a nine-year-old girl whether she thought that dead people hear the words spoken during a blessing, and she replied that "No, they don't hear, because their ears are plugged up." I then asked her whether dead people get the stuff that is offered to them, for example the rum, rice, or meat. She replied "No, they don't get it, but all they do is to wander around looking for left-over rice" – the food eaten by *olo vokatsy*.

As noted in the introduction, seventeen-year-old Brika was well aware of the difference between *angatse* and *olo vokatsy*. In this he was not exceptional, even though he was able to explain it as no other person his age. The open-ended conversations I had with him and his contemporaries suggested that the differentiation between the two beyond-death-entities is driven by the realization that *angatse*, unlike *olo vokatsy*, are invisible. Thus, whereas a ten-year-old would maintain that one cannot see *angatse* because they hide in the forest (which is what *olo vokatsy* typically are forced to do), a sixteen- or seventeen-year-old would maintain that one cannot see *angatse* because they are like air – they move about but they are invisible to the eye.

To return to the results of the death studies, we can better understand why children were more likely than adults to attribute physical properties to the deceased in the "tomb" condition. This is because, when primed to think ancestrally, children brought to mind the image of a stinky, hungry, thieving *olo vokatsy* rather than the image of an immaterial *angatse* – hence they reasoned, understandably, that the stomach needs food or that the legs move (none of the seventeen-year-olds did so). However, if this is the image that children bring to mind, their knowledge about the ancestors, although inescapable, is very different from that of the adults.

### CONCLUSION – "I DON'T KNOW, I'VE NEVER BEEN DEAD"

When considering how Vezo children come to know that some properties of the person survive after death and that, consequently, dead people remain actively involved in the lives of their descendants, one is struck by the fact that Vezo adults intentionally refrain from teaching their children what happens after death. As a result, children take their own, largely untutored steps to create *their* understanding of the afterlife. Whereas early on in this constructive process children take the view that nothing at all survives after death, they are later attracted to the idea that dead people can come back to life, body and all. By their late teens they realize that most deceased people do not escape from their abode under the sand, but that they continue their existence as disembodied but powerful spirits.

Having come this far in the story, I want to conclude by taking a critical look at one of the assumptions of my analysis, namely that if Vezo adults were differently minded – if they held different beliefs about children's lack of understanding and vulnerability – they could teach their children about the ancestors. What this scenario assumes is that adults hold a coherent body of knowledge that they could transfer to their children. In the course of anthropological fieldwork, one is compelled to search for coherence, because one's first undertaking must be to make sense of the peculiar. Coherence, however, can be both a distraction and an imposition, as I was forced to realize when I began to combine traditional ethnographic methods with a simple experimental tool such as the death interview.

For example, adults who participated in the death studies revealed that, depending on context, they can summon up different, even contrary representations of what happens to people after death – believing that nothing at all survives *and* that the *angatse* survives (Astuti & Harris, 2008; Harris, Chapter 2). Moreover, those adults who judged that something of the deceased would survive varied in the number of functions that they deemed to remain viable after death (ranging from all seven mental properties that were probed to only one). In other words, there was remarkably little agreement about what exactly the survival of the *angatse* entails, which suggests that the belief in its survival is appropriated by different people to compose very personal and idiosyncratic representations of what happens after death.

Yet even this rendition might turn out to be too much of a distraction and an imposition. For what became apparent in the course of the informal conversations that were sparked by the death interviews is that most adults hold very tentative representations of the afterlife. True, some elders had clearly spent a lot of time thinking about the ancestors' ways of being, their way of communicating, of eating, and so on. When pressed by my relentless questioning, they hardly faltered, giving evidence that they had themselves, at some point, reflected about the hows and whys, and had come up with their own answers (different, perhaps, from those of a brother or a husband I had approached a few hours earlier). Yet they were the exceptions. Most people found it hard to articulate what kind of existence the ancestors enjoy, how exactly the *angatse* acts on the living, whether dreams are a necessary vehicle for their interventions, and so on. Some were indifferent, even skeptical novices, whereas others struggled to produce a coherent account and readily gave up by asserting: "I don't know, I have never been dead."

It is hard to imagine that such hesitant knowledge could effectively be imparted to the children, even if adults were motivated to do so. This brings me to my final point about the pivotal role of ritual in ensuring that the ancestors are kept alive in children's and adults' minds: The endemic difference of opinion – or even the absence of opinion – regarding the ways of the ancestors does not stop people, children included, from coming together and actually talking and offering food, drinks, and shelter to them. When this has to happen, the focus is on performing the correct actions, on using the correct utensils, on saying the correct words on the right day and at the right time. The fact that different participants bring with them very different personal interpretations of what they are doing never seems to interfere with the smooth orchestration of the ritual. This is a remarkable achievement, based on what Bloch (2005) calls "deference." As people gather to get things done, they are likely to stop speculating or doubting or not caring about the ancestors' ways of being, their way of communicating, of eating, and so on. Instead, they defer to whoever it was that, a very long time ago, originated this way of doing things and align themselves with it.

By so doing, they not only honor the ancestors, placate their anger, and avoid their interference. They also provide the crowd of excitable children with indirect but all important testimony of the existence of invisible yet powerful entities that need honoring and placating and have the power to interfere in one's life.[4] Thus, as long as the rituals are staged, children will eventually construct an understanding of what lies beyond death that will motivate them to be interested in much more than the food.

### ACKNOWLEDGMENTS

The research on which this paper is based was supported by the Economic and Social Research Council, UK (Research Fellowship R000271254, 2002–5). I wish to thank the villagers of Betania, adults and children, for allowing me to learn with and through them. Thank you to Sean Epstein for joining me in the process and to Maurice Bloch for discussing its outcome.

### REFERENCES

Astuti, R. (1994). "Invisible" objects: Funerary rituals among the Vezo of western Madagascar. *Res. Anthropology and Aesthetics*, 25, 11–122.
    (1995). *People of the sea: Identity and descent among the Vezo of Madagascar.* Cambridge, England: Cambridge University Press.
    (2000). Les gens ressemblent-ils aux poulets? Penser la frontière homme / animal à Madagascar. *Terrain*, 34, 89–105.
Astuti, R. & Harris, P.L. (2008). Understanding mortality and the life of the ancestors in rural Madagascar. *Cognitive Science*, 32, 713–740.
Bloch, M. (2005). *Essays on cultural transmission.* London School of Economics Monographs on Social Anthropology, 75, Oxford: Berg.
Keesing, R.M. (1982). *Kwaio religion: The living and the dead in a Solomon island society.* New York, NY: Columbia University Press.
Kopytoff, I. (1971). Ancestors as elders in Africa. *Africa, 41*, 129–142.
Mead, M. (1932). An investigation of the thought of primitive children, with special reference to animism. *Journal of the Royal Anthropological Institute, 32*, 173–190.

[4] I wish to thank Paul L. Harris for suggesting this point to me.

# 2

# Death in Spain, Madagascar, and Beyond

PAUL L. HARRIS

Two different research programs have addressed children's developing conception of death. On the one hand, children have been viewed as apprentice biologists who come to view death as an inevitable part of the life cycle. According to this view, which can be traced back to Piaget, children's cognitive development moves toward an objective understanding. Piecemeal observations are increasingly coordinated into a coherent, theorylike organization. More recently, children have also been viewed as apprentice theologians who adopt a spiritual or religious view of death. Indeed, some investigators have suggested that young children are naturally disposed to assume that certain processes continue after death. Others propose that children increasingly understand and endorse the particular claims about the afterlife that are characteristic of their community. In either case, this more recent research assumes that children's developing conception of death cannot be characterized in exclusively biological terms. It embraces various transcendent elements.

I argue that each of these programs makes an important contribution to our understanding of children's ideas about death. What is needed, however, is research on the extent to which these two conceptions – the biological conception on the one hand and the religious conception on the other – coexist in the mind of any individual child. I describe two studies showing that such coexistence is found and indeed increases with age.

I conclude by discussing the implications of the findings. I ask how children – and indeed adults – adopt two different and apparently conflicting conceptions of death, and whether there is any natural tendency to think that the body and mind obey different causal laws and can be separated from one another at death.

## TWO CONCEPTIONS OF DEATH

Developmental psychologists have probed children's grasp of three biological aspects of death: its universality – all living beings must eventually die; its irreversibility – once dead, a creature cannot come back to life; and its comprehensive impact – the total cessation of all vital functions. Various studies indicate that these three concepts are progressively mastered between the ages of four and ten years (Keynon, 2001; Speece & Brent, 1992). Children's developing knowledge about the organs of the body appears to play a key role in the acquisition of this biological understanding. Slaughter and her colleagues found that preschoolers who knew about the function of hidden organs – such as the lungs or the heart – were better at recognizing the inevitability, irreversibility, and terminal impact of death (Slaughter, Jaakola, & Carey, 1999). Moreover, when children were given explicit instruction about the critical role played by various organs, their grasp of death's inevitability, irreversibility, and universality increased (Slaughter & Lyons, 2003).

These findings are consistent with the idea that children think like scientists. They gradually coordinate various observations into a theorylike understanding of a natural phenomenon. In particular, the findings of Slaughter et al. (1999) underline how an understanding of the role of normally hidden organs helps children to realize that the body is a coordinated entity in which various internal parts are critical for the maintenance of vital functions – eating, breathing, mobility, and so forth.

Despite the plausibility of this account of children's developing conception of death, a moment's reflection suggests that it is unlikely to capture all of their thinking in this domain. Survey data show that a belief in the afterlife is common among adults in North America and Western Europe. Moreover, the belief in an afterlife shows no signs of a decline over recent decades (Greeley & Hout, 1999). By implication, at some point in their development, children or adolescents come to the conclusion – notwithstanding the biological facts of death – that some form of immortality is possible. Indeed, when adolescents have been interviewed along with children about the nature of death, a progressive increase in references to the afterlife is observed with age (Brent, Speece, Lin, Dong, & Yang, 1996; Wenestram & Wass, 1987).

## CHILDREN'S ACCEPTANCE OF CONFLICTING TESTIMONY

With these somewhat conflicting findings in mind, we interviewed seven- and eleven-year-old Spanish children (Harris & Giménez, 2005). The children were all attending public schools in the metropolitan area of Madrid. In contemporary Spain, the division between church and state is recognized by public schools. Thus, the children were receiving no explicit religious instruction in school. At the same time, the children were growing up in a culture with a strong Catholic tradition.

Children were given two separate stories. Each story described the death of a grandparent, and each included an episode in which a grandchild discussed this loss with an adult. Despite their basic similarity, the two stories differed in important ways. The "doctor" story included a conversation between the bereaved grandchild and a doctor who explained that there was nothing that the doctors could do to save the life of the grandparent and that the grandparent was now dead. By contrast, the "priest" story included a conversation between the bereaved grandchild and a priest who also acknowledged that there was nothing that the doctors could do, but added that the grandparent was now with God. The stories were intended to offer children two different contexts for thinking about death: a medical context, focusing on the finality of death, and a religious context, focusing on the possibility of a life hereafter. The expectation was that the two contexts would prime two different conceptions of death – death as a biological terminus on the one hand and death as a spiritual metamorphosis on the other. The key question was whether children would opt consistently for one conception or the other – irrespective of story context – or alternatively would display first one and then the other, depending on the context at hand.

To probe for these two conceptions, children were asked to say whether various processes continued to function or not following the grandparent's death. Some questions involved the explicit mention of a particular body part, for example: "Do you think her eyes still work?" Other questions involved explicit mention of a particular mental state, for example: "Do you think she sees anything?" We anticipated that children might be willing to assert the continuation of mental processes even if they denied the continued functioning of associated body parts.

Children's replies displayed a very systematic pattern. First, although there was a general tendency to say that most processes had stopped at death, this tendency was considerably stronger among younger children than older children. Thus, the plausible assumption that children gradually consolidate a biological conception of death – according to which all vital processes cease – needs qualification. When children are probed comprehensively, they increasingly deny the possibility of total cessation as they get older. Second, children were sensitive to the story context. In the context of the doctor story, both younger and older children were likely to say that processes no longer functioned, but in the context of the priest story, they were less prone to this conclusion. Finally, irrespective of their age and the story that they had just heard, children displayed a quasi-dualist stance. They were more likely to deny the continued functioning of body parts – the eyes, the ears, and so forth – than to deny the continued functioning of associated mental processes such as seeing and hearing.

As a further probe, children were asked after each story to comment on the functioning of the body (in general) and invited to justify that judgment. Similarly, they were asked to comment on the functioning of the mind (in general) and to justify that judgment. These requests for justification were worded in an open-ended fashion: "Why is it that her body/mind is still working (doesn't work anymore)." Children typically justified claims that the mind or body no longer functions after death in biological terms, for example: "If the heart stops, the entire body stays still"; "If he is dead, nothing can work"; "Because he is dead and the body disintegrates until there is only the skeleton left." By contrast, they typically justified claims that the mind or body continues to function after death in religious terms, by referring to God, to Heaven, or to the survival of some essential part of the person, for example: "In Heaven everything can work even if she is dead. God is said to give you all that"; "The soul keeps working"; or "The spirit is out there and keeps working."

When considered in combination, children's judgments about the mind and the body and their subsequent justifications could be allocated to three different patterns: a biological pattern in which they claimed that the mind or body no longer worked and justified that claim in biological terms; a religious pattern in which they claimed that the mind or body still worked and justified that claim in religious terms; and, finally, an inconsistent pattern in which either children's claim and their justification did not fit together, or they failed to offer a justification at all.

Figure 2.1 shows the percentage of younger and older children displaying each of these three patterns depending on the story context and on whether they were talking about the body or the mind.

Inspection of Figure 2.1 reinforces the conclusions reached earlier. First, an age change is evident. As compared to younger children, older children are more likely to adopt a religious stance and less likely to adopt a biological stance. Second, the adoption of a religious stance is more frequent in the context of the priest story than the doctor story. Finally, it is more frequent for the mind than the body.

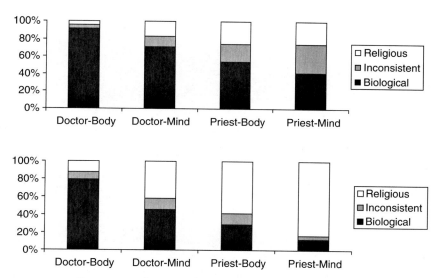

FIGURE 2.1. Percentage of younger (upper panel) and older (lower panel) children displaying a consistently biological, a consistently religious, or an inconsistent pattern, as a function of Story (Doctor versus Priest) and Process Type (Body versus Mind).

These results might be construed in the following way: The biological conception of death is widespread among younger children – especially when they talk about the body in the context of the doctor story. By contrast, the religious conception of death is widespread among older children especially when they talk about the mind in the context of the priest story. Inspection of the extremes of Figure 2.1 – the left-most bar in the upper panel and the right-most bar in the lower panel – seems to confirm this interpretation. It implies that in the course of development, the biological conception is trumped by the religious conception when measured in terms of the proportion of younger and older children who subscribe to one or the other.

In fact, however, this construal misrepresents the developmental change that takes place. This emerged clearly in a follow-up analysis. Note that children were given an opportunity to make a claim and justify that claim on four different occasions throughout the interview: with respect to the body in the context of each of the two stories, and with respect to the mind in the context of each of the two stories. Thus, for any given child, we could ask if they (i) consistently adopted a biological stance on all four occasions; (ii) consistently adopted a religious stance on all four occasions;

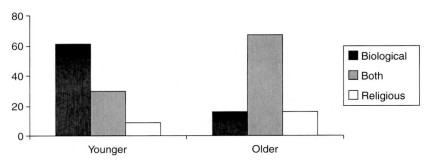

FIGURE 2.2. Percentage of younger and older children displaying a biological stance, a religious stance, or both.

or (iii) adopted both stances but on different occasions – for example, adopted a biological stance when discussing the body in the context of the doctor story but adopted a religious stance when discussing the mind in the context of the priest story.

Figure 2.2 presents the results of this breakdown. It is evident that the number of children who consistently adopt a biological stance declines with age. However, this is not because the number of children who consistently adopt a religious stance increases with age. Instead, the number of children who adopt both stances sharply increases. In other words, the acquisition of a religious conception of death supplements but does not displace children's biological conception. By implication, each of the two research programs described earlier helps us to understand children's conception of death, but neither comprises the entire picture, especially for older children.

Although the data gathered in Madrid provide considerable support for the claim that children display two different but coexisting conceptions of death, it could be objected that the data have limited validity for two different reasons. First, the age range studied was fairly narrow. So, it could be argued that if adolescents or adults had been tested they might have adopted a con-sistently religious stance – or, at least, moved further toward it. On this view, the coexistence of both conceptions is a transitional phenomenon, one that is steadily outgrown in the longer course of development. The second con-cern is that the data were collected in a community in which the Christian belief in God, Heaven, and the immortal soul is widespread. Conceivably, in a different community – a non-Christian community, for example – the pattern of judgment might be different.

With these concerns in mind, Astuti and Harris (2008) conducted a rep-lication and extension of the Madrid study among the Vezo of Madagascar.

As described in Chapter 1 by Rita Astuti, the Vezo – as is common throughout Madagascar – maintain close relations with the ancestors, who continue to influence their lives. The spirits of deceased relatives appear in people's dreams demanding food, drinks, and a well-kept tomb; if displeased by the attention they receive, they will make people ill, prevent women from bearing children, or even cause people to die. The Vezo therefore seek to appease the ancestors through ritual offerings and the construction and upkeep of monumental tombs, which both honor the ancestors and keep them safely apart from the living. Thus, although the Vezo do not subscribe to the Christian idea of Heaven, they do believe in an afterlife. Moreover, like Christians, they assume that death does not annihilate all capacities for sentient awareness. The ancestors can feel displeasure, react angrily, and be appeased.

The interview presented to the Vezo participants was similar to the one used in Madrid, but with suitable modifications. For example, in place of the "doctor" story, the "hospital" story described a man who suffered a malaria attack and was taken to a hospital where he received injections that failed to save his life. In place of the "priest" story, the "tomb" story described a man who died at home surrounded by his grandchildren, who often dream of him but are pleased to have completed the construction of his tomb. Thus, as in Madrid, the two stories differed in their central iconography – the paraphernalia of illness and medicine in the hospital story and ancestral communication and desires in the tomb story.

In line with the objectives of this follow-up study, the age range of the participants was expanded. A group of children ranging from eight to seventeen years (mean age = twelve years, eight months) was compared to a group of adults ranging from nineteen to seventy-one years (mean age = thirty-five years). In contrast to the Madrid study, each participant was presented with only one story. Afterward, they answered a series of questions similar to those used in Madrid but with notable additions.

In key respects, the replies made by Vezo children and adults echoed those that had been made in Madrid. Thus, there was an overall tendency to say that most processes had stopped. Nevertheless, as in the earlier study, participants were sensitive to the story context. They were more likely to claim that processes had stopped in the context of the hospital story than in the context of the tomb story. In addition, they were more likely to claim that bodily processes had stopped as compared to mental processes.

Recall that in Madrid older children were less likely than younger children to claim that vital processes – both bodily processes and mental processes – had stopped at death. A similar age change reappeared in

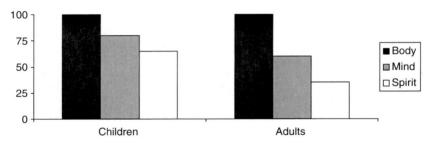

FIGURE 2.3. Percentage of Vezo children and adults claiming that the body, mind, or spirit ceases to function at death.

Madagascar, but it was more circumscribed. Adults were less likely than children to claim that mental processes had stopped, but the two age groups were equally likely to claim that bodily processes had stopped. Moreover, further analysis revealed that the age change for mental processes was true for particular mental processes rather than for all mental processes. More specifically, children and adults were equally likely to claim that perception or sensation-based mental processes (seeing, hearing, feeling hungry) cease after death, but adults were more likely than children to claim that cognitive and emotional processes (knowing, remembering, and missing one's children) continue after death. In sum, the tendency to differentiate between the fate of the bodily processes and the fate of the mental processes was more evident among adults, and that was especially true when the mental processes in question were not obviously associated with any particular body part.

One final set of questions casts further light on the way that Vezo participants think about the afterlife. After they had been asked about the continued function of various vital processes as just described, they were asked about the function of three different entities that may be roughly translated into English as body, mind, and spirit. As might be expected, given the results so far, participants who heard the hospital story as opposed to the tomb story were more likely to claim that each entity would cease to function at death. In addition, however, they differentiated among the three entities, claiming that the body was more likely to cease to function than the mind, and that the mind was more likely to cease to function than the spirit. As Figure 2.3 shows, this differentiation among the three entities was especially obvious among adults.

In summary, the findings in Madagascar confirmed and extended the pattern that had been found in Madrid. First, the Vezo participants were sensitive to the story context in much the same way as the Spanish children. In both cultural settings, a story about death that focused on its medical aspects provoked children and adults alike to claim that most if not all vital functions cease at death. By contrast, a story that highlighted connections to the afterlife led children and adults to claim that certain vital functions continue after death. Second, in both settings there was a strong tendency to distinguish between mind and body – to claim that although the body no longer functions at death, the mind continues. The data from Madagascar underline two additional features of such a dualist stance. First, this stance is more obvious among adults than children, and it is more obvious for central mental processes such as knowing and remembering than for processes like seeing and hearing that ordinarily depend on a bodily organ. Second, echoing references to the soul or the spirit by Spanish children, explicit questioning revealed that the Vezo – especially adult Vezo – are particularly likely to associate continued functioning with the spirit rather than the mind or body.

Surveying the findings across the two studies, we find a relatively consistent picture despite the marked differences in age range and cultural setting. In both Spain and Madagascar, participants adjusted to the story context. Also, in both settings, there was a greater willingness to assert the continuity of mental as compared to bodily processes. Furthermore, there was no indication among adults in Madagascar that their belief in the afterlife displaces a biological conception of death. Both conceptions were apparent depending on the story context.

Two main findings warrant further discussion. First, children and adults alike are very sensitive to the context in which a death is presented. They answer the same question differently depending on that context. It is reasonable to ask, therefore, how they arrive at such coexisting beliefs. Second, throughout both interviews there were recurrent signs that people think of the body and the mind differently. Where does this dualistic stance come from? Is it nurtured by cultural learning and more specifically by exposure to religious or supernatural beliefs about the afterlife? Alternatively, does it reflect an early cognitive stance that comes naturally to young children even before they are exposed to any religious teaching?

## COEXISTENCE

As described, participants adjusted their claims about the continuity of functioning after death depending on the story context. One possible explanation for this shifting pattern of replies is that participants endorse what they assume to be the answer expected by the interviewer. They treat the story that the interviewer has just presented as a signal in this regard. They emphasize cessation of function in the context of the doctor or hospital story and continuity of function in the context of the priest or tomb story. On this view, participants are not really reporting their own beliefs. Instead, they are trying to figure out what is expected of them. There are two reasons for doubting the validity of this interpretation. First, in Madrid older children were more likely than younger children to display both the religious and the biological stance. Yet if children were simply seeking to defer to an adult interviewer, such deference might be expected to decline rather increase with age. Still, a counter-argument is feasible. Perhaps the two age groups are equally motivated to defer, but older children are simply better at inferring what the interviewer expects. This could account for the age change observed in Spain. Accordingly, the data from Madagascar are especially important in assessing the deference hypothesis. In Madagascar, adult as well as child participants were sensitive to the story context. However, given their longstanding acquaintance with the interviewer and their familiarity with her genuine desire to learn about Vezo customs and practices, it is unlikely that the observed shift in judgment from one story context to the other, especially among adults, was prompted by an inclination to defer to her supposed knowledge or expectations. Instead, it is much more likely that participants, and especially adult participants, were offering their own best judgment in an effort to be as informative as possible.

Given these points, how can the shift be explained? A plausible explanation is that everyday thinking is primarily aimed at providing a guide for action. On this view, death is conceptualized in two different ways because there are two relatively distinct sets of pragmatic concerns that need to be satisfied. On the one hand, there are the goals that arise from the day-to-day exigencies of life: the care of children, the demands of work, the provisioning of a family. The dead person is no longer a living agent who can contribute to those immediate and pressing goals. From this mundane perspective, death is regarded as a biological terminus because it marks the cessation of the vital functions needed for such practical activities. The living person is reduced to a corpse, immobile and insensate. On the other hand, there are longer-term concerns that do not call for any day-to-day agency. The dead person cannot act in the real world, but he or she can be an interlocutor, a guide, and a beneficiary. From this perspective, the dead person is far from being an insensate corpse: He or she is someone with a stable identity, a past and a future, someone who has ties to the living, and with whom the living may eventually be reunited. Different religious traditions shape the way in which this enduring personhood is viewed. Nevertheless, they share the same basic conception of the afterlife in which the dead individual is not a corpse divested of all agency, but a person with an enduring social network.

Given that the two conceptions are ordinarily evoked in different pragmatic contexts, it is unlikely that their different implications generate any particular psychological conflicts. For example, in the context of the doctor or hospital story, the chief concern is to keep the dying person in the land of the living. This is what medicine aims to do. When this goal is not met and the person dies, the living are confronted by a corpse that needs to be buried, cremated, or otherwise disposed of. From this perspective, it is appropriate to conclude that the eyes of the dead person no longer function, and that he or she can no longer see anything. By contrast, in the context of the priest or the tomb story, a different framework, namely the standing of the dead person in the afterworld, displaces everyday mortal concerns. From this perspective, it makes sense to ascribe sentience to the person – some awareness of the life they have left behind and of the afterlife itself. Thus, although the parallel claims that, for example, the dead person no longer sees but remains able to see can be regarded as contradictory, it is unlikely that participants are aware of any contradiction. It is the corpse that cannot see. The person who has moved on to the afterlife and the corpse are not regarded as one and the same thing. The person who is with God, in Heaven, or among the ancestors may well be able to see.

These conclusions fit into a broader set of findings regarding the context-driven nature of concept formation and recruitment. The same phenomenon may be viewed under different descriptions, and a distinctive causal narrative is brought to bear with respect to each particular description. Consider, for example, deadly illnesses such as AIDS. Legare and Gelman (2008) offer persuasive evidence that children and adults in South Africa effectively think of AIDS as two partially overlapping phenomena: a purely medical, viral infection attributable to the mixing of blood products, and a sickness brought about by malevolent witchcraft. As in the case of death, participants can be prompted to invoke each of these causal narratives depending on the story context. As a related example, consider lay thinking about Darwinian theory. Many adults accept that natural selection is sufficient to explain the origins of animal species. At the same time, they conceptualize the human animal differently. They invoke some form of divine creation (Evans, 2008). Taken together, these findings underline the point that when adults think about central existential issues – the nature of death, the causes of illness, and the origin of species – they gravitate sometimes to a naturalistic explanation and sometimes to an explanation based on divine or supernatural powers. Depending on the context, they are prone to invoke both modes of explanation, but because each explanation is tied to a particular context or target, no obvious sense of contradiction or incompatibility is experienced.

### DUALISM

Throughout the interviews, both in Madrid and Madagascar, participants were more likely to claim continuity of function for the mind than for the body. Where does this dualist stance come from? There are at least three plausible hypotheses. First, dualist intuitions might come easily – even to young children. They might need no sustenance or cultivation. On this view, we would expect young children to adopt a dualist stance even before they encounter the beliefs of their community about the afterlife. A second possibility is that collective representations of the afterlife, to the extent that they emphasize the integrity of the spirit in the face of corporeal decomposition, might inculcate a dualist stance no matter what the child's natural inclinations. On this view, the dualist stance should become increasingly evident in the course of development as children come to understand and accept the beliefs of their community regarding the afterlife, but it should be absent from the thinking of young children. Third, it is possible that the distinction is available – even in early childhood – but is also elaborated and consolidated by collective representations of the afterlife. In this case, the dualist stance should be evident in early childhood, but it should also become increasingly coherent and pronounced in the course of development.

Which of these three hypotheses best fits the data from Madrid and Madagascar? The data from Madagascar provide persuasive evidence that the distinction between mind and body alters in the course of development. Recall that although both children and adults differentiated between mind and body, this differentiation was more evident among adults than children, particularly for those mental activities that typify the ancestors – knowing, remembering, and missing one's children. Indeed, as compared to children, adults were more inclined to move beyond a simple dualism and to differentiate between body, mind, and spirit. These developmental changes imply that collective representations do play an important role. Collective representations either induce the dualist stance as implied by the second hypothesis, or alternatively, collective representations elaborate and consolidate an early propensity toward dualism – as implied by the third hypothesis.

Paul Bloom (2004) has set out a sustained case for the existence of an early propensity toward dualism. He offers several interesting arguments. First, even before they learn to talk and certainly before they know anything about the religious beliefs of their community, children deploy two different modes of interpretation: one for material, physical bodies and one for social beings. In understanding the behavior of material bodies, infants invoke various physical principles. For example, they assume that a stationary object that goes out of sight will normally continue to exist in the same place and that an object with no visible means of support will fall vertically. By contrast, in understanding the behavior of social beings, infants invoke psychological principles. For example, they assume that an object that moves with apparent purpose will take the most direct path toward its goal. They readily interpret a moving object that facilitates or impedes another's movements as guided by psychological dispositions to help or hinder. Granted these two distinct explanatory systems, Bloom concludes that even babies are inclined toward dualism.

However, there is a conceptual problem with this line of argument. Strictly speaking, a dualist is someone who believes that the mind can function independent of the body – and may even survive the body. Thus, a dualist is distinguished by his or her assumptions about the basis for mental states. Admittedly, he or she may also be inclined to explain the behavior of inanimate objects in a different way from the behavior of social beings. Yet that is not a defining feature of the dualist stance. This point will become clear if we consider a modern-day materialist. Unlike the dualist, he or she will insist that mental states depend on the body and, more specifically, on the brain. Hence, once the brain ceases to function, mental life will cease as a result. However, such a materialist may also explain the behavior of inanimate physical objects according to different principles from the behavior of animate beings, including human beings. Although the materialist presumably believes that the brain is a physical object, ultimately constrained by the laws of physics, that does not mean that the type of explanation a materialist advances for brain states – or for the mental states that depend on brain states – will be fully equivalent to the type of explanation that he or she advances for the behavior of inanimate material objects. In short, dualists are defined by their beliefs about the nonmaterial basis for mental states. The fact that someone invokes one set of principles to explain why an inanimate object rolls down a slope and a different set of principles to explain why an animate being purposefully climbs a slope does not tell us whether that person is a dualist or a materialist. Similarly, the fact that babies invoke one set of principles (so called naïve physics) to predict the vertical path of an unsupported, falling object and another set of principles (so-called naïve psychology) to predict the upward path taken by a goal-directed agent does not tell us whether babies are dualists or materialists – or neither. They may well invoke one set of principles to explain apparently animate or goal-directed motion and another set to explain the mechanical motion of inanimate objects, but that differentiation is not a commitment to dualism.

One might seek to defend Bloom's proposal in the following way. Babies are equipped with two modes of interpretation, one for material objects and one for social beings. These two modes of interpretation do not entail dualism, but they do make it possible. So there is a plausible connection – albeit no necessary connection – between having two distinct modes of interpretation and being a dualist. The problem with this defense is its vagueness. If the claim is that the two modes of interpretation make dualism possible only in the sense that they are not incompatible with dualism, I would argue that the same goes for materialism, as explained earlier. If the claim is stronger, namely that the two modes of interpretation do not entail dualism but dispose children toward it rather than materialism, we need more explanation. Why exactly? It is tempting to think that the explanation is straightforward: Children rely on the interpretive system for material objects (naïve physics) when thinking about the body, whereas they rely on the interpretive system for social beings (naïve psychology) when thinking about mind. Hence, they end up with a dualist stance. However, this alleged explanation is decidedly implausible. It fails to distinguish between two different aspects of the human body. Admittedly, the human body is a material object and sometimes – for example, when it falls or collides with another body – we invoke naïve physics to explain its displacements. However, most movements of the human body call for a psychological interpretation in terms of goals and expectation, not for the type of naïve physics that we – and babies – deploy when interpreting the behavior of inanimate material objects. In short, looking at the interpretive stance of the young infant we might expect them to think that animate bodies and mental states are deeply and intimately connected – as indeed they are.

Bloom's second argument is that the propensity toward dualism offers an explanation for a widespread conception of the afterlife. Citing Boyer (2001), he writes: "Indeed, a belief that the world teems with ancestor spirits, the souls of people who have been liberated from their bodies through death, is common cross culturally" (p. 149). There are, however, several indications that people conceive of the afterlife in a less disembodied fashion than is implied by this characterization. First, as we saw earlier, it is true that children and adults claim less continuity of function for the body than the mind after death. Nevertheless, when they are presented with the priest narrative, children in Spain did not assert that all bodily functions cease – they claimed that some functions continue. Similarly, when presented with the tomb narrative in Madagascar, children and adults did not claim that all bodily functions cease – they claimed that one or two functions continue. Second, despite Christian beliefs in the immortality of the soul, Heaven is rarely construed as a meeting place for completely disembodied spirits. Family members expect to "see" and "recognize" one another. The angels have wings. The saints have haloes. Mark Twain's mordant parody of the Christian heaven – *Captain Stormfield's Visit to Heaven* turns on the assumption that new arrivals have to make various bodily – not just spiritual – adjustments to their new abode (Twain, 2004). Third, scholarly analysis of early Christian texts shows that even if the soul was routinely assumed to be different from the body, the connection between them throughout the afterlife was repeatedly analyzed and debated (Bovon, 2010). For example, the Second Coming, when allegedly the dead will be resurrected, does not imply a perpetual severance of the soul from the body, but rather the possibility of their eventual reunification. In sum, the vision of death that we might expect if dualism came naturally is not borne out when we take a closer look at common representations of the afterlife. Whether they have entered heaven or taken their place among the ancestors, the dead are rarely seen as pure souls, liberated from all corporeal functions. In key respects, they remain connected to the embodied persons that they once were and may yet become again.

Bloom's third argument is that children are naturally disposed to engage in dualist thinking because they easily understand fairy stories or myths in which a person retains the same mind or mental states but magically acquires a new body. In fact, however, scrutiny of the available evidence shows that young children have a good deal of trouble in seeing the implications of such metamorphoses. For example, Johnson (1990; Study 1) asked young children to think about the implications of a brain transplant: a pig whose brain is replaced by that of a child. Across a range of questions, there was a sharp age change between five and seven years. Five-year-olds frequently claimed that the pig would retain the behaviors and mental states of a pig rather than acquire those of a child (e.g., love sleeping in sloppy mud; remember being a pig; think of itself as a pig). Only seven-year-olds systematically claimed that the pig would acquire the behaviors and mental states of a child rather than retain those of a pig (e.g., love sleeping in a bed; remember being a child; think of itself as a child). In a similar study,

Gottfried, Gelman, and Schultz (1999) asked children about the effects of a brain transplant between one animal and another. Their findings paralleled those reported by Johnson (1990). Kindergartners failed to appreciate the effects of a transplant whereas older children systematically realized that a transplant would lead to a change in the animal's thoughts and memories.

A plausible explanation for this age change is that five-year-olds are capable of dualistic thinking, but because the metamorphosis in the afore-mentioned studies was couched in terms of a brain transplant and they know little about the person-specific functions of a given brain, they did not grasp its implications. On this argument, five-year-olds would do better if they were invited to contemplate a mind transplant rather than a brain transplant. Certainly, this would be a much more direct test of Bloom's proposal that children are naturally inclined to conceive of the mind as potentially distinct from the body. To examine this possibility, Corriveau, Pasquini, and Harris (2005) gave five- and seven-year-olds stories that involved either the magical transplantation of one creature's brain or mind to another's body. Two main results emerged. First, as expected, children did better in anticipating the consequences of a mind as compared to a brain transplant. Nevertheless, seven-year-olds responded more accurately than five-year-olds. For example, only about one-third of the five-year-olds correctly answered a set of four identity questions about a mind transplant whereas three-quarters of the five-year-olds were able to do so. In sum, although it is true that older children are able to grasp the kind of meta-morphoses explored by Homer, Kafka, and the brothers Grimm – a human being knowingly imprisoned in the body of an animal, an insect, or a frog – younger children often have difficulty in grasping their implications. For them, a disjunction of mind and body is hard to understand.

None of the aforementioned arguments against Bloom's proposal is deci-sive, but, in any case, they pertain to only indirect reasons for accepting that young children are natural dualists. The most direct way to establish that claim is to assess whether young children think that the mind can function independent of the body and its parts. Investigators have probed children about this in two ways. First, they have asked children how far various men-tal states are possible in the absence of a brain. Second, they have asked very young children – who may not have received any religious instruc-tion – whether mental functioning continues independent of the body after death.

Bloom (2004) notes that young children have a very limited conception of the brain's role in mental life. For example, five- and six-year-olds do not systematically realize that the brain is necessary for simple motor actions (e.g., walking or grabbing something), involuntary reactions (e.g., coughing or blinking), or indeed for perceptual acts (e.g., seeing and hearing) (Johnson & Wellman, 1982). This limited appreciation of the critical role of the brain in all sorts of activities might lead young children to dualism – to the conclusion that mental and brain activity are separate types of events. In turn, that dualist conclusion might support their belief in the continuation of mental processes after death. More specifically, young children might assume that mental activity can continue even though brain activity comes to a complete halt. However, closer scrutiny of the empirical findings on children's understanding of the brain reveals a more complicated and interesting picture. Young children are not, in fact, completely unaware of the contribution made by the brain to mental activity. Rather, they have too narrow a conception of the role of the brain.

When children ranging from five to fifteen years of age were asked whether the brain is needed for prototypically cognitive acts – thinking and remembering – they all agreed, irrespective of age, that the brain is needed (Johnson & Wellman, 1882; Studies 1 and 2). Indeed, in a study targeting kindergartners, just over half of the four-year-olds and almost all of the five-year-olds were quite systematic in claiming that the brain is needed for cognitive acts such as thinking and remembering (Johnson & Wellman, 1882; Study 3). These results are important for two reasons. First, they show that young children are far from being full-fledged dualists. They claim that the brain is needed for higher-order processes such as thinking – even if they fail to realize its involvement in perceptual acts such as seeing and hearing or motor acts such as walking and blinking. Second, the pattern of results underlines the fact that children's insights into brain function have little connection to their beliefs about what processes do and do not continue after death. More specifically, if children's (limited) dualism led them to think that certain mental activities are possible after death, it would incline them to believe that seeing and hearing are possible, given their supposed independence from brain functioning, whereas thinking and remembering are not, given their dependence on brain function. In fact, however, young children – and indeed adults – are inclined to think that a variety of mental processes are possible after death. They certainly do not stipulate that thinking and remembering are impossible because the brain no longer functions. In short, there is actually considerable tension between children's beliefs about the brain and their beliefs about life after death. They recognize that the brain is needed for cognitive processes like thinking and remembering, but they assert that those same cognitive processes continue after death. By implication, children's early ideas about the relationship between mind and brain, far from contributing to their conception of the afterlife as implied by Bloom, are simply ignored or overridden when they think about what is possible in the afterlife.

In summary, Bloom's arguments do not offer a watertight case for the proposal that afterlife beliefs, particularly the belief that certain mental processes will continue after death, can be traced back to an early propensity toward dualism. Nevertheless, persuasive empirical evidence in favor of that proposal has been reported by Bering and his colleagues. Using a puppet story about the death of a mouse, they questioned kindergartners as well as older elementary school children about which vital functions do or do not continue after death (Bering & Bjorklund, 2004). Across three studies, both age groups typically judged that various biological or bodily functions of the mouse – brain processes, for example, or the need to eat food – would cease at death. By contrast, children often said that purely mental functions of the mouse – for example, his love for his mother or wanting to go home – would continue after death. In a follow-up study conducted with Spanish children attending either a Catholic school or a public secular school, very similar results emerged, save that children attending the Catholic school claimed continuity for all functions more often than children attending the secular school (Bering, Hernández Blasi, & Bjorklund, 2005).

Bering et al. (2005) interpret these data in terms of three interacting components: an early propensity toward dualism – similar to that proposed by Bloom (2004) – and two competing forms of cultural learning that serve to either prune or maintain children's beliefs in the continuity of vital processes. On the one hand, children's growing biological knowledge gradually undermines the default assumption that vital functions continue. On the other hand, their exposure to religious teaching serves to protect that default assumption at least for mental processes. Thus, Bering favors the third hypothesis set out earlier – the proposal that cultural learning shapes and consolidates a preexisting dualist stance.

Taken together, the various studies reported by Bering and his colleagues are provocative. The youngest children tested were in kindergarten and ranged from three to six years of age. So it is tempting to assume that the questions tap their untutored dualism and, more specifically, their assumption that psychological functions survive death. However, there is a major caveat. Bering and Bjorklund (2004) report that the American children they tested rarely used any explicitly religious terms (e.g., Heaven, God, spirit), but their Spanish data (Bering et al., 2005) showed that the environment that children were living in – notably whether they attended a Catholic or a secular school – influenced the extent to which they made afterlife claims. By implication, children's cultural environment does impact their thinking about death, even during the kindergarten years. In other words, it is not safe to assume that children who are in kindergarten display only natural or untutored assumptions about death. Even if they are still in kindergarten, they may be influenced by adult assumptions about death. Indeed, it is reasonable to speculate that no matter what type of school they attend, children in Spain or North America will be exposed to adult discourse about death, and that discourse might induce or sustain a belief in continuity after death, particularly the continuity of psychological functions. How might this come about?

First, although kindergarten children in Spain and North America may well encounter a dead creature first-hand – a dead squirrel or a dead insect – it is likely that their most meaningful and emotionally charged encounters are based on their hearing about the death of a pet, a family member, or someone known in the immediate community. What they will be told at this age about these deaths will rarely attest to the biological story of complete cessation. For example, they will rarely be told that their dead grandmother or their dead pet does not remember them or feels nothing toward them. More likely, children will be invited to think about and maintain an emotional connection with the deceased. Indeed, it is reasonable to argue that the maintenance of such an emotional connection is a normal feature of bereavement and grief as described in Chapter 4 by Margaret Mahon. Note also that such palliative discourse will not generally take the corpse as its referent. Instead, children will be invited to remember the qualities of the person or creature when they were alive, rather than to dwell on the dead corpse that the person has become. It would not be surprising if children conclude, on the basis of such discourse, that even if death terminates many biological functions – after all, dead creatures do not move, breathe, eat, or display any signs of sentience – the social relationships and all that those relationships presuppose in terms of thoughts, desires, and feelings can and should endure in some fashion or another.

This analysis makes two predictions. First, it implies that young children will be especially inclined to endorse the continuity of those psychological functions that connect the dead person as a social being to the living. Consider, for example, one of the questions posed by Bering and his colleagues about the dead mouse: "Does he still love his Mom?" This question provoked especially widespread continuity responding and not just among kindergartners. The majority of elementary school children and even the majority of adults claimed that this emotion would continue beyond death.

By contrast, children and adults alike were less likely to say that the mouse was still scared of the predatory, mouse-eating alligator.

The second prediction is that children who are not exposed to talk about the afterlife of the dead will be unlikely to display a dualist stance. Consider, for example, young children growing up in the Vezo community. Although they may be present during burial ceremonies and rituals, they are given little information about their import. Indeed, as described by Rita Astuti in Chapter 1, adults believe that it is dangerous for young children to learn about the world of the ancestors. At the same time, Vezo children can observe the biological facts of death for themselves. They are likely to be present when fish, birds, or oxen are killed for food or in the context of a ritual. Thus, young Vezo children are likely to understand the way that death terminates obvious vital functions such as movement, breathing, and sentience; but they are not likely to have any insight into what lies beyond the tomb in the eyes of the adult community, namely the ancestral afterlife. To assess these expectations, Vezo children aged five and seven years of age were interviewed about the death of a bird and the death of a person (Astuti & Harris, 2008). As in the studies described earlier, they were asked a mix of questions about the extent to which various bodily and mental questions would continue after death. The findings were clear-cut. There was no trace of any dualist thinking by either age group. There was, however, a clear age change. The younger children replied unsystematically whether they were asked about mental or bodily functions. The seven-year-olds, on the other hand, claimed that most functions would cease at death, and they made that claim just as often for mental functions as for bodily functions.

In summary, children and adults are more likely to expect mental processes to continue after death than bodily processes. This dualist tendency is, if anything, more obvious among adults than children, indicating a role for cultural learning. By contrast, the proposal that very young children naturally adopt a dualist stance is not well supported. That stance may be apparent among young children in Europe and North America, but it is not found among young Vezo children. By implication, its early appearance is not attributable to a cognitive default, but rather to children's exposure to, and acceptance of, the afterlife beliefs of their community.

## CONCLUSION

By going beyond children's developing grasp of the biological lifecycle to probe their ideas about the afterlife, we arrive not just at a richer understanding of children's understanding of death, we also arrive at a richer understanding of the nature of cognitive development. I underline two points.

Neither in Spain nor in Madagascar is there evidence that the emerging spiritual or religious conception of death ends up displacing an earlier biological conception. Instead, the two conceptions coexist. Much influential research on cognitive development has focused on the notion of conceptual displacement – for example the displacement of early, intuitive ideas about the shape of the earth by later, scientifically accurate ideas about its sphericity. Research on children's understanding of death shows, however, that such displacement is far from inevitable. The child's mind is a bit like a city. There are ancient structures. Alongside those, there are more modern and recently built structures. Both may be habitable and in daily use.

Dualistic thinking about death is clearly widespread – it is found in Christian and non-Christian cultures, and it is found among adults as well as children. Nevertheless, we found no trace of dualistic thinking among young Vezo children, arguably because they are shielded from the life of the ancestors. Further collaboration between developmental psychologists and anthropologists is likely to help us understand both the frequency of dualistic thinking and its absence.

### ACKNOWLEDGMENTS

I thank Jesse Bering, Paul Bloom, Carl Johnson, and Michael Schleifer for very helpful discussion of this chapter, especially concerning the possible link between an early propensity toward dualism and the belief in an afterlife.

### REFERENCES

Astuti, R. & Harris, P.L. (2008). Understanding mortality and the life of the ancestors in Madagascar. *Cognitive Science, 32*, 713–740.

Bering, J.M. & Bjorklund, D.F. (2004). The natural emergence of reasoning about the afterlife as a developmental regularity. *Developmental Psychology, 40*, 217–233.

Bering, J.M., Hernández Blasi, C., & Bjorklund, D.F. (2005). The development of "afterlife" beliefs in religiously and secularly schooled children. *British Journal of Developmental Psychology, 23*, 587–607.

Bloom, P. (2004). *Descartes' baby.* New York, NY: Basic Books.

Bovon, F. (2010). The soul's comeback: Immortality and resurrection in early Christianity. *Harvard Theological Review, 103*, 387–406.

Boyer, P. (2001). *Religion explained.* New York, NY: Basic Books.

Brent, S.B., Speece, M.W., Lin, C., Dong, Q., & Yang, C. (1996). The development of the concept of death among Chinese and U.S. children 3–17 years of age: From binary to "fuzzy" concepts? *Omega, 33,* 67–83.

Corriveau, K., Pasquini, E.S., & Harris, P.L. (2005). "If it's in your mind, it's in your knowledge": Children's developing anatomy of identity. *Cognitive Development, 20,* 321–340.

Evans, E.M. (2008). Conceptual change and evolutionary biology: A developmental analysis. In S. Vosniadou (Ed.), *International handbook of research on conceptual change* (pp. 263–294). New York, NY: Routledge.

Gottfried, G.M., Gelman, S.A., & Shultz, J. (1999). Children's understanding of the brain. From early essentialism to biological theory. *Cognitive Development, 14,* 147–174.

Greeley, A.M. & Hout, M. (1999). Americans' increasing belief in life after death: Religious competition and acculturation. *American Sociological Review, 64,* 813–835.

Harris, P.L. & Giménez, M. (2005). Children's acceptance of conflicting testimony: The case of death. *Journal of Cognition and Culture, 5,* 143–164.

Johnson, C.N. (1990). If you had my brain, where would I be? Children's understanding of the brain and identity. *Child Development, 61,* 962–972.

Johnson, C.N. & Wellman, H.M. (1982). Children's developing conceptions of the mind and brain. *Child Development, 53,* 223–234.

Keynon, B.L. (2001). Current research in children's conceptions of death: A critical review. *Omega, 43,* 63–91.

Legare, C.H. & Gelman, S.A. (2008). Bewitchment, biology, or both: The co-existence of natural and supernatural explanatory frameworks across development. *Cognitive Science, 32,* 607–642.

Speece, M.W. & Brent, S.B. (1992). The acquisition of a mature understanding of three components of the concept of death. *Death Studies, 16,* 211–229.

Slaughter, V., Jaakola, R., & Carey, S. (1999). Constructing a coherent theory: Children's biological understanding of life and death. In M. Siegal & C. Peterson (Eds.), *Children's understanding of biology, health, and ethics* (pp. 71–96). Cambridge: Cambridge University Press.

Slaughter, V. & Lyons, M. (2003). Learning about life and death in early childhood. *Cognitive Psychology, 46,* 1–30.

Twain, M. (2004). *The best short stories of Mark Twain.* New York, NY: The Modern Library.

Wenestram, C.G. & Wass, H. (1987). Swedish and U.S. children's thinking about death: A qualitative study and cross-cultural comparison. *Death Studies, 11,* 99–121.

# 3

## Ambivalent Teaching and Painful Learning:
## Mastering the Facts of Life (?)

BENJAMIN BEIT-HALLAHMI

These reflections on death awareness in children and adults are informed by observations about the human capacity to account for all events through anthropocentrism, that is, creating pleasant fantasies sometimes known as religion. Death has always been the most important challenge to our natural anthropocentrism. Still, our intuitive way of placing each one of us, and humanity as a whole, at the center of the universe, although constantly challenged, is never defeated. More recently, humanity has managed to develop some nonanthropocentric ideas about nature and our place in it, including death, but these new ideas may coexist with more traditional notions.

My reflections will be presented in a series of binary oppositions: traditional death awareness versus modernity; the wish to protect versus the duty to educate; mature understanding versus Innocence; basic research versus the grief context; biological death versus the bypassing of the biological; and universality versus death of self.

### TRADITIONAL DEATH AWARENESS VERSUS MODERNITY

Modern culture has been described and criticized as a web of ideas that avoids at any cost the recognition of death as part of life. There have been charges that modernity means the belief in the abolition of death. One major critic of modernity stated: "Our modern model of death was born and developed in places that gave birth to two beliefs: first, the belief in a nature that seemed to eliminate death; next, the belief in a technology that would replace nature and eliminate death" (Ariès, 1981, p. 595). Prior (1997) stated, "... in the modern world, the explanation of death (one of the great imponderables of life) in terms of a set of distinct and limited number of disease forms helps to generate the illusion that death can somehow be

41

controlled," (p. 188) and ignored the fact that life expectancy has gone up dramatically and that most infectious diseases have been controlled.

The denial of death is often considered one aspect of our being cut off and alienated from nature and from natural processes. Gorer (1965) stated: "The natural processes of corruption and decay have become disgusting, as disgusting as the natural processes of birth and copulation were a century ago.... ugly facts are relentlessly hidden; the art of the embalmers is an art of complete denial" (p.51). According to Gorer, with the decline of the belief in immortality, the finality of death and the dissolution of the physical body, too frightful to face, had to be denied through other means. Thus, American mortuary practices include embalming and the preparation of the corpse for institutionalized "viewing," which requires the services of beauticians and hairdressers. The "viewing" ritual is the chance to say farewell and preserve an image of the dear departed at his or her best, which sometimes demands real ingenuity. Morticians are proud of their ability to take a mangled body and head and make them not just presentable, but attractive. Industrialization, urbanization, the decline of the family, and secularization are said to have created the sanitized and commodified American way of death (Farrell, 1980). A British observer, Jessica Mitford (1963), is often credited with first diagnosing this phenomenon, but it was actually another Briton, Evelyn Waugh (1948), who first satirized the American institution of the commercial funeral in *The Loved One*, which was made into a fine film in 1965.

The modern way of handling mortality consists of distancing daily life from the physical events of dying, death, and the disposal of dead bodies, coupled with full recognition of the finality of death, and with no illusions about the survival of the self or personal identity. We can observe a historical process of moving away from being involved in handling the dead, which used to be a task shared by all, to the modern anonymity and professionalization of final disposal. The way death is talked about to children is said to follow these modern ideologies and ideals, and so modern culture has been accused of making extraordinary efforts to hide the reality of death from both children and adults.

There is no doubt that the facts of life were within sight of children during most of humanity's existence. The reality of suffering and mortality was never hidden. When traditions of processing the dead were being developed tens of thousands of years ago, children were always in close proximity. In the small human communities of the Stone Age and in all human communities until recent times, death occurred in the family. Children witnessed every phase of dying, death, disposing of the corpse, and mourning rituals.

This was especially true when other children were the dead, and the death of children used to be a common occurrence. This is still true for tens of millions of children today.

In traditional cultures, all ceremonies of processing the dead are public and involve the family and the community (see, for example, Chapter 1 by Rita Astuti). Thus, among the Amazonian Yanamomo, children, as part of the whole community, take part in the *reahu* (funeral feast), where the ashes of dead relatives are consumed in plantain soup (Hames, 1995). Among the South Fore of New Guinea, mortuary practices once involved women cannibalizing the bodies of dead relatives, especially their brains, with their own children in tow. That is why both women and children fell victim to the *kuru prion* disease (Gajdusek, 1973). These are extreme and unusual examples, but in many other cultures, the dead are buried at or very close to home, and their remains are kept in sight.

Throughout history, an encounter with the reality of death for children has meant seeing a family member's dead body, most often another child. What should be emphasized is that death in childhood used to be so common that children used to know it intimately. The revolution in human existence that we have recently experienced has for the first time decisively connected death to old age. This truly amazing change in the lives of humans and its effects on the way we think about death is noted in the following statement:

> The problem of the *meaning* of death is coming ... to be concentrated about death occurring as the completion of a normal life cycle ... This central, irreducible problem *is becoming disentangled from* the problem of adjusting to deaths that occur earlier in the life cycle, particularly in infancy and early childhood, which was more general in the premodern period. (Parsons & Lidz, 1967, p. 137)

What we are being told here is nothing short of astounding. Humans had to deal with the meaning of death for many millennia, when they were faced with concrete deaths in large numbers among the young and the very young. Now all this has changed. The success of biomedicine over the past two centuries has changed the basic meaning of life and death for children (and for adults). Not only our way of thinking about death, but also the reality of dying, has been transformed. Modernity means not only the medicalization of birth and dying, but that birth itself is no longer surrounded by death. The meaning of birth itself has changed with the connection between sex and procreation, now under human control in both contraception and fertilization. On the one hand, biomedicine has separated sexuality from procreation, and on the other, it has severed the intimate connection between childhood and death through the medicalization of birth and infancy. This is a revolution in the human life experience that we are still in the process of assimilating.

These stunning changes are related to the fact that more and more people no longer believe in souls; thus they no longer believe that souls are powerful, or that souls of the departed need to be cared for. Biomedicine, which has done much to decrease, if not eliminate, suffering and anxiety has undoubtedly affected the power of religion, because the level of everyday anxiety about what used to be common misfortunes was reduced, and supernaturalist claims about causes of suffering were rejected. It is the recognition of death in its irreversibility and universality that has led humanity's efforts to alleviate suffering and delay death. Today we know that certain suffering can be totally prevented if it is the result of just human action, and that nature-caused suffering can be reduced. Death cannot be abolished, but it can be delayed, and this is what medicine and the life sciences are all about.

The whole idea of teaching children about death is a modern, secular idea, reflecting the fact that children no longer witness death as a common occurrence. The great tragedy is that the biomedical revolution has still not reached most of the world's children, and so what was the reality of death and death awareness in the First World hundreds of years ago is still the reality for most of humanity. Most of the research on death awareness and children has been done among the fortunate segment of humanity that has enjoyed the benefits of the biomedical revolution.

The CIA World Fact Book provides a list of 224 nations and territories ranked by life expectancy. Canada is number eight, Israel is number thirteen, and the United States, where biomedicine is mostly profit-driven, is number fifty. We know that in those nations ranked below fifty, children are more likely to witness death just the way they have done since time immemorial. For them death is a physical reality, never hidden or denied. They learn its cultural meanings, but what they need more than explanations is access to biomedicine. In Swaziland, with a life expectancy at birth of 31.99 years, ranked 224, no one is talking about death denial. This is a luxury only those at the top can enjoy.

### THE WISH TO PROTECT VERSUS THE DUTY TO EDUCATE

Do we want children to know the whole truth about dying and death? Do we want to share the whole truth about evil and suffering short of death, and do we always want to share the whole truth about sex?

In the twenty-first century, we are not only better at hiding death through medicalization, we are also much better at delaying it; and we are able to protect our children not only by denial, but by offering real help. Even when children witness the physical reality of death and dying, they still have to learn its meaning, cultural and biological. In earlier times and in many traditional cultures today, children saw the dying and dead but learned that biological changes were not the end of the self.

Today, to become an adult, you must realize the finality, irreversibility, and universality of death. We would expect a twelve-year-old in any culture to have that knowledge, unless serious cognitive disabilities are in evidence (Kastenbaum & Costa, 1977; Kenyon, 2001). This is then a developmental milestone, but unlike other milestones in the acquisition of cultural knowledge, learning about death is never celebrated, and teaching about death is always done with a heavy heart. Both are marked by ambivalence, anxiety, confusion, and denial.

Most often "the facts of life" mean sexuality and procreation, but we know that death is really the most important fact of life. Learning about death could indeed be compared to learning about sexuality. In both cases, even with the assimilation and absorption of facts, we are left with an emotional force field surrounding them, dominated by anxieties and confusion. Part of what is conveyed to the child in the case of death, as in the case of sex, is our own anxiety coupled with the wish to protect those in our charge. Children are assumed to be innocent when they lack the adult knowledge of sexuality or death.

The idea of childhood as a time of innocence, ending with the painful discovery of sex and death, is best known in our culture through the myth of the Garden of Eden. There, discovering the facts of life is punished as a sin and leads humankind to eternal damnation. Many similar stories are told all over the world, expressing the idea that death and suffering are meted out to humanity because of ancient sins.

The Garden of Eden myth of painful awakening from innocence brings to mind a gripping and powerful tale about a young man raised in the luxury of a royal palace without a worry in the world, and who one day is shocked to discover that disease, old age, and death exist. This loss of innocence leads him to give up family ties and worldly possessions in search of the meaning of human existence, and transforms him into the founder of a new religion.

Prince Siddhartha Gautama, son of Suddhodana, the ruler of Kapilavatthu at the foothills of the Himalayas, married and the father of one son, renounced the princely life at age twenty-nine. The prince's life started with loss when his mother died after his birth. The king consulted a soothsayer about his son's future and was told that he would become either a great king or a savior of humanity. The father was determined to shield the child from anything that might result in entering the religious life, and so Siddhartha was prevented from being exposed to suffering. Only beauty and health surrounded him, as he was not permitted to see the elderly, the sickly, the dead, or anyone devoted to religion.

Siddhartha grew up to be a strong and handsome young man. When it came time for him to marry, he won the hand of a beautiful princess by beating all competitors at sports. Yashodhara and Siddhartha got married when both were sixteen. As Siddhartha continued living in the luxury of his palaces, he grew restless and curious about the world and finally demanded to see his people and his lands. The king made sure that only young and healthy people should greet the prince. As he was led through Kapilavatthu he saw a couple of old men who had accidentally wandered into the scene. Amazed and bewildered, he chased them to find out what they were. Then he came across some people who were severely ill. Finally, he came across a funeral pyre, and for the first time in his life he saw death. He also saw a monk who had renounced all the pleasures of the flesh and had a peaceful look on his face. This series of discoveries transformed Siddhartha. After kissing his sleeping wife and newborn son Rahula goodbye, he sneaked out of the palace at midnight and began to practice the austerities and self-mortifications of an ascetic.

This fantasy is about all of us, and we find ourselves in Siddhartha's story as both children and parents. As parents we are all King Suddhodana, Siddhartha's loving father, who wishes to protect his son from the trauma he is destined to face. As children and adults, we are all Siddhartha, who represents all of humanity in its journey of bitter discovery. We can easily imagine ourselves as this young man walking through the marketplace in Kapilavatthu, surrounded by his father's loyal servants, who are charged with blocking his view so that he would not encounter any unpleasant sights. Two motifs stand out: the father's responsibility for hiding the facts of life from his son, and the immediate discovery of these facts as soon as the son enters the real world (cf. Beit-Hallahmi, 1976). The Buddha legend reminds us that in order to keep children from learning the reality of suffering, we must erect high walls and keep them in virtual imprisonment.

Should children be grateful to modern parents for delaying the moment of truth and shielding them from the harsh facts of life? As children, we have been through Siddhartha's discoveries and disillusionment. Who among us would not have wished to delay knowing the facts of death until age twenty-nine? The problem is that we have all discovered the facts of life and death too early. Too soon have we seen suffering and death, and too soon have we realized that death awaits all of us. No one is a prince, but we all undergo the process of princely disillusionment.

For our discussion, the most important aspect of the myth is the wish to shield children from the reality of death, which seems to be an ancient and permanent part of parental consciousness. The expression *ad usum Delphini* ("for the use of the *Dauphin*") referred to Greek and Roman classics that Louis XIV had expurgated of offensive or improper parts, mostly sexual, to be read by his heir apparent, the *Dauphin*. What was hidden from Prince Siddhartha was not sex, but aging, illness, pain, and death.

The Siddhartha story combines the fantasy of a pain-free childhood with the reality of recognizing death and suffering to be a permanent part of existence. The father is at the center in this parable of betrayal, mourning, and disillusionment. Siddhartha's father wanted to protect his child, but then Siddhartha found himself alone and unprepared when facing the discovery of suffering and death. The response to parental betrayal is not only the rejection of the father and of princely life, but also the desertion of his own nuclear family following this crisis. One moral of the story here is that parents should not try to hide the truth of life and death from children, because children will perceive it as a betrayal. A story about a father who is determined to hide the reality of suffering and death from his son was naturally absurd when it was first being told probably 2,000 years ago, but it expressed a universal yearning on the part of all parents. It telescopes a long natural process in a concentrated, dramatic way. The normal developmental process, which is gradual, is actually denied by presenting it as sudden, and the moment of discovery becomes a major crisis.

The discovery of death is indeed (as the Siddhartha story reminds us) the worst disillusionment we face in life, both ontogenetically, as individuals, and phylogenetically, as humanity. Humanity's understandable emotions about this cognitive task have never been expressed better than in this myth. The moment of discovery leads the Prince to reassess and renegotiate his relationship with the world and with his father. The Siddhartha story is an absurd fantasy, like all mythology, but we are entranced with it because we can find ourselves in it (cf. Beit-Hallahmi, 2010).

MATURE UNDERSTANDING VERSUS INNOCENCE

As adults, we know about the facts of life – about birth, death, and all that leads from one to the other – or so we believe. Growing up means gaining full knowledge of those secrets kept from children about pleasure and pain, sex and death; and it also means disillusionment as we discover the facts of life and are disabused of the innocence-ignorance of childhood.

Despite the anxieties involved on all sides, there is a seemingly uniform and universal process by which children learn the facts of death. An adult understanding for our purposes means grasping the biological meaning of death as internal to the organism (Safier, 1964). This, as endorsed by Kastenbaum and Costa (1977) means knowing "the concept of both life and death as internal to the organism" (p. 232). We don't expect children or most adults to understand the physiology of death (Nuland, 1994), but we do expect them to demonstrate that they know it's an inherently biological process.

Systematic observations have shown that children are aware of death quite early on, and that recognition of the finality, universality, nonfunctionality, and causality of death occurs between the ages of seven and ten (Adams & Deveau, 1995; Barrett & Behne, 2005; Orbach, Gross, Glaubman & Berman, 1986; Slaughter & Lyons 2003; Slaughter, Jaakola & Carey, 1999; Speece & Brent, 1984; Speece & Brent, 1992). There is some evidence that ideas of death develop separately for humans and for animals, and those about humans develop first (Smilansky, 1987).

The exposure hypothesis, implicit and explicit in the research literature, suggests that illness, loss, direct observation of dying, or living in a violent environment will affect the development of death awareness. The evidence about the effects of life-threatening illness seems equivocal (Clunies-Ross & Lansdown, 1988; Jay, Green, Johnson, Caldwell & Nitschke, 1987), and the experience of parental loss does not seem to contribute to achieving a mature conceptualization (Smilansky, 1981, 1987).

Israel has been rightly perceived as one society where children grow up with exposure to violent death, and much research has been done on Israeli children. As is well known, the state of Israel has been at a state of permanent war with the indigenous population of West Asia since its beginnings (Beit-Hallahmi, 1992, 1993; Bunzl & Beit-Hallahmi, 2002). This situation creates a "widespread confrontation with death" (Smilansky, 1987, p. 19) and a pervasive anxiety about the collective future.

Research has shown that Israeli children perform better than children in the United States in all grade levels with respect to two components, that of irreversibility and the combined death concept scores. No significant differences were noted for the remaining factors of causality, inevitability, and old age (Schonfeld & Smilansky, 1989; Smilansky, 1989). In a study of Israeli children living with their families on an airbase and whose fathers serve as pilots and navigators, it was found that such children, even at age four and five, were far more advanced in their death concepts compared to city children (Smilansky, 1987). This difference was explained in terms of the greater exposure to death in the case of children from aircrew families. These children live in a close-knit neighborhood, where cases of death in accidents or in combat reverberate through the community. They become aware of the danger their fathers are exposed to through their mothers and through the constant talk around them. It should be noted that most of the children in the Israeli studies come from a more secularized, Westernized background.

McWhirter, Young, and Majury (1983) reported that children in Northern Ireland achieved a mature conception of death earlier than expected. Wenestam and Wass (1987) found considerable similarities in the ways that Swedish and U.S. children depicted death. However, more Swedish children depicted traditional practices and symbols, and more U.S. children depicted violent causes of death, presumably reflecting media images that children are exposed to in the United States.

Support for the exposure hypothesis seems more clear-cut when we look at the effects of collective violence and violent imagery, in which powerful social learning seems to show its effects. In the case of individual illness, what may affect the findings are individual differences in resilience.

BASIC RESEARCH VERSUS THE GRIEF CONTEXT

Why is teaching about the biological reality of death important? The humanist answer is that the promotion of illusions must be rejected in principle, regardless of their supposed benefits. However, it can be argued that learning about death is not a matter of enlightenment, cognition, or intellectual achievement, but in reality is a preparation for the inevitable losses and mourning we are going to face in life. With respect to children, the case for knowing biological reality as necessary for adjustment to loss has been presented from a perspective of urgency and necessity (cf. Haine, Ayers, Sandler & Wolchik, 2008).

The explicit stance here is that a child raised with denial will experience shock similar to the crisis described in the Siddhartha myth. Children being raised with death denial will not be ready for death and loss when they have to face it, but those with mature knowledge will cope better with the task of bereavement.

Smilansky (1987) states that mastering the reality of death and its full meaning are prerequisite for optimal mourning, followed by recovery, in children. She then elaborates on the need to avoid illusions and explains how each component of mature conceptualization will play a role in coping. Without achieving the conviction of finality and irreversibility, real mourning is illusory, and the child will suffer. Understanding causality is important to avoid blame. If death has resulted from disease, accident, or bullets, you cannot blame the dead for their fate. Realizing the universality of death will also reduce blaming the dead and blaming oneself, which does appear in children after the loss of a parent. Work with Israeli orphans seems to indicate that their loss has found them unprepared to cope, and this suggests that death education should be attempted formally at a young age (Smilansky, 1987). Slaughter and Griffiths (2007) found some support for the hypothesis that teaching children about death and dying in biological terms may be effective in alleviating their fear of death.

In this context, the most dramatic claim has been that distorted notions of death may be tied to self-destructive actions in children. Cuddy-Casey and Orvaschel (1997) reported that suicidal children may possess distorted and less mature concepts of death. Such distortions may even make death look more attractive and less permanent to some suicidal children.

## BIOLOGICAL DEATH VERSUS THE BYPASSING OF BIOLOGY

The encounter with death has been hypothesized as the starting point of all religions:

> The testimony of the senses, the gruesome decomposition of the corpse, the visible disappearance of the personality – certain apparently instinctive suggestions of fear and horror seem to threaten man at all stages of culture with some idea of annihilation, with some hidden fears and forebodings. And here into this play of emotional forces, into this supreme dilemma of life and final death, religion steps in, selecting the positive creed, the comforting view, the culturally valuable belief in immortality, in the spirit independent of the body, and in the continuance of life after death (Malinowski, 1925, pp. 49–50).

Freud (1915) presented a highly similar hypothesis about the encounter with death and the beginnings of religion and culture (cf. Beit-Hallahmi, 1996; Freud, 1927). It was William James (1902/1961) who already stated that "Religion, in fact, for the great majority of our own race, *means* immortality and nothing else" (p. 406). The main implication of the belief in the world of the spirits, common to all religions, is the denial of death as final, and that is one of religion's main attractions (Beit-Hallahmi, 1989; Beit-Hallahmi & Argyle, 1997).

Religion, whether it be shamanism or Protestantism, rises from our apprehension of death. To give meaning to meaninglessness is the endless quest of religion ... Clearly we possess religion, if we want to, precisely to obscure the truth of our perishing.... When death becomes the center, then religion begins. (Bloom, 1992, p. 29)

Frazer described religion, with "the almost universal belief in the survival of the human spirit after death" (Frazer, 1933–6, p. v) at its center, as resulting from the fear of the dead, which is the fear of death itself. Frazer (1933–6) stated that he was

> not concerned with the belief in immortality as it is taught in the higher religions ... [but with] that momentous belief as it meets us in what I call primitive religion, by which, roughly speaking, I mean the religion of the backward or uncivilized races; in other words, savages and barbarians. (p. 4)

He was soon forced to admit that so-called civilized cultures harbored beliefs indistinguishable from those of "savages and barbarians." The terror of death leads to the creation of powerful psychological and cultural mechanisms, and the survival value of denial and evolutionary optimism is clear (Beit-Hallahmi & Argyle, 1997). The denial of death does have an adaptive value for humans and human culture. Religious ideas, which are about death, and which humans rely on most often when facing death, express denial most directly and clearly.

What is conspicuous in most critiques of modern culture is the notion that the denial of death is somehow a modern, recent development. The supernaturalism that is part of religion is not considered denial. Omitted is the fact that the most common way of denying death is the religious one. Religious claims about an immortal soul and a bodily resurrection, taken seriously by billions, are ignored. Modernity means secular self-reflection and self-critique. This critical tendency misses the mark when it assumes that there are no continuities in the human condition. This is supposedly a description of something uniquely modern, but such a trite portrayal may fit any individual and any culture we can imagine.

The seeming complexity and diversity of mortuary practices in different times and places can still be understood as expressions of denial and avoidance. If modern Westerners are deniers, so were ancient Egyptians, who put so much energy into the preparation of the dead for a long future believed to lie ahead of them.

Within the religious framework, death is not a singular event occurring only once in the history of the individual, but rather a transition from one form of existence to another. All religions state that death itself is only a passage, a transition point in the existence of the soul as it comes out of a particular human body. Different religions offer differing accounts of the soul's farther movements, whether up to heaven (or down to hell), or to another human body, a nonhuman body, or an inanimate object. Most religions promise a return of the particular soul (or even a particular body) to earthly and much improved existence, but this safe trip through eternity is reserved only for loyal followers of a specific doctrine.

What religious traditions offer us are not just claims about "the future of the dead" (McCullers, 1940, p. 188), but also explanations about the causes of death. Religions explain not only death, but quite often particular concrete deaths tied to angry gods and spirits. Humans have been most likely to explain disease and death as resulting from divine retribution and the acts of evil spirits (Murdock, 1980). Humans would rather believe that disease and misfortune are caused by the will of the gods and the spirits and not by impersonal pathogens. The supernaturalist way of explaining our lives and deaths easily triumphs over the naturalist one, because ideas about the "spiritual" causation still dominate humanity's thoughts about health and illness. A.D. White (1896/1993) suggested that it was human frustration with the inability of religious means for stopping illness that led to the coming of biological research.

Could any ideology other than religion enable humans to face death? Some secular ideologies such as nationalism clearly do that, but they do not ever promise fallen heroes immortality or resurrection. Religion offers an individual and a collective victory over death. The individual victory comes with the soul's survival of bodily death. The collective victory will come with cosmic salvation, the Eschaton, the coming of a messiah, and the end of human existence in this vale of tears: "One short sleep past, we wake eternally/ And Death shall be no more: Death, thou shalt die!" (Donne, 1610)

The future of religion may be the future of the belief in immortality; yet on June 7, 1933, James George Frazer (1933–6), an unbeliever, expressed his expectation that in the long run science will undermine that belief:

> ... an impartial observer might be tempted to conclude that the spirits of the dead exist only in the imagination of the fond and foolish portion of mankind; but this conclusion, so little consonant with the natural wishes, and perhaps the instincts, of humanity, is not likely to be ever popular, and it seems probable that the great majority of our species will continue to acquiesce in a belief so flattering to human vanity and so comforting to human sorrow.... But the batteries of science have an ever longer range, and on this side they may yet make a deep breach in the frowning bastions of faith. (pp. v–vi)

Religions offer us an elegant solution in which physical death is just part of the story and the self lives on as the soul. Are children or adults in religious cultures troubled by what outsiders like us regard as an inconsistency? This may happen only when they become aware of the issue. Religious accounts of the soul offer a way of bypassing the seeming opposition by contrasting the ephemeral body with our own consciousness and our own personality, which are eternal.

One thing that biological thinking eliminates is the religious notion of human biological superiority, according to which both human creation and human death are unique. The biological conception of death, with its finality and irreversibility, is a decidedly secular idea that goes against the religious claim that death is not really the end, and not all researchers and educators are ready to embrace it (cf. Klatt, 1991). It is clear that the mature conceptualization discussed by researchers is totally secular (Smilansky, 1987).

Does the opposition between biology and religion have an impact on children's development? Do traditional religious teachings undermine children's attainment of the notions of irreversibility, finality, universality, and causality because of their culturally learned illusions about eternal souls? Does this opposition mean that children (and adults) in traditional cultures do not attain a realistic ("mature") concept of death, because they take part in rituals of communication with the spirits of dead family members?

Bowlby (1980) suggested that religious beliefs about the afterlife and reincarnation will inhibit the acquisition of accurate death concepts, because religious claims run counter to those cognitive achievements and specifically to the concepts of finality and irreversibility. The question of interference or competition from religious ideas has been investigated. Kenyon (2001) stated that practices that emphasize noncorporeal continuity or an afterlife appear to influence children's concept of irreversibility. Brent, Lin, Speece, Dong, and Yang (1996) found that a higher percentage of Chinese children than American children understood the concepts of irreversibility and nonfunctionality, and American children provided more nonnaturalistic explanations for death. This was explained as the result of exposure to Christian ideas. We also find some evidence that modernization and secularization affect the achievement of a mature biological understanding. Florian and Kravetz (1985) compared children coming from four religious traditions. There were clear differences, with the rank order of achieving biological conceptualization being Jewish, Christian, Moslem, and Druze. This was interpreted as the result of differences in the degree to which children had internalized the Western (biological) concept of death and was correlated with the degree of secularization in each cultural group (cf. Wass, Guenther, & Towry, 1979).

These findings, which suggest an opposition between biological and religious conceptions of death, are seriously challenged by another approach that claims that these conceptions are context dependent. Both children and adults differentiate between biological ideas about the end of the physical body and its vital processes and religious ideas about the continuing existence of the soul. Recent cross-cultural research has shown that children as well as adults use biological and religious concepts in different contexts and as parts of two different modes of discourse (Astuti & Harris, 2008; Harris, Chapter 2; Harris & Giménez, 2005; Harris & Koenig, 2006; Kenyon, 2001; Richert & Harris, 2006). Moreover, religious ideas appear later than biological ones. What we observe are contextualized cognitions, learned in specific contexts, and then used in specific ways and in culturally approved contexts. In all cultures, the biological, pragmatic view of dead bodies coexists with the belief in an afterlife in which human souls may live forever and even human bodies may function in modified form (Harris, Chapter 2). The work by Harris and his colleagues teaches us an important lesson about the selective and context-dependent way in which humans use religious ideas. As we know quite well, religious ideation, although illusory, does not automatically hamper adjustment and sometimes even aids it. This is possible precisely because of its selective use (Beit-Hallahmi & Argyle, 1997).

UNIVERSALITY VERSUS DEATH OF SELF

We can imagine a line separating innocent (or ignorant) children on one side, and on the other side, all those children and adults who understand the finality, irreversibility, and universality of death. This imaginary line of separation pervades the literature. This concept of transformation from childhood to maturity is reflected in some religious writings: "When I was a child, I spake as a child, I understood as a child, I thought as a child: but when I became a man, I put away childish things" (1 Cor. 13:11). This seems like a naïve view today, and here is a modern retort by Edna St. Vincent Millay: "Childhood is not from birth to a certain age and at a certain age the child is grown, and puts away childish things. Childhood is the kingdom where nobody dies." Are we sure that adults or children over the age of twelve really know the truth about death and accept it? The existence of so many cultural fantasies about immortality prove that they do not (cf. Beit-Hallahmi, 2010). Some have diagnosed an adult "acceptance gap" between cognition and emotion:

> On the intellectual–conscious level we accept death, since we are cognizant of "reality" and are therefore reminded that at any moment "we may be struck down." The unconscious-emotional level does not allow us to "feel" death, however and it thereby provides a "delusion of invulnerability" which compels us to deny death by conceptualizing it as infinitely distant. (Dumont & Foss, 1972, p. 106)

This gap between cognition and emotion in the acceptance of death among adults is reported by researchers who found that children and adults are not always so different (Brent & Speece, 1993; Kenyon, 2001).

Yet there is an illusion and a gap in the way we think about death that is permanent and inevitable. Here we look at a universal illusion that cannot be blamed on supernaturalism. What happens when we realize that death is not just universal, but personal, and is going to reach us and become our final destination? Can we apply the general, mature knowledge of death to ourselves?

Sigmund Freud (1915) stated that there is a clear psychological distinction between the attitude toward one's own death and toward the loss of others by death, so that even as adults we deny our own death.

Wittgenstein (1921/1974) famously observed that "Death is not an event in life. Death is not lived through" (p. 6,431), but Freud (1915) described the basic cognitive issue: "It is indeed impossible to imagine our own death; and whenever we attempt to do so we can perceive that we are in fact still present as spectators" (p. 289). The final disappearance of one's self is simply inconceivable. As a result,

> the adult person assumes the rational idea (knowledge) of death as the irrevocable end of physical existence. This idea, when made conscious, is most of all loaded with anxiety or fear. And it can be called normal that one tries to cope with this anxiety by means of the mechanism of repression or denial. (Corvelyn, 1996, p. 63)

When others die, there can be many kinds of reactions. The knowledge of death as the end coexists with a basic fantasy of immortality about the self. This "makes it psychologically understandable that man doesn't show in fact much concern about death and finitude in his everyday life, in spite of his rational knowledge about it. This kind of narcissism gives him a sound vitality" (Corvelyn, 1996, p. 62). This strategy of narcissistic denial may be the only choice before us: "The major coping mechanism is negation or denial. This coping strategy is not pathological, it makes life livable, even under the worst of circumstances" (p. 61). These statements refer to adults, but we may wonder about the age in which this illusion takes shape.

The personal immortality illusion looks like one of those "childish things" that adults never give up.

We have observed here two kinds of dual cognitions held simultaneously and operating in context. One has to do with the fuzzy religious denial of death, which operates by teaching children to hold beliefs about the eternal soul separate from the ephemeral physical body. The other is that of universal, natural narcissism, which creates an illusion of personal immortality once we learn that the facts of life and death apply to all humans. In these cases of duality and seeming gaps, which do not seem to cause real difficulties, both children and adults naturally operate within the universe of multiple cognitions. They easily cope with the opposition between supernaturalism and the finality of death, as well as the opposition between the universality of death and the immortal self.

We may now generalize about basic cognitive processes and observe that both children and adults can easily learn to entertain two seemingly inconsistent or contradictory ideas (or more) in their mind (cf. Harris, Chapter 2). It is likely that they are not bothered and don't think about them at the same time, but in a particular context or with some mental effort, they can handle the seeming contradiction. Only sometimes or rarely will this precipitate a crisis (Beit-Hallahmi, 2006–7; Freud, 1928). We know that humans easily compartmentalize what are experienced as contradictory cognitions, and it is an effective way of handling them without expending much psychic energy.

## CONCLUSION

In the world we know, viewing a dead body normally takes place after a long process of knowing about death in less concrete terms. The Siddhartha moment of sudden shock is no longer possible. We are all Suddhodana, Siddhartha's father, wishing to shield him from learning about death too early. Parents have always wanted to provide such protection for their children, but unlike the mythical king, we can offer our children both the opportunity to witness death only rarely and to prolong their own lives. The modern denial relies on biomedical technology, which has eliminated the connection between death and childhood.

Death still needs to be explained, and the biological understanding of our finality still has to compete with supernaturalist illusions. Modernity is self-critical, self-questioning, and self-doubting, and some may envy what look like the certainties of past times; but we know very well that those who promised eternal life could not deliver lower infant-mortality rates. The need to teach children about dying will be felt more strongly as biomedicine advances, while at the same time no technological progress will relieve the universal fear of death.

### ACKNOWLEDGMENTS

My colleagues Amiram Raviv, Israel Ohrbach, and Shimshon Rubin provided important help during the preparation of this chapter. The support of the University of Haifa Research Authority and the University of Haifa Library made the work possible.

### REFERENCES

Adams, D.W. & Deveau, E.J. (Eds.), (1995). *Beyond the innocence of childhood.* Amityville, NY: Baywood Publishing Co.

Ariès, P. (1981). *The hour of our death.* New York, NY: Alfred A. Knopf.

Astuti, R. & Harris, P.L. (2008). Understanding mortality and the life of the ancestors in Madagascar. *Cognitive Science, 32,* 713–740.

Barrett, C. & Behne, T. (2005). Children's understanding of death as the cessation of agency: A test using sleep versus death. *Cognition, 96,* 93–108.

Beit-Hallahmi, B. (1976). "The Turn of the Screw" and "The Exorcist:" Demoniacal possession and childhood purity. *American Imago, 3,* 296–303.

(1989). *Prolegomena to the psychological study of religion.* Lewisburg, PA: Bucknell University Press.

(1992). *Despair and deliverance: Private salvation in contemporary Israel.* Albany, NY: SUNY Press.

(1993). *Original sins: Reflections on the history of Zionism and Israel.* New York, NY: Interlink.

(1996). *Psychoanalytic studies of religion: Critical assessment and annotated bibliography.* Westport, CT: Greenwood Press.

(2006–2007). Triggering metamorphosis: Freud and Siddhartha. *Annual of Psychoanalysis, 34–35,* 151–163.

Beit-Hallahmi, B. (Ed.). (2010). *Psychoanalysis and theism: Critical reflections on the Grunbaum Thesis.* Lanham, MD: Jason Aronson.

Beit-Hallahmi, B. & Argyle, M. (1997). *The psychology of religious behaviour, belief and experience.* London, England: Routledge.

Bloom, H. (1992). *The American religion: The making of a post-Christian nation.* New York, NY: Simon & Schuster.

Bowlby, J. (1980). *Attachment and loss: Vol. 3. Loss, sadness and depression.* New York, NY: Basic Books.

Brent, S.B., Lin C., Speece, M.W., Dong, Q., & Yang, C. (1996). The development of the concept of death among Chinese and U.S. children 3–17 years of age: From binary to "fuzzy" concepts? *Omega: Journal of Death and Dying, 33,* 67–83.

Brent, S.B. & Speece, M.W. (1993). "Adult" conceptualization of irreversibility: Implications for the development of the concept of death. *Death Studies, 17,* 203–224.

Bunzl, J. & Beit-Hallahmi, B. (2002). *Psychoanalysis, identity, and ideology: Critical essays on the Israel/Palestine case.* Boston, MA: Kluwer.

Clunies-Ross, C. & Lansdown, R. (1988). Concepts of death, illness and isolation found in children with leukaemia. *Child: Care, Health, and Development, 14,* 373–386.

Corveleyn, J. (1996). The psychological explanation of religion as a wish-fulfilment. A test-case: the belief in immortality. In H. Grzymala–Moszczynska & B. Beit-Hallahmi (Eds.), *Religion, psychopathology, and coping.* Amsterdam, Netherlands: Rodopi.

Cuddy-Casey M. & Orvaschel, H. (1997). Children's understanding of death in relation to child suicidality and homicidality. *Clinical Psychology Review, 17,* 33–45.

Dumont, R.G. & Foss, D.C. (1972). *The American view of death: Acceptance or denial?* Cambridge, MA: Schenkman.

Farrell, J. (1980). *Inventing the American way of death, 1830–1920.* Philadelphia, PA: Temple University Press.

Florian, V. & Kravetz, S. (1985). Children's concepts of death: A cross cultural comparison among Muslims, Druze, Christians, and Jews in Israel. *Journal of Cross-Cultural Psychology, 16,* 174–189.

Frazer, J.G. (1933–1936). *The fear of the dead in primitive religion* (Vols. 1–3). London, England: Macmillan.

Freud, S. (1915). Thoughts for the times on war and death. In Freud, S. *The standard edition of the complete psychological works of Sigmund Freud, 14* (pp. 274–301). London, England: Hogarth Press.

    (1927). Future of an illusion. In Freud, S. *The standard edition of the complete psychological works of Sigmund Freud, 21* (pp. 3–56). London, England: Hogarth Press.

    (1928). A religious experience. In Freud, S. *The standard edition of the complete psychological works of Sigmund Freud, 21* (pp. 167–172). London, England: Hogarth Press.

Gajdusek, D.C. (1973). Kuru in the New Guinea Highlands. In J.D. Spillane (Ed.), *Tropical neurology* (pp. 270–282). New York, NY: Oxford University Press.

Gorer, G. (1955). The pornography of death. *Encounter, 5* (4), 49–52.

Haine, R.A., Ayers, T.S., Sandler, I.N., & Wolchik, S.A. (2008). Evidence-based practices for parentally bereaved children and their families. *Professional Psychology: Research and Practice, 39,* 113–121.

Hames, R. (1995). Yanomamö: Varying adaptations of foraging horticulturalists. In C.R. Ember & M. Ember (Eds.). *Just in time anthropology* (pp. 103–131). New York, NY: Simon & Schuster.

Harris, P.L. & Giménez, M. (2005). Children's acceptance of conflicting testimony: The case of death. *Journal of Cognition and Culture, 5,* 143–164.

Harris, P.L. & Koenig, M. (2006). Trust in testimony: How children learn about science and religion. *Child Development, 77,* 505–524.

James, W. (1902/1961). *The varieties of religious experience.* New York, NY: Collier.

Jay, S., Green, V., Johnson, S., Caldwell, S., & Nitschke, R. (1987). Differences in death concepts between children with cancer and physically healthy children. *Journal of Clinical Child Psychology, 46,* 301–306.

Kastenbaum, R. & Costa, P.T. Jr. (1977). Psychological perspectives on death. *Annual Review of Psychology, 28,* 225–249.

Kenyon, B.L. (2001). Current research in children's conception of death: A critical review. *Omega: Journal of Death and Dying, 43,* 63–91.

Klatt, H.J. (1991). In search of a mature concept of death. *Death Studies, 15,* 177–187.

Malinowski, B. (1925). Magic science and religion. In J. Needham (Ed.), *Science Religion and Reality* (pp. 19–64). London, England: The Sheldon Press.

McWhirter, L., Young, V., & Majury, J. (1983). Belfast children's awareness of violent death. *British Journal of Social Psychology, 22,* 81–92.

McCullers, C. (1940). *The heart is a lonely hunter.* Boston, MA: Houghton Mifflin.

Mitford, J. (1963). *The American way of death.* New York, NY: Simon & Schuster.

Murdock, G.P. (1980). *Theories of illness: A world survey.* Pittsburgh, PA: University of Pittsburgh Press.

Nuland, S.B. (1994). *How we die: Reflections on life's final chapter.* New York, NY: Knopf.

Orbach, I., Gross, Y., Glaubman, H., & Berman, D. (1986). Children's perception of various determinants of the death concept as a function of intelligence, age, and anxiety. *Journal of Clinical Psychology, 15,* 120–126.

Parsons, T. & Lidz, V. (1967). Death in American society. In E.S. Schneidman (Ed.), *Essays in self-destruction* (pp. 133–140). New York, NY: Science House.

Prior, L. (1997). Actuarial visions of death: Life, death and chance in the modern world. In P.C. Jupp & G. Howarth (Eds.). *The changing face of death: Historical accounts of death and dying* (pp. 177–193). New York, NY: St. Martin's Press.

Richert, R. A. & Harris, P. L. (2006). The ghost in my body: Children's developing concept of the soul. *Journal of Cognition and Culture, 6,* 409–427.

Safier, G. (1964). A study in relationships between life-death concepts in children. *Journal of Genetic Psychology, 105,* 238–295.

Schonfeld, D. & Smilansky, S. (1989). A cross cultural comparison of Israeli and American children's death concepts. *Death Studies, 13,* 593–604.

Slaughter, V. & Griffiths, M. (2007). Death understanding and fear of death in young children. *Clinical Child Psychology and Psychiatry, 12,* 4, 525–535.

Slaughter, V., Jaakola, R., & Carey, S. (1999). Constructing a coherent theory: Children's biological understanding of life and death. In M. Siegal & C.C. Peterson (Eds.), *Children's understanding of biology and health* (pp. 71–96). New York, NY: Cambridge University Press.

Slaughter, V. & Lyons, M. (2003). Learning about life and death in early childhood. *Cognitive Psychology, 46,* 1–30.

Smilansky, S. (1981). Different mourning patterns and the orphan's utilization of his intellectual ability to understand the concept of death. *Advances in Thanatology, 5,* 39–55.

   (1987). *On death: Helping children understand and cope.* New York, NY: Peter Lang.

Speece, M.W., & Brent, S.B. (1984). Children's understanding of death: A review of three components of a death concept. *Child Development, 55,* 1671–1686.

(1992). The acquisition of a mature understanding of three components of the concept of death. *Death Studies, 16,* 221–229.

Wass, H., Guenther, Z., & Towry, B. (1979). United States and Brazilian children's concepts of death. *Death Studies, 3,* 41–55.

Waugh, E. (1948). *The loved one: An Anglo-American tragedy.* Boston, MA: Little, Brown & Co.

Wenestam, C. & Wass, H. (1987). Swedish and U.S. children's thinking about death: A qualitative study and cross-cultural comparison. *Death Studies, 11,* 99–121.

White, A.D. (1896/1993). *A history of the warfare of science with theology in Christendom.* Buffalo, NY: Prometheus Books.

Wittgenstein, L. (1921/1974). *Tractatus logico-philosophicus.* London, England: Routledge.

# 4

## Death in the Lives of Children

MARGARET M. MAHON

Childhood bereavement comprises as many different experiences as there are children who are bereaved. The HIV/AIDS epidemic has had a tremendous impact on the number and experiences of bereaved children. Around the world, 13–15 million children have been orphaned by HIV/AIDS (UNAIDS 2009; Wessner 2009). In Africa, more than 12 million children are orphans due to HIV/AIDS. Unprecedented numbers of children are being raised by grandparents, and 13.5% of older people are living with their grandchildren, though not their children (Cheng & Siankam, 2009). Researchers have projected that one-third of children in Africa will be orphaned due to AIDS by 2010 (Wessner, 2009). The HIV/AIDS epidemic has worldwide implications, though there are tremendous geographic differences in the effects of HIV/AIDS. Regardless, HIV/AIDS does not affect a majority of children in the world.

Children experience the deaths of parents, siblings, or friends. Children are affected by what they see on television, whether in cartoons, on adult television shows, or on the news. Death is even a surprisingly common theme in Disney movies (Cox, Garrett, & Graham, 2005). When there is an international disaster such as the bombings in Mumbai (November 2008), the 2004 Madrid train bombings, or the September 11, 2001, hijackings and attacks, the events and their aftermaths are played and replayed. Children exposed to these events absorb them or not. They have an important reaction to them or not. The same is true of children who observed the killing of John F. Kennedy and Lee Harvey Oswald, Martin Luther King, or Robert F. Kennedy, or who saw the coverage of the bodies sent home in body bags during the Vietnam War. Media has changed children's exposure to death, but death has always been a part of the lives of children.

61

The same event affects children differently; no single variable determines how a child responds to death. It is simplistic and counterproductive to suggest, "An 11-year-old will respond this way ..." or "A boy is more likely to. ..." Children respond to death based on factors such as age, developmental level, the nature of the relationship with the person who died, the security of the child's ongoing relationships, life experiences, personality factors, and others. Although no child's reaction can be predicted precisely, understanding what is known about childhood bereavement and what might help the child and family can facilitate healthy bereavement.

Internationally, more than 9 million children younger than five years old die each year (UNICEF, 2009b). However, in the twenty-first century children who die young are much more likely to be from economically deprived countries. In prior generations, the death of children was far more common. Death rates of children are reliable surrogate indicators for health-care discrepancies between cultures. The death of a child has become a rarity in some environments while remaining commonplace in others. The same is true for children's experiences of the death of someone close to them; in some regions it is common; in others, extremely rare.

In this chapter, some dimensions of death in the lives of children will be described. This will include a focus on the experiences of dying children, family responses to the death of a child, and children's responses to other deaths. Because encounters within the health-care system are a tremendous determinant of experiences of dying and death, the effects and responsibilities of health-care providers will be explored, as will health-care providers' opportunities to support families in which a member is seriously ill or has died.

## CHILDREN'S UNDERSTANDING OF DEATH

For decades, many have believed that children accurately understand death by about mid-school age, or about ten to twelve years of age. More recently, researchers and clinicians have recognized that the concept of death develops in the same way as other concepts: gradually, and at a wide variety of ages. Some children accurately understand death at five years of age, and others at age twelve. Children's understanding of death is discussed elsewhere in this volume.

Too often, information about someone's serious illness or dying is withheld from children because of incorrect beliefs about children's abilities to understand the implications of death. It may be easier for adults to believe that children are incapable of understanding death and are therefore too young to grieve. Incorrect beliefs about children's understanding of death and ability to grieve are also common in professionals who work with children, for example, health-care providers, educators, and counselors (MacPherson & Emeleus, 2007; Mahon, Goldberg, & Washington, 1999b; Price, 2007). Some misunderstandings exist because of a reliance on older science, others because it is unfathomable for adults to imagine that children should experience the pain of grieving. Wrong beliefs can lead to inaction or the provision of poor advice and ultimately can isolate children.

Children can understand death. For the purposes of this chapter, it is recognized that healthy children as young as five years of age (and some younger) can have an accurate understanding, although some children do not have an accurate understanding of death until age twelve; the wide span is reflective of the various components that comprise a full understanding of death and its implications (Hunter & Smith, 2008; Mahon, 1993; Mahon, Goldberg, & Washington, 1999b). For most children, age is an appropriate surrogate for developmental level, although for some children develop-mental level is a more accurate predictor of their understanding. An accurate understanding of death does not mean that a child will have more intense reactions to death. Rather, an accurate or inaccurate understanding means that a child may have *different* reactions.

There is an ongoing question about the role of experience in children's understanding of death. Experience with death has been posited to advance children's understanding of death (e.g., Sood, Razdan, Weller, & Weller, 2006). Experiences with death may advance children's knowledge of rituals and other environmental factors. With the exception of their own termi-nal illnesses (Bluebond-Langner, 1978), however, experience with death is not likely to advance children's overall understanding of death (Hunter & Smith, 2008; Mahon, 1993).

Experience may inform a child about the events and routines associated with illness. Consider the child whose parent, grandparent, or sibling is hos-pitalized, or who might even be hospitalized herself. A child who has been to a hospital is likely to have more realistic expectations about the hospital environment than the child who has not (Mahon, 1994). A lack of experience may result in fears that are worse than reality. Knowledge and experience do not necessarily translate to accurate understanding or to advances in a child's development. Experiences with serious illness or death, including seeing someone in the hospital, participation in death-related rituals, or even seeing the body of someone who has died will not lead to an accurate understanding of death in a child who is not developmentally ready. Rather, the experience fits with the child's existing schema or the child's current understanding.

Finally, children who have experienced the death of a close family member or other person close to them may not have an accurate understanding of death (Hunter & Smith, 2008; Mahon, 1993; Mahon, Goldberg, & Washington, 1999a). Similarly, even direct family communication about death is not related to a more advanced understanding of death (Hunter & Smith, 2008). Experiences with death, then, do not lead to an accurate understanding of death.

The science related to children's concept of death and the roles of various experiences will continue to evolve. More will be learned about factors that affect children's understanding of death. It is the responsibility of those caring for dying or bereaved children, including specialists and primary-care providers, to be aware of the range of normal, healthy responses in children and to provide appropriate guidance to families and to children about dying and death.

## WHEN A CHILD IS DYING

### Causes of Death

The causes of death of children vary widely around the world. Ninety-nine percent of children's deaths occur in countries with low and middle incomes (Global Health Council, 2009). In 2008, about one-half of all deaths of children under age five occurred in Africa and 42 percent occurred in Asia (You, Wardlaw, Salama, & Jones, 2009). Communicable diseases are the most common cause of death of children under five.

In 2007, the mortality rate for children around the world was sixty-eight per one thousand live births (UNICEF, 2009b). The rate for the least developed countries was one hundred thirty per one thousand live births; the rate for developing countries was seventy-four per one thousand live births; the rate for developed countries was six per one thousand live births (UNICEF, 2009b). Children in rural areas are at greater risk than children in urban areas (UNICEF, 2009a).

Differences in causes of death and death rates lead to different needs of children across borders and boundaries. Very little research, however, has been done on the experiences and understandings of children of less affluent cultures. The focus of this section will be the experiences of dying children who receive care in developed countries.

### The Dying Child's Experiences

Of children who die in the United States, approximately half die within the first year of life. Of the other half, approximately half (26 percent overall) die suddenly, due to trauma such as falls, gunshot wounds, child abuse, or motor vehicle crashes (ChIPPS, 2001; Hoyert, Kung, & Smith, 2005). Opportunities for timing and targets of intervention vary based in part on the causes of the child's death.

The course of a child's illness is often tumultuous, framed by hopes of a cure and fears that the child will die. Some diseases with which children live for many years are potentially fatal. These include cancer, HIV/AIDS, cystic fibrosis, the muscular dystrophies, complications of prematurity, metabolic disorders, and many others. The courses of these diseases are often predictable, though the timing may not be. This knowledge of a disease trajectory provides many opportunities for interventions with children and families. Although children and their families cannot always be promised life, they can be assured that the child's care will include aggressive symptom management, decision making that involves the child, and honest communication.

*Palliative Care*
Palliative care is an ideal mechanism to provide this scope of care to children. Palliative care refers to care "to prevent and relieve suffering and to support the best possible quality of life for patients and their families, regardless of the stage of the disease or the need for other therapies.... Palliative care can be rendered along with life-prolonging treatment or as the main focus of care" (National Consensus Project, 2009). Palliative care, then, is not only about care for the child who is dying; it should also complement curative therapies. The goals of palliative care includes the relief of suffering and allowing the child to live as well as possible for whatever time the child has (Bluebond-Langner et al., 2007; Drake et al., 2003; Kane, Hellsten, & Coldsmith, 2004; Liben, Papadatou, & Wolfe, 2008).

Clinicians caring for seriously ill children, researchers in the field, and parents of ill children recommend a "blended approach," that is, the provision of palliative-care services concurrently with disease-related treatments (Bluebond-Langner et al., 2007; IOM, 2003; Kane & Hilden, 2007; Liben et al., 2008). In the American Academy of Pediatrics (AAP) (2000) statement, "Palliative care for children," it was also recommended that palliative care be integrated with curative therapies, specifying that palliative care should be "[o]ffered at diagnosis and continued throughout the course of illness, whether the outcome ends in cure or death" (Frager, 1997). The dimensions of palliative care include aggressive symptom management, assistance with decision making, and the provision of excellent end-of-life care (Mahon & Sorrell, 2008).

*Symptom Management*
Children differ from adults in their diseases, their symptoms, and their responses to treatment (Hinds, Schum et al., 2005). Over the past several decades, understanding of pain and other symptoms in children and the knowledge of how to treat them has proliferated. It is the responsibility of primary and specialist pediatric health-care providers to treat most of these symptoms (AAP, 2000) and to get help from palliative-care specialists when more specialized knowledge is needed.

For many children, the worst part of any disease is needle sticks. Whether injections, drawing blood, or more invasive procedures like spinal taps, most children (and many adults!) dread it. Despite the fact that simple technologies exist to manage the pain and distress of needle sticks (e.g., Samson et al., 2007; Zempsky et al., 2008), interventions are seldom made to alleviate this component of disease burden. Carbajal and colleagues reported that neonates in the ICU underwent an average of sixteen painful procedures a day, receiving "specific analgesia for a median of 20% (IQR 8–36%) of the painful procedures" (2008, p. 63). Analgesic therapy was often non-pharmacologic, and 79.2 percent of the procedures were accompanied by no "specific pre-procedural analgesia." When the knowledge exists to manage pain and other symptoms, it should be used.

In developed countries around the world, children often die having lived the ends of their lives with a significant symptom burden, most frequently including pain, difficulty in breathing, anxiety, and other symptoms (Drake et al., 2003; Goldman, Hewitt et al., 2006; Hechler et al., 2008; Wolfe et al., 2008). This frequently includes the use of intensive-care technology that has no chance of saving the child's life. Rather, these technologies prolong an inevitable and too often burdensome dying. Children often die in intensive-care units.

Discussions about when children are dying are often delayed or held only within hours of death. Opportunities for hospice care are late. Although there are undoubtedly circumstances in which children can benefit from the use of a certain few technologies, the commonality of ventilator use and the delay in discussions about when cardiopulmonary resuscitation is not indicated suggest a lack of focus on the imminence and inevitability of the child's death.

The advent of palliative care has improved care for many children, however, suffering is still too common. Even with aggressive implementation of palliative care, several areas of care are inadequate. Over almost a decade of the implementation of palliative care at very good medical centers, there remains no improvement in the percentage of families for whom there was a documented discussion about a terminal prognosis, and no change in the time before death when life-prolonging therapies were discontinued (Wolfe et al., 2008).

A primary goal of palliative care is to alleviate suffering and to allow an optimal quality of life for children and their families (Kane, Hellsten, & Coldsmith, 2004; Liben, Papadatou, & Wolfe, 2008). Symptom management is an extremely important means to allow children to live well. An early integration of palliative care improves symptom management for children (Mack & Wolfe, 2006). Certainly this imposes a mandate for access to palliative care for all seriously ill children.

### THE CHILD'S EXPERIENCES

Over the past fifty years, treatments for childhood diseases have increased almost exponentially. Diseases that would have been rapidly fatal may even be cured. Children live well for many years with diseases from which they would have died in earlier decades. This greater ability to cure has led some people to believe that a death in childhood is somehow an aberration. Still, all diseases cannot be cured. Some children are born too soon to survive. Certain injuries are fatal.

More treatments (e.g., more drugs, transplants, surgeries, or experimental therapies) do not necessarily mean better care. Not uncommonly, especially in the United States, children receive therapies from which they are extremely unlikely to gain benefits. It is not uncommon for parents to seek out and aggressively pursue therapies not only unlikely to save the child's life, but that also impose a significant burden on the child, often without any commensurate benefit (Bluebond-Langner, Belasco, Goldman, & Belasco, 2007; Mack, Joffe, Hilden et al., 2008).

This aggressive, single-minded pursuit of a cure has a profound effect on the child's experience of his or her own dying. Children who know the only goal is a cure may feel unable to discuss their thoughts and fears. It is not uncommon to hear of children who approached a parent or even a physician, nurse, or other health-care provider to talk about whether they will die. A common response is, "Don't talk like that! You have to be positive."

Eight-year-old Gregory had lived with a serious illness for several years. He approached his parents several times in an attempt to discuss his dying; they uniformly refused to hear Gregory's questions and concerns. Gregory was in the clinic for an out-patient treatment. He turned to the parent sitting next to his chair and urgently said again, "I think I'm going to die." As the parent protested, Gregory died.[1]

---

[1] This vignette and others throughout the chapter are from the author's experiences with children and families.

This refusal of some parents to discuss the possibility of death with children almost seems to be magical thinking. These parents seem to believe that discussing death would make it happen, and conversely, that positive thinking will lead to a cure. Indeed, parents have reported that they fear that thinking about a child's death will make it happen (Hinds, Birenbaum, Clarke-Steffen et al., 1996; Hinds, Birenbaum, Pedrosa, & Pedrosa, 2002). Their attitude conveys a strong message to children: "You cannot or should not talk about it." This can lead to extreme isolation for the dying child. Parents who feel so constrained about verbalizing their thoughts and fears are also likely to feel isolated.

This avoidance is common in health-care providers. Bluebond-Langner described "mutual pretense" and the use of "distancing strategies" (1978, p. 206). Mutual pretense was originally described by Glaser and Strauss (1965), who wrote about it as a technique used by health-care providers, patients, and families to avoid discussion of difficult topics. Glaser and Strauss identified the systemic implications of mutual pretense. For example, if there were a tacit agreement that a patient's terminal diagnosis be discussed, that patient was likely to receive less nursing care. Avoiding this discussion meant avoiding any contract.

Bluebond-Langner (1978) described mutual pretense as allowing all involved in the dying of a child to maintain the socially proscribed roles, including that the child will have a future. This allows the parent to continue to function as one who molds and nurtures the child. Parents and health care providers often purposefully engage in mutual pretense with children to try to protect the child and themselves from the pain and suffering of the child's illness and dying. Children engage in mutual pretense to allow others to maintain the façade. That is, children make decisions to allow adults to maintain the pretense.

The reality is, dying children know they are dying. In some of the most important work in this field, Myra Bluebond-Langner (1978) described the processes through which children go as they come to understand the illness, its treatment, and the trajectory of the disease. Specifically, in her study, regardless of the child's age, children's understanding evolved from recognizing "it" as a serious illness to recognizing the disease as a series of relapses and remissions that would lead to death. Simultaneously, children's self-concept over the course of the disease evolved from being a child who was seriously ill to becoming a child who was dying. This evolution of understanding occurred independent of age.

Although other experiences do not advance children's understanding of death, it is different for those who are dying. As is true for adults, children who are dying are aware of their impending death, even without being told. Avoiding or denying this reality has implications for the child and for the family.

## Communication

Many adults in the child's life may not be comfortable with the concept of honest and direct communication. A realistic and important guideline is to focus on the needs of the child, though these may differ from the desires of the parents. Children need information, just as the parents need to be informed. As with much of pediatrics, discussions should be guided by the child's questions. Given that children are often acutely aware of adults' discomfort, the health-care team should assure that the child and family have frequent opportunities to discuss the child's condition with someone who is knowledgeable and open.

Children often want to plan their own funerals or to develop some other way to ensure they are not forgotten. Although these encounters are never easy, they can be extremely rewarding, allowing the child a sense of peace and reassurance. Children often want to know what dying will be like. Providers can give that information (Wolfe, 2004). Many children want to have a say in how they will die.

Talking with a child about his or her impending death is not easy. Regardless, in many ways it is easier than the incredible amount of energy it takes to keep secrets. Perhaps surprisingly, once the reality of the child's dying is in the open, there are more opportunities to enhance the child's living. Children do not speak solely about their dying. Rather, they often focus on living. What they want often depends on their age or developmental level. Support for the terminally ill child must include the recognition of childhood first, with the overlay of how the illness shapes the child's life. Family is likely to be very important to the child, but friends are also extremely important. Children and young adults strive to be "just like everyone else." Ways of allowing normalcy during a child's dying (e.g., playing video games, listening to music, visiting with friends), even as death is near, can be a great gift, not just to the child who is dying, but also to peers who will ultimately be bereaved.

Bluebond-Langner (1978) provided excellent guidance about how to communicate with dying children. Information should not be forced on children. Rather, children tend to be very specific about what they want to know. They "test" adults in their environment to determine who is willing to be honest with them and to identify who insists on mutual pretense.

Children want to talk about their impending death, but this does not become their sole focus. To have the reality of death in the open can be unburdening. Kreicbergs and colleagues (2004) interviewed parents in Sweden whose child had died from cancer. Of responding parents, 34 percent had spoken with the child about death, whereas 66 percent had not. Not a single parent who had spoken with the child about death regretted it. Of those who had chosen not speak with the child about death, 27 percent regretted the decision, often because of a belief that the child knew he or she was dying.

Providers should encourage honesty, though some will be challenged because of their own discomfort with a child's dying. Parents cannot be expected to be experts to guide the child and to address his or her questions and concerns. Children deserve information. Finally, children can be promised presence. Children are often reassured by knowing that they will never be alone. This does not mean immediate proximity, but rather that the child has someone available at all times. This often includes the presence of friends, siblings, and parents.

### The Parents' Experiences

The experience of having a child die is often posited as the worst or most stressful event one can experience. As is true for children, however, many factors determine the parents' actual experiences. Perhaps first among these is the nature of the child's dying. Although some factors certainly put parents at risk for complicated bereavement, some of the perceptions about what makes bereavement more difficult actually vary between bereaved parents. Upon exiting a support group meeting, a mother stated, "I don't know how those parents do it. Their children's deaths were so prolonged! They were tortured!" It is not uncommon to hear parents whose children have died following a long illness say, "At least I had her with me for as long as possible. I know we did everything we could."

The notion of "doing everything" seems especially common in the United States. Three-year-old Mark was at a party in a neighbor's yard. He fell into the pool; by the time he was discovered, he had been submerged for several minutes. Paramedics arrived and continued the resuscitation efforts begun by two adults at the party. Mark was taken to the hospital where prolonged resuscitation efforts continued. Several times, one of the younger physicians came out and said to the family, "We really don't think this is going well. What do you want us to do?" Invariably, the family replied, "Do everything." After several hours, another physician joined the younger one in yet another one of his conversations with the family. A chaplain joined them. The senior physician began, saying, "We've been working on your son for a long time. I don't think we're going to be able to save him. We really should stop." There was a prolonged pause. Finally, the father said, "If you stopped now, could you use his organs for transplant? Could you give his organs to someone else?" The physician replied, "No. It's been too long. We wouldn't be able to use his organs." The father replied, "Okay, good. Then you can stop. If the organs aren't good enough for someone else, you can stop."

It was essential to this father that he be assured that his child's death was inevitable, that there truly was "nothing else to be done." Then the father would tell the team to discontinue resuscitative efforts.

Many challenges and opportunities become clear with this vignette. First, the family was not asked to make a decision for which they were qualified. The question, "What do you want us to do?" calls for medical, specifically pediatric, trauma expertise. Second, the focus on what the family wanted is not ideal. Rather, the focus should have been on what was medically possible for the child. Although many factors affect the decisions parents make, the skill and knowledge of clinicians should shape decision making (Truog, Christ, Browning, & Meyer, 2006). In this case, rather than stating vaguely, "Things aren't going well," the neurologic and cardiovascular diagnoses should have been stipulated as a foundation for what clinical options existed, and which were no longer possible.

Upon a child's arrival in the emergency department, the focus is clear. For a previously healthy child, every effort must be made to save his or her life (Baren & Mahon, 2003). When it becomes clear that this life cannot be saved, it is incumbent on physicians and other providers to keep the focus on what is medically indicated for the child. Parents should not be asked to make medical decisions. Providers can structure the interactions with families to assure them every effort has been made to save the child, but that the medical team was unable to do that. Providers are required to recognize when efforts are futile and when resuscitation should be stopped (Baren & Mahon, 2003).

Similar principles apply to interactions with parents of children dying from other diseases. Other illnesses, such as cystic fibrosis or some of the muscular dystrophies may have an inevitable outcome, but the course of the child's disease is likely to include similar hopes and fears and the desire for more time.

Parents rely on health-care providers, especially physicians, for accurate information about a child's disease (Mack, Wolfe, Cook, et al., 2009). Most parents want as much information as possible about the disease and about its prognosis (Hinds et al., 2001; Mack, Wolfe, Grier, et al., 2006). Still, parents who have lived with and cared for a child with an illness that will or might be terminal acquire an expertise. These parents often recognize before anyone that "something is different," "something is wrong." Parents become the expert about the child and the child's response to the disease and its treatments. (This is different from being an expert about the disease, and does not exonerate physicians and others from the responsibility of providing timely and precise information.) Parents of healthy children not uncommonly assert that they know their child better than anyone else. The knowledge of the parents of a child with a chronic illness may come with additional responsibility: Parents, especially mothers (usually the primary caregiver) of chronically ill children sometimes believe that their knowledge is what protects or saves the child.

When parents realize a disease might be fatal, they live with fear that the child will die. Some parents become hypervigilant, monitoring the child's activities, worrying every time the phone rings, or fearing that a minor illness could have fatal consequences (Farnsworth, Fosyth, Haglund, & Ackerman, 2006). Parents live with apprehension and uncertainty for the course of the child's illness (Monterosso & Kristjanson, 2008). Bonner and colleagues (2006) described four factors that clinicians should consider in working with families in which a child is seriously ill. The factors include: guilt and worry, unresolved sorrow and anger, long-term uncertainty, and emotional resources. Bluebond-Langner (1996) described family adaptation to living with a chronic illness as the establishment of a "new normal." Though a disease such as cystic fibrosis, certain muscular dystrophies, or other diseases are almost always fatal, this new normal allows families to focus on how to live with the diseases rather than to focus on the dying.

As with children's responses to illness, family responses will vary based on a variety of factors having to do both with the individuals who comprise the family as well as how the family functions as a unit. Families can be taught certain skills to improve their functioning. Parental adjustment affects the child's adjustment as well as the overall experience of the illness (Bluebond-Langner, 1996).

The time after diagnosis is likely to be followed by a significant disruption, followed by a time during which new patterns of family functioning emerge (Kazak et al., 2004). Although many of the parental responses to a child's serious illness are negative, Bonner and colleagues (2006) emphasized that parents identified emotional resources as a strength, and that all parents in their study were able to identify some emotional resources within themselves.

Once these new patterns have become routine, as different as they are from how life was before, the families come to view the new functioning as normal (Deatrick et al., 2006). In more than twenty years of research with families living with a child's chronic and/or terminal illness, Deatrick, Knafl, and colleagues have described a range of patterns of family functioning or Family Management Style (FMS) (e.g., Deatrick & Knafl, 1990; Knafl, Breitmayer, Gallo, & Zoeller, 1994; Knafl & Deatrick, 2002). Family Management Styles include thriving, accommodating, enduring, struggling, and floundering (Deatrick et al., 2006, p. 21). Family Management Styles have been explored across illnesses; the dimensions vary somewhat depending on the specific illness. Family views of the child range from normal to tragic. FMS is affected by and affects individual functioning and family unit functioning.

It is not possible to predict how families will function at the time when an illness is recognized as terminal. Some have known this time was inevitable, others still believe that the child will not die. Some feel that this time has come far too soon; others recognize that this was the inevitable end of an arduous journey.

Parents come to recognize the time of dying in many different ways. Health-care providers sometimes wait to discuss the proximal reality of the child's death until the parent shows signs of being ready to have the discussion (Wolfe, 2004). Researchers have repeatedly described a great lag between physician recognition of the proximal reality of the child's death and that of the parents.

Mack and colleagues (Mack, Cook, Wolfe, et al., 2007) reported that parents of seriously ill children are more optimistic than physicians. They noted that parental optimism does not exist in isolation. Rather, "physicians' confidence in their estimates of prognosis was a determinant of parent's knowledge" (p. 1360). Parents cannot be expected to know what they are not told. The tools exist to recognize when death is inevitable. Physicians and other health-care providers have a responsibility to be honest with families. This includes proactive efforts to communicate information, and *not* waiting until parents (or children) request information.

Parents of children with cancer recognized that the child was dying an average of 106 days before the child's death. Physicians, however, recognized the child's impending death 100 days earlier, about 206 days prior to the child's death (Wolfe, Klar, Grier, Duncan, Salem-Shatz et al., 2000). Hechler and colleagues (2008) reported that parents became aware of their child's impending death nine weeks prior to the death; only half of these parents came to this awareness because of a discussion with the health-care team. In other cases, this recognition by families does not come until days before the child's death (Kane & Primono, 2001).

Parents can only make decisions based on what they know. Information about the child's condition does not belong to the health-care team. Providers sometimes withhold information from parents because they believe the information is too complicated, because it is "bad news," or because they "don't want to take away hope" (Hinds, Drew et al., 2005). Developing an accurate, specifically timed prognosis can be difficult in children (Bluebond-Langner et al., 2007; Hinds, Schum et al., 2005; Mack & Wolfe, 2006; Wolfe, Klar, Grier et al., 2000), though the inevitability of the child's death can be clear even from the time of diagnosis. Regardless, 47 percent of pediatric oncologists reported that they would not indicate a discussion of DNR (do not resuscitate) until the parents introduced the topic (Hilden et al., 2001).

Though providers' decisions to withhold information are often made with good intent, this can have deleterious effects (Mack, Wolfe, Grier, Cleary, & Weeks, 2006). Providers have a responsibility to share information necessary to make decisions in the best interest of the child. Certainly the inevitability and proximal reality of the child's death is relevant for decision making. Parents need and desire information about the condition and the prognosis (Baker et al., 2007; Hinds, Drew et al., 2005; Mack, Hilden, Watterson et al., 2005; Mack, Wolfe, Grier, Cleary, & Weeks, 2006). Involvement of the palliative-care team earlier in the course of the child's illness can facilitate the content and process of treatment decision making across the disease trajectory (Kane & Hilden, 2007).

Even when they recognized that their child was dying and that a cure was no longer possible, 38 percent of parents in one study described pursing curative efforts (Mack et al., 2008). Of those, a majority later acknowledged not only that the child accrued no benefit, but more, that the child sustained significant suffering during this futile therapy.

Though some parents are never able to face the reality of the child's impending death, many others describe acute awareness of the reality of the child's dying. Their parenting and caregiving changes; caring for a child who is dying is perceived as different from caring for the same child with a chronic illness, but is described similarly across cultures (Davies et al., 1998).

Parents can often only address the reality for brief periods of time. Otherwise, they avoid the reality so that they can continue to function as they need, including being able to care for the child (Hinds et al., 1996).

Too often when parents seem reticent, health-care providers try to force the issue, repeatedly refocusing the conversation on the child's dying. They label parents as "in denial." In fact, true denial is *extremely* rare. Parents facing the death of a child are confronting a horrific nightmare. When evaluating the parents' understanding, providers can weigh several factors. Have these parents accurately integrated information over the course of the child's illness? Though they speak of the next family vacation, does their decision making in the moment reflect an understanding of the child's current clinical condition? Wishful thinking in the presence of child-centered decision making is often an appropriate and hopeful strategy.

## Decision Making

### Components of Decision Making

Decision making is a part of every child's disease trajectory. Parents vary in the extent to which they choose or are able to participate in decision making. Optimal clinical decision making cannot begin, however, with parents' preferences. Clinical decision making must always begin with a focus on the facts of the child's condition. How advanced is the disease? What is the known trajectory of the child's condition? Based on these facts, the goals of care can be established. Broadly speaking, is the goal of care that this child will be cured? Will he or she live many years with a chronic disease? Should care focus on keeping the child as comfortable as possible for whatever time remains? It is only after the facts have been established that the options can be delineated.

Decision making is an ongoing part of any person's health care. Because there is often a right answer, it might be easy to overlook that a decision is even being made. When a child is a certain age, for example, immunizations are required. The routine nature of the intervention almost obviates a structured decision-making process.

Clinical decision making, then, must be structured by the clinical experts. Those who are the most knowledgeable about the disease are responsible not only for describing the state of the child's disease, but also for delineating the options that exist for this child. The manifestations of sickle cell disease or cystic fibrosis or spinal cord injury differ between children; thus, the goals of care and treatment options for two children with the same condition may differ.

Decision making is an ongoing process. Participation depends on understanding. When health-care providers ask or expect families to be involved in decision making, they are (or should be) asking the participants to be informed. Being informed implies not just knowledge of a child's diseases, but also of the *goals of treatment*. There are overall goals of treatment, and there are treatment-specific goals of treatment.

The goals of treatment for a child with sickle cell diseases, cystic fibro-sis, spinal cord injury, or certain other diseases are not a cure. These are diseases with which the child will live for his or her entire life. The overall goal of treatment likely includes that the child will live as well as possible, will be like other children of the same age, and will have few complications of the disease. If a child with any of these diseases develops an infection, the overall goal of treatment does not change. The specific goal of treatment for the infection is different and more specific; it is to cure the infection and to minimize the complications of the infection and its treatment.

It is far too common for parents to believe that they have made a deci-sion that *caused* a child's death, for example, not insisting on aggressive use of technology or not finding a clinical trial in time. Clinicians can structure questions in such a way as to make it clear that any limits on the options for this child exist because of the disease, rather than due to any parental action or inaction. For example, the parent of a child with muscular dystro-phy may be confronted with the prospect of the child's impending inability to breathe unaided. The physician might ask, "What have you noticed about Jason's breathing lately?" Based on the parent's responses, the clinician can specify first the child's actual respiratory status, often including numbers such as pulmonary function tests or other indicators. The team can then put the current information into the overall disease trajectory: "You have seen Jason's breathing change, even in the short time since he was here last. We are at the point where it is time to consider whether Jason would benefit from the use of a ventilator." (In several types of the diseases, Jason would be able to participate in this discussion. If able, he should be included.)

Even this decision is not clear. The type of muscular dystrophy is a con-sideration when weighing varying options. Some children can live for years with assisted ventilation; they are still able to be up in a wheel chair, interact well with others, play, and enjoy. For other variations of the diseases, this level of decline in respiratory status indicates that death is likely to happen soon, independent of technological intervention.

In each case, decision making must include weighing the benefits of the treatment against its burdens. Parents rarely have the knowledge and expe-rience to do this. Hinds and colleagues reported that parents found decision making more difficult after being told of the side-effects of an experimental medication (Hinds, Drew, Oakes et al., 2005). Regardless, health-care providers must provide information not only about what a technology can do, but what it cannot accomplish. The decision in these cases is not about whether the child will die, but about how (and perhaps) where the child will die. Again, children may have important preferences, often having to do with adverse events, hospitalization, or recognitions of futility, that should be included in decision making (Hinds, Drew, Oakes et al., 2005).

Health-care providers are often uncomfortable with decision-making processes around end of life care, particularly discussions with families about a patient's – especially a child's – impending death (Davison et al., 2006; Sulmasy et al., 2008). Parents, however, rely on and trust especially the physician's participation and guidance in decision making (Mack, Wolfe, Cook et al., 2009). Parents of children in neonatal intensive-care units in several countries have described that they do not necessarily need to be involved in the decision-making process. Rather, they trust that the physician has heard the parents' preferences in their ongoing conversations, and that this knowledge of parents' preferences is weighed as the physician makes decisions (Orfali, 2004).

The parent of a child who is dying has often been managing the child's condition, including providing medical therapies for months or even years. The parent has become expert in many areas of the child's care. When the transition has been made so that decisions are about the end of the child's life, there are changes in parents' perceptions of the process. Just as parenting becomes different, so too does decision making. Parents describe end-of-life decision making as the most difficult type of decision making (Hinds, Schum, Baker, & Wolfe, 2005).

Discussions about care at the end of a child's life are not distinct. Rather, they are an extension of decisions that have been made over the course of the child's illness. Trust built over the course of the child's illness will be of great importance during end-of-life care. Decisions will still be framed by medical facts, by pathophysiological realities. The goals of care, however, will likely shift.

Based on a series of studies with families in which a child was seriously ill, Hinds and others have developed a model for decision making (see Figure 4.1) (Nuss, Hinds, & LaFond, 2005; Hinds & Kelly, 2010). Relational factors and trust are important to all involved in end-of-life decision making, including the child, parent(s), the physician, and other members of the health-care team. This model provides guidance for what to consider and what to address in end-of-life discussion with families. Several of the factors, including trust, information, time to understand, and monitoring changes in the child's status are based on the recognition that decision making is a process; belief in and respect for the others' understanding of these dimensions accrue over time.

Because parents often feel unable to engage in prolonged discussion about the end of the child's life (Hinds & Kelly, 2010), the model can also provide a roadmap to guide the content of ongoing discussion. It is a

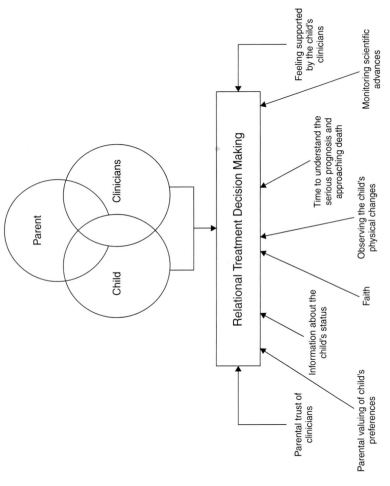

FIGURE 4.1. Relational model of end-of-life treatment decision making: Depicting the factors that influence parental decision making. From Hinds and Kelly (2010), adapted from Nuss, Hinds, and La Fond (2005).

practical way for an interdisciplinary team to focus. It does not, however, indicate a sharp delineation of roles. For example, faith should not be the sole purview of the chaplain. The outcome of using a model that focuses on relational factors and building trust lead to outcomes focused on symptom management, quality of life, and concurrence in decision making (Hinds & Kelly, 2010). It is interesting to note that these components are completely concordant with a palliative-care focus.

Each of the dimensions of decision making, then, indicate an opportunity for health-care providers. Ongoing involvement of those who have been involved in the child's care is very important. Families often feel abandoned when the health-care team with whom they have been involved for months or years say, "There is nothing else we can do," and transfer the family to hospice. Although hospices can provide excellent care to people who are dying, though less often to dying children, this results in a new group of providers at an already tumultuous time for the child and family. Ideally, the physician and health-care team who have been providing care for the child and family will at least collaborate with a hospice team if one becomes involved.

For many children, end-of-life decision making includes a decision to withdraw or withhold potentially life-prolonging treatments. It is crucially important that the discussion be structured so that parents do not believe they are making a decision "to pull the plug" or to cause the child's death. Providers and parents must understand the decision is not about causing death, but rather about allowing an inevitable death and choosing not to impose burdensome treatments (e.g., ventilator support, CPR) on the child.

The decision-making process may be confounded by disagreements between health-care providers, not necessarily about *this* child's care, but rather about broader principles of end-of-life care (IOM, Field, & Behrman, 2003). In developed countries, this often involves the use of technologies. Comfort with broadly recognized principles of withdrawing and withholding technologies can guide professional decision making and can inform an interdisciplinary focus to the child's care (see Table 4.1). An interdisciplinary focus broadens the resources for the child and family.

*Children's Roles in Decision Making at the End of Life*
Recognizing that dying children almost always know that they are dying provides an opportunity and a responsibility to include the child in decision making. Children are often quick to offer an opinion; their preferences frequently include requests such as the presence of certain people and the proximity of a pet or a blanket. Often children want to die at home.

TABLE 4.1. *Principles of withdrawing and withholding life-prolonging therapies*

1. There is no difference between withdrawing and withholding a life-prolonging therapy.
2. Providers should never start a therapy they are not willing to discontinue.
3. The goals of care both for a specific therapy and for the child's overall care should be specified.
4. Medical indications should be considered first when determining clinical options.
5. If the efficacy of a particular therapy is unknown, a trial of that therapy is often reasonable.
6. Though specific therapies may be withdrawn, the child's care should be uninterrupted, often with aggressive attention to symptom management.
7. There is a tremendous difference between allowing a death and causing a death.

Mahon, M.M. (2009). Withdrawing and withholding life prolonging therapies for children. *University of Pennsylvania Center for Bioethics Handbook.* V. Ravitsky, A. Caplan & A. Fiester, Eds. University of Pennsylvania Press.

Children's questions about death provide further indications about what they want as well as about what the goals of care can be. Children commonly ask, "Will it hurt?"

In a study with adolescents, parents, and physicians, Hinds and colleagues (Hinds, Oakes, Furman et al., 2001) described factors that influenced adolescents' decision making. Fifty-two adolescents identified the following factors as important: "doing what others think I should" (n = 14), "having previous experiences with life support" (n = 13), "religious beliefs" (often having to do with life after death) (n = 8), "having a personal [uniformly negative] preference about life support" (n = 6), and "no treatment is working" (n = 4).

Able children who are invited to participate in decision making most frequently base decisions about end-of-life care on relationships. Children who are involved in decision making about end-of-life care are clear that they will die (Hinds, Drew, Oakes et al., 2005). Factors that influenced decision making for ten- to twenty-year-olds in the United States and Australia (n = 20) included avoiding adverse events and information from health-care providers. Specifically, when asked, "What kinds of things did you think about when you were trying to make this decision?" participants described: "thinking about my relationships with others" (n = 19), "avoiding adverse events" (n = 14), "wanting no more" (n = 13), "ready to die and go to heaven" (n = 10), "seeing others die" (n = 10), "believing treatment now is futile" (n = 6), "seeking a chance for a cure [by enrolling in a Phase 1 clinical trial]" (n = 4; 7 had been given the opportunity to enroll) (Hinds, Drew, Oakes et al., 2005, p. 9149).

Some children's responses reflected the beliefs of others. One theme was, "I would feel like a quitter" (Hinds, Drew et al., 2005, p. 9148). Curative treatment was seen by many children as an opportunity to be home and to be with family or friends (Hinds, Drew et al., 2005).

Parents identified different factors in their decision making, including prolonging the child's life, trusting and feeling supported by staff, and making a decision based on the child's preferences. Children sometimes made a decision based on their parents' preferences, even though it contradicted their own preferences.

There are occasions when children will refuse a treatment that their parents want. Though this circumstance is rare, it must be met with deliberation and careful consideration. Many parents want the child's life to be as long as possible. Children are more likely to focus on living well when a cure is no longer possible. Children have a right to participate in decision making about their own illness (AAP, 2000) and are capable of doing so (Hinds, Oakes et al., 2001). A child's refusal to participate in treatment or in research must be considered. A child's refusal for treatment or dissent often must be binding if the minor is mature (IOM, 2003).

End-of-life decisions are likely to have to do with which treatments should be started and which treatments should be discontinued. A very common decision point is the development of a DNR or do not attempt resuscitation (DNAR) order. It is the provider's responsibility to bring up the topic. Too often however, these discussions occur only hours before the child's death (Hinds, Schum et al., 2005).

## CHILDREN AS SURVIVORS

*Saying Good-bye*

Acknowledging the reality of an impending death provides an extremely important opportunity within families. A child saying good-bye to a dying parent is exceedingly difficult, but can be very beneficial for the child. "Being deprived of any chance to say a last good-bye can be torture for children" (Crenshaw, 2006–2007, p. 330).

When a parent is seriously ill, even a very young child is often acutely aware of differences in the parent. The relationship between the child and parent is reshaped during and because of the parent's illness (Saldinger, Cain et al., 2004). The relationship between the child and the parent is affected by factors on both sides: The parent's ability to interact may be limited due to illness, and the child may have responses to the illness (loss of hair, weakness, "being sick") that are separate from the responses to the parent. "Yet the hunger for attachment in the children is painfully clear" (Saldinger, Cain et al., 2004, p. 926). Even if not prepared to say good-bye, a parent can assure the child that he or she is loved.

Saying good-bye or offering reassurances is not always possible; many deaths are sudden. The funeral can be constructed as the opportunity to say good-bye. The child can be given the opportunity to write a note, draw a picture, or describe a favorite memory. Some children have made plans to continue a relationship with their parent (Sheehan, 2007). Even without a plan, many survivors believe that the person who died is still present in their lives and take comfort from that presence (Schultz, 2007).

Certain factors have been posited to affect children's bereavement responses including gender, gender relative to the person who died, ethnicity, culture, time since death, cause of death, family structure, socioeconomic factors, religion, and spirituality. The data on these findings are mixed and often complex (Collins & Doolittle, 2006; Corr, 2006–2007; Hufton, 2006; Lawrence et al., 2005–2006; Mahon, 1993; Neimeyer, Baldwin, & Gillies, 2006; Pelton & Forehand, 2005; Servaty-Seib & Pistole, 2007; Wolchik, Tein, Sandler, & Ayers, 2006; Worden, 1996). Factors predicting long-term effects are complex, multifactorial, and nonlinear with multiple interrelationships (Wolchik et al., 2006). As a result, consideration of these factors to predict or explain the bereavement responses of any individual child is most often unrealistic.

Certain factors are likely to affect the child's bereavement responses in predictable ways. These include developmental-level, parental relationships, whether the child had a chance to say good-bye, and understanding the child's emotions (Christ & Christ, 2006; Mahon, 1993; Turner et al., 2007).

In this context, "bereavement" is used to describe the overall adaptation process necessitated by the death of someone close. Grief is used to describe the emotional reaction to loss and as such is broader than a reaction to death. (Consider losing one's home, one's job, or one's cell phone; each can engender grief, however, the scope and magnitude vary.) Mourning encompasses the most intense emotions of grief and has also been used to describe the rituals following a death (Stroebe, Hansson, Schut, & Stroebe, 2008). Bereavement, then, is a reaction to a loss, specifically a loss through death; it encompasses grief and mourning.

The goal of bereavement is not to "get over" or to "recover" from the death. Rather, the goal of bereavement is to put the person who died in a new place in the survivor's life (Worden, 1996). This learning to live without the physical presences of the person who died but with the continued influences of the person who died is complex, painful, arduous, and ongoing. Children work to remain connected with the person who died (Silverman & Worden, 1992). Bereavement is an ongoing adaptive process with cognitive and affective dimensions; the social context (including the person who died) is an inseparable, albeit mutable part of bereavement (Silverman, Nickman, & Worden, 1992). When a child has died, siblings may imagine the child who has died growing as the surviving children grow. Parents often do the same thing, imagining what the child would be like as he or she got older (Price, 2007).

Three themes are common in childhood bereavement: prolonged pain, gradual acclimation to a different life, and tainted experiences (what was normal or routine is no longer so; "events that would have been joyful milestones [are] overshadowed") (Mahon, 1999, p. 308). Bereavement is the process of adapting to life without the person who died. These three themes will differ for each bereaved child but are likely to be generally present across their adaptation.

Parents are the most important source for support and guidance in the bereaved child's life. Parents most often want to do what is best for children, to support their bereavement. However, parents are often without the resources to guide them in guiding their children. In most circumstances, if the child is bereaved, the parent, too, is bereaved. A parent's grief and a parent's psychological resources are often important mediators of the child's bereavement adaptation.

*Emotions*

Children's grief is qualitatively different from that of adults (Sood et al., 2006). One cannot evaluate a child's responses by watching the child; that is, emotions cannot be judged by appearances. Children make specific decisions to hide their emotions from their parents (Mahon & Page, 1995). For example, if a child's parent or sibling has died, the surviving child is often acutely aware of the surviving parent's or caregiver's grief. When a parent has died, the greatest stressor for the newly bereaved child is the surviving parent's distress (Kwok et al., 2005). Children are very sensitive to parental grief (Kaufman & Kaufman, 2005). In an attempt to protect the parent, the child chooses to hide pain, tears, and loneliness. This can lead to parental unawareness of the child's grief. The parent's grief may also impede the parent's ability to recognize the child's grief. Though others may be unaware, the child's pain may last for years, and perhaps a lifetime. Though likely to diminish over time, there may be upsurges of pain throughout life.

The specific emotions children experience may not differ from those of adults (Schultz, 2007), however, children may be unable to tolerate intense emotions for a long period of time (Sood et al., 2006). Children experience profound sadness and can be overwhelmed by the intensity of their feelings. As a result, some children are experts at "dosing" themselves with their grief. They confront the grief, feel it for a while, but when it becomes too overwhelming, they retreat to the distraction of familiar and comforting behaviors, such as reading a book or being involved in a physical activity.

This absorption in a "normal" behavior is sometimes confusing to adults. One father whose son had been hit by a car was devastated by what he believed to be his daughter's indifference: "I thought she loved him! But all she can do is walk with her friends, laughing, like nothing happened." The man's anguish was palpable. The daughter was incredibly sad about her brother's death, but she explained, "Sometimes I just can't deal with it. My friends let me be me. When I want to cry, they let me. But when I don't want to talk about it, that's okay, too."

Children's most prevalent emotion following the death of a parent is sadness (Christ, Siegel, & Christ, 2002; Eppler, 2008; Worden, 1996). Depending on the circumstances, factors besides the death also evoke sadness. Though some who write about childhood bereavement equate grief and sadness, grief is broader, encompassing more emotions than sadness. The sadness of grief is likely a far deeper grief than any sadness the child has ever experienced.

Children may be angry at the person who died for abandoning them. They are often ashamed at this feeling, somehow getting the message that not only is it bad to be angry, but it is *really* bad or wrong to be angry at someone who died. Children sometimes also feel anger at people whom they perceive as disrespecting their grief.

Twelve-year-old Angie died suddenly from an acute infectious illness. The next day at school, all the children were brought into the gymnasium before classes and were told of Angie's death. The morning was spent informally. Class lessons were largely suspended; grief counselors were available to children. To varying degrees based on their relationship with Angie, the students cried, reminisced, and spoke of how she would be remembered. (As is not unexpected in that age group, she immediately became the most popular girl in the school and had been everyone's best friend.) Several of the students had known Angie their entire lives; there was a group of about five children who had been extremely close. By lunchtime, the principal made an announcement: "That's enough time to grieve. It's time for everyone to get back to work." Although the principal certainly had to ensure that the work of the school got done, the apparent cavalier attitude with which she did so and the seeming disregard for the students' feelings was hurtful and confusing for students. Several remained angry for a very long time.

Isolation is a very common feeling in bereaved children (Crenshaw, 2006–2007; Davies et al., 2007). For school-aged children and older, being like their peers is extremely important. Although acutely aware of the absence of the person who died, many choose to hide their emotions so they do not seem different. Adolescents often hide emotions in public but may seek outlets such as diaries (Sheehan, 2007). School-aged children and adolescents often identify a very select few people with whom they are comfortable sharing their grief.

Following Angie's death, a teacher approached one of the students who had been close friends with Angie. The teacher explained that her sister had died when she was very young, so the teacher believed that she understood at least some of the pain that the friend was experiencing. The teacher offered to be available if the student ever wanted to talk. The bereaved student rarely availed herself of this offer of support, but knowing that "at least she understands" was a great source of comfort.

Children are acutely aware that others evaluate their bereavement responses as good or bad, right or wrong. (Consider the father who took his daughter's reaction to her brother's death as a sign that she didn't love her brother.) Some adults take it upon themselves to admonish children about their responsibilities to their parents: "Your mother is very sad right now, so you have to be extra good" (Mahon & Page, 1995, p. 20). This is typical of what children perceive as attempts to establish hierarchies of grief; the grief of parents is commonly viewed as worse than a child's grief could be. Other children have described adults calling the house to ask the child how the parent is doing: "Oh no, I don't want to disturb your mother. Just tell me how she is doing." In these conversations, there is rarely an inquiry about how the bereaved child is.

Guilt is extremely common in bereaved children (Mahon & Page, 1995; Worden, 1996). For many children, guilt is about the last interaction with the person who died: "I never said good-bye." "I was so mad at him the last time I saw him." "They told me she was going to die, but I didn't believe them. They'd said it so many times before."

Isolation is a very common component of childhood bereavement. The child's grief is not recognized or devalued. When a child was dying, the ill child received, usually of necessity, a majority of the family's attention and perhaps resources. This may engender envy when the child is alive and guilt after the child has died. Believing these feelings inappropriate, the surviving child keeps them secreted away, compounding the isolation. Some children seek physical isolation for brief periods in their grieving but then feel guilty about that as well. As one child described, "[After the sibling died] I went to my room and stayed all day, and I locked my door, which wasn't very – because everyone else was going through the same thing.... They were downstairs together and I just couldn't.... I refused to come out and they were disappointed.... It was selfish" (Mahon & Page, 1995, p. 19). This not only represents the evaluative nature of children's grief, but also their acute awareness of others' grief. This is not commonly seen in adults.

Uncertainty is also common in bereaved children. A death during childhood is often not only the child's first experience with death, but also the parent's first exposure. A death engenders tremendous upheaval. If a parent has died, children specifically fear what will happen if the other parent or surrogate caregiver were to die. What would happen to them? This can also engender feelings of powerlessness (Crenshaw, 2006–2007). This lack of surety and lack of power can further result in "misunderstandings" and "frightened fantasies" (Saldinger, Cain et al., 2004, p. 917). Some children begin to imagine many terrible things that might happen. "After all, who would have thought this terrible thing could happen? If my father could die, other horrible things could happen." This manifests as anxiety in some children (Worden, 1996). Some children may not even be sure of their own survival (Christian, 2007).

One of the challenges of intervening with bereaved people is not to presume that one knows their story, their responses. Allowing someone who is grieving to tell his or her own story, perhaps with structured questions ("Tell me what happened when ... ?"; "What was it like for you when ... ?") can help reveal what is important. There is one exception with children. The vast majority of children feel guilty about something. Thus, saying to a child (well into a relationship, not as an initial approach), "Many children whose father [or mother, sister, brother, etc.] has died have told me that they feel guilty about something related to the death. Do you feel guilty about anything?" Only one child has ever denied feeling guilty about anything.

Children's prolonged pain is multifaceted and complex. They are often very aware of all of their emotions, though they might dose their confrontation of the grief (Mahon, 1999). This rich awareness can lead to ambivalence, to being of two minds. Children are aware of their own deep, sometimes overwhelming pain. Conversely, they also recognize pain in others and want to alleviate that if they can. Children take pride in being able to comfort a parent, a not uncommon goal of bereaved children. An adolescent reported, "I take care of my mom and my sister.... Nobody takes care of me" (Mahon & Page, p. 20).

Children also not uncommonly have difficult experiences with friends. Those with whom they had felt close before often turn out to be unavailable to support the bereaved sibling, often failing even to acknowledge the death. This inability to provide support of any kind further compounds the child's isolation.

All of these emotions are normal, functional components of grief; none of these emotions is pathognomonic for unhealthy grief. To be healthy, grief has to be painful. It is not uncommon to see overt symptoms of grief including behavioral symptoms for one to two years after the death of someone close to the child (Fernandez et al., 2007; Wolchik, Tein, Sandler, & Ayers, 2006; Worden, 1996).

Part of the difficulty in determining whether grief is pathological is the almost complete absence of reliable and valid tools to measure grief (Currier, Holland, & Neimeyer, 2007). With the exception of the work by Hogan and DeSantis (1996), there are no tools to help either clinicians or researchers in a definitive categorization (Currier et al., 2007).

*Secondary Losses*
Any death has broad implications in the lives of survivors. For children, certain deaths can have many and extensive ripples. A secondary loss is "a physical or psychosocial loss that coincides with or develops as a consequence of the initial loss" (Rando, 1993, p. 20). Understanding the impact of a death on the life of a child is incomplete unless one considers secondary losses (Mahon, 1999). In many families, the mother is the person most responsible for daily routines, for rituals, and for celebrations. If their mother dies, children may experience not only the death of their mother, but also the person who knew what they liked in their lunch box, who knew how to make Friday nights a special family celebration, and who always made birthday cakes a particular way. Much of this has to do with the tainted experiences of childhood bereavement. Birthdays and Friday nights still happen, however, the experience is overshadowed by the lack of the mother's presence, and the event is "not the same" because of the absence of interventions the mother would have provided.

If the person who provides most or all of the family income dies, secondary losses may include tremendous cutbacks in style of living. Fewer fiscal resources may mean that the family has to move. When the father of two young children died suddenly, both children and the mother moved in with her parents. The mother slept on the sofa and the two children shared a bedroom, whereas previously they had been in separate rooms. The move also necessitated changing schools and taking a bus to school.

The children lost contact with many of their friends and had many new routines in their lives. Their father's death meant that the children had to adapt not only to life without their father and going through the prolonged pain engendered by that loss, but they also lost their home, privacy, daily routines, school, access to their friends, and more. Although none of these were perceived to be as painful as the death of their father, each was a loss engendering its own grief response. Finally, the mother, who had not been employed before, took a job at a much lower wage than the family's prior income. There was no foreseeable return to the lifestyle the family had before, and of greatest difficulty, the mother was less available to the children. The children did have more support from their grandparents and grew closer to them, though that adaptation took several years.

*Funerals*

In almost all cultures, an individual's death is marked by ritual. This ritual serves many purposes, some for the dead (e.g., the Muslim practice of opening an east-facing window to allow for the release of the spirit, or the Christian Sacrament of the Sick) and many for the living. Funerals often serve religious, social, and personal purposes. Funerals honor the person who died but also acknowledge the transitions that are occurring in the lives of the survivors, and they provide a structured environment for support of the bereaved (Collins & Doolittle, 2006).

Many families have developed their own death-related rituals over generations, either independent from or in the context of religious or cultural customs. As with many other rituals, the roles of those involved in funerals and other postdeath rituals are learned. Thus, "greater experience with death and specifically with funerals seems to put individuals in a better position to make sound choices about the funeral and help cope with its emotional demands" (Hayslip, Booher, Scoles, & Guarnaccia, 2007, p. 103).

Coupled with the intense emotions of the bereaved, the sheer work of planning and managing a funeral may be even more intense and overwhelming to the inexperienced. In a study of 348 bereaved adults, Hayslip and colleagues (2007) found that younger adults had more problems with funerals than middle-aged or older adults, as did those with less experience with death and with funerals.

Funerals and other death-related rituals in the twenty-first century have changed from earlier generations, sometimes being more subdued or otherwise less emotive (Clark & Franzmann, 2006). There is no evidence, however, that the needs of families have similarly contracted. Thus, societal changes may leave families without supports on which they could have relied decades earlier (Ariès, 1981). Funeral directors, then, may be an important resource for families and specifically for children. There is tremendous variability in the skills, resources, and willingness of funeral directors to intervene with bereaved children (Mahon, 2009). Some make specific efforts to include the child in discussions and to create time and space for the child (with an adult there to support the child) to have time with the body. Funeral directors have described that their efforts to assist the child were hindered by parents trying to protect the child. Other parents were described as forcing the child to be close to the body of the person who died when the child was clearly not ready to do so.

It can be very helpful to have an adult at the funeral specifically to help the bereaved children. That is, most people in the surviving child's immediate family will be acutely grieving. Many younger children may not be able to sit through the service, either due to its length, to unfamiliarity with the rituals, or even as a result of discomfort with the intense emotions around them. If there is an adult with whom the child is comfortable and who is not grieving as acutely, that adult can be with the child, taking her or him out if necessary. In this way, there is the greatest chance of meeting the child's needs.

## Bereavement Support

There is no single formulaic approach to interventions with bereaved children (Saldinger, Cain et al., 2004). Some people believe that bereaved children will invariably benefit from psychotherapy or participation in a support group. For some children, support groups are helpful and can result in normalization at a time when children feel very different (Davies et al., 2007). Other children find that they get the support they want and need from other sources. In a meta-analysis exploring the impact of grief therapies with children, Currier and colleagues (Currier, Holland, & Neimeyer, 2007) concluded that there is no significant impact of specific bereavement interventions on children, and that they "do not appear to produce the outcomes that are expected from professional psychotherapeutic interventions" (p. 257). The authors suggest that overuse of therapy may come from a tendency to "pathologize" grief and bereavement (p. 258).

Children are readily able to identify factors that helped them following a death. Following the death of a sibling, mothers were most commonly described as helpful, either for their general availability or their willingness to talk about the person who died. Fathers were only episodically identified as helpful, though some children described fathers as generally helpful and also helpful in specific instances. Siblings and friends were also described as helpful (Mahon & Page, 1995). Bereaved siblings found people helpful who were willing to accept their feelings, whatever they might be at the moment. Further, people who do not judge or evaluate a child's grief are valued supports. People who are helpful not only listen to the child, but they recognize the child's grief and seek out opportunities to be supportive. Although wanting their grief to be recognized, bereaved children also want to be "normal," that is, like everyone else. Not only can friends provide bereavement support, but they can also provide the dimension of normalcy that still allows children to be like everyone else (Nolbris & Hellström, 2005).

### Continuing Bonds

Relationships do not end with death; continued relationships are a healthy part of the bereavement process. Continuing bonds can be supported not only by encouraging the child to remember, but also to participate in the process. Adults who knew both the person who died and the surviving child can ask questions that foster memories and allow for the survivors to share memories as well as feelings.

If the child's relationship with the person was not good, the process of continuing bonds as well as the surviving child's bereavement is challenged (Packman et al., 2006). Regardless, death should not be an opportunity to re-create history. Adults should not pretend that the person who died was not a bully if she was, or that he was not manipulative if he was. Continuing bonds cannot and should not be forced. Continuing bonds are fluid, evolving over time (Packman et al., 2006). As the surviving child matures, he or she may come to understand what was incomprehensible in childhood. Forgiving a person who caused harm can only be done by the person who was hurt. It is not automatic and cannot be expected.

### CONCLUSION

The dying and death of a child and childhood bereavement are complex, ongoing processes. There is not one right way to accomplish the adaptation of bereavement. In recent years, knowledge about how to support dying children and their families has increased exponentially. Similarly, understanding the complexity of childhood bereavement and prolonged pain, including gradual acclimation and tainted events, allows us to attend to factors that are important to children and to families.

## REFERENCES

American Academy of Pediatrics Committee on Bioethics and Committee on Hospital Care. (2000). Palliative care for children. *Pediatrics, 106*, 351–357.

Ariès, P. (1981). *The hour of our death.* New York: Oxford University Press.

Baker, J., Barfield, R., Hinds, P., & Kane, J. (2007). A process to facilitate decision making in pediatric stem cell transplantation: The individualized care planning and coordination model. *Biology of Blood and Marrow Transplantation, 133*, 245–254.

Baren, J.M. & Mahon, M.M. (2003). End-of-life issues in the pediatric emergency department. *Clinical Pediatric Emergency Medicine, 4*, 265–272.

Bluebond-Langner, M. (1978). *The private worlds of dying children.* Princeton, NJ: Princeton University Press.

——— (1996). *In the shadow of illness: Parents and siblings of the chronically ill child.* Princeton, NJ: Princeton University Press.

Bluebond-Langner, M., Belasco, J.B., Goldman, A., & Belasco, C. (2007). Understanding parents' approaches to care and treatment of children with cancer when standard therapy has failed. *Journal of Clinical Oncology, 25*, 2414–2419.

Bonner, M.J., Hardy, K.K., Guill, A.B., McLaughlin, C., Schweitzer, H., & Carter, K. (2006). Development and validation of the parent experience of child illness. *Journal of Pediatric Psychology, 31*, 310–321.

Carbajal, R., Rousset, A., Danan, C., Coquery, S., Nolent, P., Ducrocq, S., ... Bréart, G. (2008). Epidemiology and treatment of painful procedures in neonates in intensive care units. *Journal of the American Medical Association, 300*, 60–70.

Children's International Project on Palliative/Hospice Services (ChIPPS). (2001). A call for change: Recommendations to improve the care of children living with life-threatening conditions. Alexandria, VA: National Hospice and Palliative Care Organization. Retrieved from http://www.nhpco.org/files/public/ChIPPSCallforChange.pdf.

Cheng, S.T. & Siankam, B. (2009). The impacts of the HIV/AIDS pandemic and socioeconomic development on the living arrangements of older persons in sub-Saharan Africa: A country-level analysis. *American Journal of Community Psychology, 44*, 136–147.

Christ, G.H. & Christ, A.E. (2006). Current approaches to helping children cope with a parent's terminal illness. *CA: A Cancer Journal for Clinicians, 56*, 197–212.

Christ, G.H., Siegel, K., & Christ, A.E. (2002). "It never really hit me ... until it actually happened." *JAMA, 288*, 1269–1278.

Christian, C. (2007). Sibling loss, guilt and reparation: A case study. *International Journal of Psychoanalysis, 88*, 41–54.

Clark, J. & Franzmann, M. (2006). Authority from grief, presence and place in the making of roadside memorials. *Death Studies, 30*, 579–599.

Collins, W.L. & Doolittle, A. (2006). Personal reflections of funeral rituals and spirituality in a Kentucky African American family. *Death Studies, 30*, 957–969.

Corr, C.A. (2006–2007). Parents in death-related literature for children. *Omega, 54,* 237–254.

Cox, M., Garrett, E., & Graham, J.A. (2005). Death in Disney films: Implications for children's understanding of death. *Omega, 50,* 267–280.

Crenshaw, D.A. (2006–2007). An interpersonal neurobiological-informed treatment model for childhood traumatic grief. *Omega, 54,* 319–335.

Currier, J.M., Holland, J.M., & Neimeyer, R.A. (2007). The effectiveness of bereavement interventions with children: A meta-analytic review of controlled outcome research. *Journal of Clinical Child and Adolescent Psychology, 36,* 253–259.

Davies, B., Deveau, E., deVeberm B., Howell, D., Martinson, I., Papadatou, et al. (1998). Experiences of mothers in five countries whose child died of cancer. *Cancer Nursing, 21,* 301–311.

Davies, B., Collins, J., Steele, R., Cook, K., Distler, V., & Brenner, A. (2007). Parents' and children's perspectives of a children's hospice bereavement program. *Journal of Palliative Care, 23,* 14–23.

Deatrick, J. & Knafl, K. (1990). Management behaviors: Day-to-day adjustments to childhood chronic conditions. *Journal of Pediatric Nursing, 5,* 1, 15–22.

Deatrick, J.A., Thibodeaux, A.G., Mooney, K., Schmus, C., Pollack, R., & Davey, B.H. (2006). Family management style framework: A new tool with potential to assess families who have children with brain tumors. *Journal of Pediatric Oncology Nursing, 23,* 19–27.

Drake, R., Frost, J., & Collins, J.J. (2003). The symptoms of dying children. *Journal of Pain & Symptom Management, 26,* 594–603.

Eppler, C. (2008). Exploring themes of resiliency in children after the death of a parent. *Professional School Counseling, 11,* 189–196.

Farnsworth, M.M., Fosyth, D., Haglund, C., & Ackerman, M.J. (2006). When I go in to wake them … I wonder: Parental perceptions about congenital long QT syndrome. *Journal of the American Academy of Nurse Practitioners, 18,* 284–290.

Fernandez, M.A.P., Labrador, F.J., & Raich, R.M. (2007). Prevalence of eating disorders among adolescent and young adult scholastic population in the region of Madrid (Spain). *Journal of Psychosomatic Research, 62,* 681–690.

Frager, G. (1997). Palliative care and terminal care of children. *Child and Adolescent Psychiatric Clinics of North America, 6,* 889–909.

Glaser, B.G. & Strauss, A.L. (1965). *Awareness of dying.* Chicago: Aldine Publishing.

Global Health Council. (2009). Where do child deaths occur? Retrieved from http:// www.globalhealth.org/child_health/child_mortality/where_occur/.

Goldman, A., Hewitt, M., Collins, G.S., Childs, M., Hain, R., for the United Kingdom Children's Cancer Study Group (2006). Symptoms in children/ young people with progressive malignant disease: United Kingdom Children's Cancer Study Group/Paediatric Oncology Nurses Forum survey. *Pediatrics 117:* e1179-e1186

Hayslip, B., Booher, S.K., Scoles, M.T., & Guarnaccia, C.A. (2007). Assessing adults' difficulty in coping with funerals. *Omega, 55,* 93–115.

Hechler, T., Blankenburg, M., Friedrichsdorf, S.J., Garske, D., Hübner, B., Menke, A., et al. (2008). Parents' perspectives on symptoms, quality of life, characteristics of death and end-of-life decisions for children dying from cancer. *Klinische, Pädiatrie, 3,* 220, 166–174.

Hilden, J.M., Emanuel, E.J., Fairclough, D.L., Link, M.P., Foley, K.M., Clarridge, B.C., et al. (2001). Attitudes and practices among pediatric oncologists regarding end-of-life care: Results of the 1998 American Society of Clinical Oncology Survey, *Journal of Clinical Oncology, 19,* 205–212.

Hinds, P.S., Birenbaum, L.K., Clarke-Steffen, L., Quargnenti, A., Kreissman, S., Kazak, A., et al. (1996). Coming to terms: Parents' response to a first cancer recurrence in their child. *Nursing Research, 45,* 3, 148–153.

Hinds, P.S., Birenbaum, L., Pedrosa, A.M., & Pedrosa, F. (2002). Guidelines for the recurrence of pediatric cancer. *Seminars in Oncology Nursing, 18,* 1, 50–59.

Hinds, P.S., Drew, D., Oakes, L.L., Fouladi, M., Spunt, S.L., Church, C., et al. (2005). End-of-life preferences of pediatric patients with cancer. *Journal of Clinical Oncology, 23,* 9146–9154.

Hinds, P.S. & Kelly, K.P. (2010). Helping parents make and survive end-of-life decisions for their seriously ill child. *Nursing Clinics of North America.*

Hinds, P.S., Oakes, L., Furman, W., Quargnenti, A., Olson, M.S., Foppiano, P., et al. (2001). End-of-life decision making by adolescents, parents, and healthcare providers in pediatric oncology: Research to evidence-based practice guidelines. *Cancer Nursing, 24,* 122–134.

Hinds, P.S., Schum, L., Baker, J.N., & Wolfe, J. (2005). Key factors affecting dying children and their families. *Journal of Palliative Medicine, 8, Suppl 1,* S70–78.

Hogan, N.S. & DeSantis, L. (1996). Basic constructs of a theory of adolescent sibling bereavement. In D. Klass, P.R. Silverman, & S.L. Nickman (Eds.) *Continuing bonds.* (pp. 235–255). Philadelphia: Taylor & Francis.

Hoyert, D.L., Kung, H.C., & Smith, B.L. (2005). Deaths: Preliminary data for 2003. *National Vital Statistics Reports, 53*(15). http://mchb.hrsa.gov/mchirc/chusa_05/healthstat/children/graphs/0315cmH.htm.

Hufton, E. (2006). Parting gifts: The spiritual needs of children. *Journal of Child Health Care, 10,* 240–250.

Hunter, S.B. & Smith, D.E. (2008). Predictors of children's understandings of death: Age, cognitive ability, death experience and maternal communicative competence. *Omega, 57,* 143–162.

Institute of Medicine Committee on Palliative and End-of-Life Care for Children and Their Families. (2003). M. Field & R. Behrman (Eds.) *When children die: Improving palliative and end-of-life care for children and their families.* Washington, DC: National Academy Press.

Kane, J.R., Hellsten, M.B., & Coldsmith, A. (2004). Human suffering: The need for relationship-based research in pediatric end-of-life care. *Journal of Pediatric Oncology Nursing, 21,* 180–185.

Kane, J.R. & Hilden, J. (2007). Tools to aid decision making in the care of pediatric patients with cancer. *The American Society of Clinical Oncology, 2007 Educational Book.* 188–192.

Kane, J.R. & Primono, M. (2001). Alleviating the suffering of seriously ill children. *American Journal of Hospice & Palliative Medicine, 18,* 161–169.

Kaufman, K.R. & Kaufman, N.D. (2005). Childhood mourning: Prospective case analysis of multiple losses. *Death Studies, 29,* 237–249.

Kazak, A.E., McClure, K.S., Alderfer, M.A., Hwang, W., Crump, T.A., Le, L.T., et al. (2004). Cancer-related parental beliefs: The Family Illness Beliefs Inventory (FIBI). *Journal of Pediatric Psychology, 29,* 7, 531–542.

Knafl, K., Breitmayer, B., Gallo, A., & Zoeller, L. (1994). Family response to childhood chronic illness: Description of management styles *Journal of Pediatric Nursing, 11,* 315–326.

Knafl, K. & Deatrick, J. (2002). The challenge of normalization for families of children with chronic conditions. *Pediatric Nursing, 28,* 46, 48–53.

Kreicbergs, U., Valdimarsdóttir, U., Onelöv, E., Henter, J.I., Steineck, G. (2004). Talking about death with children who have severe malignant disease. *New England Journal of Medicine, 351,* 1175–1186.

Kwok, O.M., Haine, R.A., Sandler, I.N., Ayers, T.S., Wolchik, S.A., & Tein, J.Y. (2005). Positive parenting as a mediator of the relations between parental psychological distress and mental health problems of parentally bereaved children. *Journal of Clinical Child and Adolescent Psychology, 34,* 260–271.

Lawrence, E., Jeglic, E., Matthews, L.T., Pepper, C.M. (2005–2006). Gender differences in grief reactions following the death of a parent. *Omega, 52,* 323–337.

Liben, S., Papadatou, D., & Wolfe, J. (2008). Paediatric palliative care: Challenges and emerging ideas. *Lancet, 371*(9615), 852–864.

Mack, J.W., Cook, E.F., Wolfe, J., Grier, H.E., Cleary, P.D., & Weeks, J.C. (2007). Understanding of prognosis among parents of children with cancer: Parental optimism and the parent-physician interaction. *Journal of Clinical Oncology, 25,* 1357–1362.

Mack, J.W., Hilden, J.M., Watterson, J., Moore, C., Turner, B., Grier, H.E., Weeks, J.C. & Wolfe, J. (2005). Parent and physician perspectives on quality of care at the end of life in children with cancer. *Journal of Clinical Oncology, 23,* 9155–9161.

Mack, J.W., Joffe, S., Hilden, J.M., Watterson, J., Moore, C., Weeks, J.C. & Wolfe, J. (2008). Parents' views of cancer-directed therapy for children with no realistic chance for cure. *Journal of Clinical Oncology, 26,* 4759–4764.

Mack, J.W. & Wolfe, J. (2006). Early integration of pediatric palliative care: For some children, palliative care starts at diagnosis. *Current Opinions in Pediatrics, 18,* 10–14.

Mack, J.W., Wolfe, J., Grier, H.E., Cleary, P.D., & Weeks, J.C. (2006). Communication about prognosis between parents and physicians of children with cancer: Parent preferences and the impact of prognostic information. *Journal of Clinical Oncology, 24,* 5265–5270.

Mack, J.W., Wolfe, J., Cook, E.F., Grier, H.E., Cleary, P.D., & Weeks, J.C. (2009). Peace of mind and sense of purpose as core existential issues among parents of children with cancer. *Archives of Pediatric and Adolescent Medicine, 163,* 519–524.

MacPherson, C. & Emeleus, M. (2007). Children's needs when facing the death of a parent from cancer: Part one. *International Journal of Palliative Nursing, 13,* 478–485.

Mahon, M. (1993). Children's concept of death and sibling death from trauma. *Journal of Pediatric Nursing, 8,* 335–344.

(1994). Death of a sibling: Primary care interventions. *Pediatric Nursing, 20,* 293–295, 328.

Mahon, M.M. (1999). Secondary losses in bereaved children when both parents have died: A case study. *Omega, 39,* 297–314.

(2009). Funeral directors and bereaved children: Beliefs and experiences. *Death Studies, 22,* 828–847.

(2009). Withdrawing and withholding life prolonging therapies for children. In V. Ravitsky, A. Caplan, & A. Fiester (Eds.), *University of Pennsylvania Center for Bioethics Handbook.* Philadelphia, PA: University of Pennsylvania Press.

Mahon, M.M., Goldberg, E.Z., & Washington, S.K. (1999a). Concept of death in a sample of Israeli Kibbutz children. *Death Studies, 23,* 43–59.

Mahon, M.M., Goldberg, R., & Washington, S. (1999b). Discussing death in the classroom: Beliefs and experiences of educators and education students. *Omega, 39,* 99–121.

Mahon, M.M. & McAuley, W.J. (2010). Oncology nurses' personal understandings about palliative care. *Oncology Nursing Forum.*

Mahon, M. & Page, M.L. (1995). Childhood bereavement after the death of a sibling. *Holistic Nursing Practice, 9,* 3, 15–26.

Mahon, M.M. & Sorrell, J.M. (2008). Palliative care for people with Alzheimer's Disease. *Nursing Philosophy, 9,* 110–120.

Monterosso, L. & Kristjanson, L.J. (2008). Supportive and palliative care needs of families of children who die from cancer. *Palliative Medicine, 22,* 59–69.

National Consensus Project for Quality Palliative Care. (2009). *Clinical Practice Guidelines for Quality Palliative Care* (2nd ed.) Retrieved from http://www.nationalconsensusproject.org.

Neimeyer, R.A., Baldwin, S.A., & Gillies, J. (2006). Continuing bonds and reconstructing meaning: Mitigating complications in bereavement. *Death Studies, 30,* 715–738.

Nolbris, M. & Hellström, A.L. (2005). Siblings' needs and issues when a brother or sister dies of cancer. *Journal of Pediatric Oncology Nursing, 22,* 227–233.

Nuss, S.L., Hinds, P.S., & LaFond, D.A. (2005). Collaborative clinical research on end-of-life care in pediatric oncology. *Seminars in Oncology Nursing, 21,* 2, 125–134.

Orfali, K. (2004). Parental role in medical decision-making: fact or fiction? A comparative study of ethical dilemmas in French and American neonatal intensive care units. *Social Science & Medicine, 58,* 2009–2022.

Packman, W., Horsley, H., Davies, B., & Kramer, R., (2006). Sibling bereavement and continuing bonds. *Death Studies, 30,* 817–841.

Pelton, J. & Forehand, R. (2005). Orphans of the AIDS epidemic: An examination of clinical level problems of children. *Journal of the American Academy of Child and Adolescent Psychiatry, 44,* 585–591.

Price, S.K. (2007). Social Work, siblings, and SIDS: Conceptual and case-based guidance for family system interventions. *Journal of Social Work in End-of-Life & Palliative Care, 3*, 3, 81–101.

Rando, T.A. (1993). *Treatment of complicated mourning.* Champaign, IL: Research Press.

Saldinger, A., Cain, A.C., Porterfield, K., & Lohnes, K. (2004). Facilitating attachment between school-aged children and a dying parent. *Death Studies, 28*, 915–940.

Samson, D., Minville, V., Chasser, C., Nguyen, L., Pianezza, A., Fourcade, O., Samii, K. (2007). Eutetic mixture of local anesthetic (EMLA®) decreases pain during humeral block placement in nonsedated patients. *Anesthesia & Analgesia, 105*, 512–515.

Schultz, L.E. (2007). The influence of maternal loss on young women's experience of identity development in emerging adulthood. *Death Studies, 31*, 17–43.

Servaty-Seib, H.L. & Pistole, M.C. (2007). Adolescent grief: Relationship category and emotional closeness. *Omega, 54*, 147–167.

Sheehan, D. (2007). *Interaction Patterns Between Parents With Advanced Cancer In Hospice and Their Adolescent Children.* Dissertation, University of Akron.

Silverman, P.R., Nickman, S., & Worden, J.W. (1992). Detachment revisited: The child's reconstruction of a dead parent. *American Journal of Orthopsychiatry, 62*, 494–503.

Silverman, P.R. & Worden, J.W. (1992). Children's reactions in the early months after the death of a parent. *American Journal of Orthopsychiatry, 62*, 93–104.

Sood, A.B., Razdan, A., Weller, E.B., & Weller, R.A. (2006). Children's reactions to parental and sibling death. *Current Psychiatry Reports, 8*, 115–120.

Stroebe, M.S., Hansson, R.O., Schut, H., & Stroebe, W. (Eds.). (2008). *Handbook of bereavement research and practice: Advances in theory and intervention.* Washington, DC: American Psychological Association.

Sulmasy, D.P., He, M.K., McAuley, R., & Ury, W.A. (2008). Beliefs and attitudes of nurses and physicians about do not resuscitate orders and who should speak to patients and families about them. *Critical Care Medicine, 36*, 1817–1822.

Truog, R.D., Christ, G., Browning, D.M., & Meyer, E.C. (2006). Sudden traumatic death in children: "We did everything, but your child didn't survive." *Journal of the American Medical Association, 295*, 2646–2654.

Turner, J., Clavarino, A., Yates, P., Hargraves, M., Connors, V., & Hausmann, S. (2007). Development of a resource for parents with advanced cancer: What do parents want? *Palliative & Supportive Care, 5*, 135–145.

United Nations Children's Fund (UNICEF). (2009a). *Fact of the week – 107.* Retrieved from http://www.unicef.org/factoftheweek/index_50515.html.

United Nations Children's Fund (UNICEF). (2009b). *The state of the world's children 2009.* Retrieved from www.unicef.org/sowc09/. Under five mortality rates. http://www.unicef.org/sowc09/docs/SOWC09_U5MR_rankings.pdf.

United Nations AIDS Program. (2009). *Report on the global AIDS epidemic. Joint United Nations Programme on HIV/AIDS.* Retrieved from http://search. unaids.org/Results.aspx?q=orphans+in+Africa&x=0&y=0&o=html&d=en &l=en&s=false.

Wessner, D. (2009). *HIV/AIDS orphans in sub-Saharan Africa. The AIDS pandemic.* Retrieved from http://the-aids-pandemic.blogspot.com/2009/02/hivaids-orphans-in-sub-saharan-africa.html.

Wolchik, S.A., Tein, J.Y., Sandler, I.N., & Ayers, T.S. (2006). Stressors, quality of the child-caregiver relationship, and children's mental health problems after parental death: The mediating role of self-system beliefs. *Journal of Abnormal Child Psychology, 34,* 221–238.

Wolfe, J., Hammel, J.F., Edwards, K.E., Duncan, J., Comeau, M., Breyer, J., et al. (2008). Easing of suffering in children with cancer at the end of life: Is care changing? *Journal of Clinical Oncology, 26,* 1717–1723.

Wolfe, J., Klar, N., Grier, H.E., Duncan, J., Salem-Schatz, S., Emanuel, E.J., & Weeks, J.S. (2000). Understanding of prognosis among parents of children who died of cancer. Impact on treatment goals and integration of palliative care. *Journal of the American Medical Association, 284,* 2469–2475.

Wolfe, L. (2004). Should parents speak with a dying child about impending death? *New England Journal of Medicine, 351,* 1251–1253.

Worden, W. (1996). *Children and grief. When a parent dies.* New York, NY: Guilford Press.

You, D., Wardlaw, T., Salama, P., & Jones, G. (2009). Levels and trends in under-5 mortality, 1990–2008. *The Lancet, 375*(9709), 100–104.

Zempsky, W.T., Bean-Lijewski, J., Kauffman, R.E., Koh, J.L., Malviya, S.V., Rose, J.B., et al. (2008). Needle-free powder lidocaine delivery system provides rapid effective analgesia for venipuncture or cannulation pain in children: Randomized, double-blind comparison of venipuncture and venous cannulation pain after fast-onset needle-free power lidocaine or placebo treatment trial. *Pediatrics, 121,* 979–987.

# 5

## Talking to Children about Death
## in Educational Settings

VICTORIA TALWAR

Children are exposed to death at home, at school, and in the media. It has been estimated that approximately 4–7 percent of children experience the death of a parent by the time they are sixteen years old (Hogan & DeSantis, 1996; McCarthy & Jessop, 2005). Others will experience the death of a sibling, a grandparent, or other family member. The death of a loved one affects not only the child, but also has a ripple effect on the rest of the children in the classroom. Alternately, the class as a whole may experience the death of a member of the school community (e.g., teachers or staff) or the death of an individual in the media (e.g., Michael Jackson). In other cases, children may be exposed to the media reports of a national or global tragedy (e.g., the earthquake in Haiti). Children who experience death will have a range of reactions in a variety of settings, including school, where they spend much of their time (Corr, Nabe, & Corr, 2003). Thus, schools are a critical setting for children who are dealing with death and loss.

Talking to children about death is a common problem faced by educators who are confronted with children's questions. It is a challenging subject and one that is often ignored and avoided. Death is associated with negative feelings such as discomfort, sadness, anger, and fear. How someone speaks to children about death depends on that individual's own beliefs and attitudes. This chapter will address how adults in educational settings deal with such discussions with children, including the taboos associated with talking about death, educational professionals' beliefs and attitudes toward discussing death with children, and the place of death education in the classroom and school.

### THE TABOO TOPIC

Adults are often reluctant to discuss death with children. It has been suggested that in our modern society, advances in medical technology has made experiencing the death of close ones less frequent (see Beit-Hallahmi's Chapter 3, this volume; and compare Astuti's Chapter 1 for a discussion of death in nonmodern societies). Adults themselves may have fewer direct encounters with death, because death often occurs in hospitals and because life expectancy is greater than in the past. Therefore, adults may have difficulty in drawing on past experience when talking to children, which may increase their discomfort. However, others suggest that especially in urban settings, children may have increased exposure to death. Increases in suicide and homicide rates among young people, urban violence, and health pandemics (e.g. HIV virus) may all lead to exposure to death (Aspinall, 1996). Regardless, of whether children's exposure has increased or decreased, death remains a part of children's lives whether it be the death of a pet, a grandparent, family member, or, more remotely, a death in the media.

Nevertheless, death remains an uncomfortable topic. Some argue that in modern Western society there is a taboo status concerning the topic of death and bereavement (Holland, 2008). We may wish to avoid both the reality of our own death and that of others. The topic is not one we usually relish, and the contemplation of it can be unpleasant to us. This may be particularly strong where children are concerned. For instance, McGovern and Barry (2000) reported that discussing death was a taboo subject for both teachers and parents, and they reported feelings of discomfort when talking to children about death (McGovern & Barry, 2000). However, this reluctance can make death confusing for children who are trying to understand this reality in terms of the biological conceptions of what happens to the body, but also in terms of larger questions about life. The desire to avoid the topic with children may stem from a wish to protect children from the impact of death or a belief that death has no real meaning for children (Holland, 2008). These beliefs are often predicated on the notion that children cannot understand death or deal with it emotionally (Schoen, Burgoyne, & Schoen, 2004).

There is a general assumption among educators and even some psychologists that young children cannot understand concepts like death and that it is wrong to burden them with such concepts and explanations (Mahon, Goldberg, & Washington, 1999). Many think that it is better to wait until later childhood to discuss death so as to not unduly upset young children. These assumptions stem from Piaget (1929), who suggested that young children do not have a clear conception of death. Some contemporary grief counselors cite Piagetian stages and age ranges as definitive in exploring children's understanding of death (Golman, 1994; Wolfelt, 1996).

However, Piaget has underestimated what young children can understand about death (Schleifer & Talwar, 2009). Contrary to Piaget's contention, children between three and five years of age can develop an understanding of irreversibility (death is final), universality (death comes to all), and causality (death is due to the termination of internal bodily functions) (Sharp, Candy-Gibbs, Barlow-Elliot, & Petrun, 1985). Speece and Brent (1984) reviewed thirty-five studies on children's understanding of death and reported that the majority of five- to seven-year-olds had achieved an understanding of these major components of death. Although investigators may disagree about the exact timetable and sequence of development, most document a progressive mastery of the biological aspects of death between three and eleven years of age (Bering & Bjorklund, 2004; Kenyon, 2001; Slaughter & Lyons, 2003; Speece & Brent, 1996). Thus, children are capable of understanding and benefiting from a discussion about death at an early age.

However, this is not commonly understood by many adults, who fear children are too young to understand such a weighty topic and tend to underestimate children's ability to comprehend death (Mahon, Goldberg, & Washington, 1999; Vianello & Lucamente, 1998; for a discussion of talking to children about death in medical settings, see Mahon's Chapter 4, this volume). In a recent survey of education professionals that included teachers (n = 59), school psychologists (n = 30), student teachers (n = 60), and graduate students in school psychology programs (n = 48), we examined attitudes to discussing death with children in educational settings (Renaud, Talwar, & Schleifer, 2010). Participants were from the Canadian provinces of Quebec and Ontario. We asked participants about children's developing understanding of death and the different components of death (i.e., its inevitability, universality, irreversibility, and causality) at different ages (preschool, early elementary, late elementary, and adolescence). The majority of participants thought that preschoolers did not have an understanding of the inevitability of death, its universality, its irreversibility, or its causality. Most participants believed that children do not develop an understanding of inevitability, universality, and irreversibility until six years of age or older. Half of the participants believed that children between six and eight years of age do not understand that death is caused by the breakdown of bodily functions, and that they acquire this knowledge at nine years of age and older. Thus, most participants judged that children do not develop a basic cognitive understanding of death until the end of elementary school. These misconceptions may hinder adults from discussing death with young children. Yet such discussions can help children construct their conceptual understanding of death. Furthermore, early experiences of death may create an increased impetus in children's desire to understand what happens at death and may increase their need for help from adults to resolve their feelings about death.

## CHILDREN'S EXPERIENCE WITH DEATH

Children will respond in different ways to loss depending on their age, experience, personality, and the context of the loss they have experienced. Grieving in children can last longer than it does in adults. Children may feel isolated, experience academic decline, act out, become aggressive, or seek attention (Grollman, 1990). Young children may show regressive behavior by becoming clingy and manifesting their anxieties in behaviors such as bedwetting and thumbsucking. Teenagers' responses to grief may be manifested in substance abuse, promiscuity, delinquency, and truancy from school. Young children who do not yet have an understanding of causality may believe they or their thoughts or behaviors are somehow responsible for the death and may feel guilty as a result.

Children need help to see that grieving is part of a normal process. Children may experience intense and varied emotions in grieving, such as sadness, guilt, and anger, and these emotions should be discussed (Schleifer & Talwar, 2009). It is important that adults recognize that children are not too young to grasp what has happened at death and are capable of mourning the person who has died (Cruchet, 2009; Holland, 2008). There is often a misconception that all children are "resilient" and are able to recover from losing someone without adult help. In our survey of educational professionals, a number of participants believed that children are resilient when it comes to dealing with death and were reluctant to address the topic with children. However, many other participants did recognize that children may not be able to resolve their feelings about death by themselves without some help from an adult.

Children can mourn the death of someone in healthy or unhealthy ways. Healthy mourning is characterized by "a timely resolution of the loss during which the child reorganizes his or her life memories and new attachments after a period of yearning for the lost one characterized by weeping and anger ... by withdrawal and sadness" (Hurd, 1999, p. 19). Hurd (1999) found that when a child loses a parent, there are several key factors that predict their healthy mourning: their relationship with the deceased parent, the emotional availability of the surviving parent, participation in the funeral, and the quality of the child's support network, which includes the child's school and peers. Children from homes that discuss death usually integrate their memories of the one lost and their feelings about the loss in a healthier way than those who discourage emotional displays (Mahon et al., 1999). Thus, children need to discuss death in supportive settings that allow them to express feelings and ask questions.

### TALKING TO CHILDREN ABOUT DEATH

Inadequate and unrealistic communication about death is the most significant situational factor causing children to have difficulty resolving their feelings of grief and adjusting to the loss of the loved one (Siegel, Mesagno, & Christ, 1990). Children need to be encouraged to express their feelings of anger, sadness, and ambivalence as well as to ask questions about the death to develop a better understanding of what has happened. For many children, the first death they will experience may be the death of a grandparent. In such cases, parents will also be affected and may be unable to respond to their children's questions or needs (Papadatou, Metallinou, Hatzichristou, & Pavlidi, 2002). Parents' reluctance to discuss death may be due to a desire to protect children from harm and emotional upset as well as their inability to cope with their own feelings of grief. Due to these unresolved feelings, parents may try to conceal the details of the death or deflect children's attention (Talwar, 2009).

When parents do not appropriately address children's questions about death and emotions of loss, children can become depressed (Takeuchi et al., 2003). Thus, a child may come to school with these questions or unaddressed needs, which can impact their academic performance, their behavior, and interactions with others at school. School staff need to be aware of the nature and range of bereavement reactions in children so that they can respond to the needs of the child. The teacher or school psychologist may be responsible for answering the students' questions about what happens when an individual dies.

The majority of teachers, when asked, recognize that discussing death and death education are important issues in schools (Holland, 2001; Mahon, Goldberg, & Washington, 1999). In our survey, participants' feelings about having to discuss death with children were mixed. Whereas the majority of participants agreed that children need help to understand death and that it is natural for children to have questions about death, they felt less certain about whether they could help by discussing death with children. As with parents, teachers' and school personnel's feelings of unease and their own unresolved feelings about death may lead them to avoid discussions of death (Reid, 2002). Yet it is important that teachers are comfortable

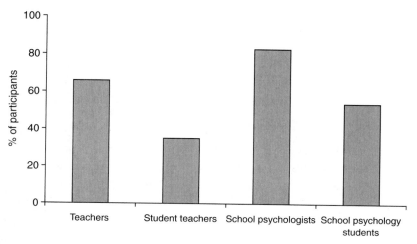

FIGURE 5.1. Percentage of educational professionals who have spoken to children about death.

with the topic of death in order to support pupils (Cullinan, 1990). Teachers who are comfortable with the topics of dying and death are more likely to intervene appropriately (Mahon, Goldberg, & Washington, 1999).

Interestingly, in our survey there were differences between psychologists and teachers. Whereas both indicated that, overall, they did not feel very comfortable with discussing the topic of death, school psychologists and graduate students in school psychology strongly endorsed the idea that children need help to understand death. Teachers and student teachers, on the other hand, were more cautious about children's need for direct help. This may reflect differences in training. When asked what made them feel qualified to discuss death with children, more school psychologists referred to specific clinical and professional training compared to teachers. Teachers often expressed a desire for more training on this issue and felt that training would help them to know "what was the right thing to say."

Indeed, school staff often report feeling concerned about not "doing the right thing" and are wary of causing "upset" by discussing death with children (Holland, 2001; Lowton & Higgenson, 2003). In our survey, approximately half of the participants indicated that they had spoken to children about death. Almost all school psychologists said that they had spoken to children about death, whereas student teachers had the least amount of experience in talking about death (see Figure 5.1).

We asked participants to reflect on their feelings about these conversations and on how successful they thought they had been in discussing death with children. Of those that had talked to children about death, less than half felt completely comfortable talking to children about death. These participants often recognized a general reluctance to discuss such difficult topics. For instance, one teacher commented, "We often perceive death as a 'white elephant' and that it is not okay to talk about it. When we do this, children begin to perceive this as well, and that is not a healthy way to deal with it." However, they also recognized that it is important to respond to the needs of the student and that it is an issue that everyone has to deal with. One student teacher commented, "I think that it is important to be open about discussing death in order to help [the student] with healing and acceptance." Others also commented on the need to be open to student-centered conversations that allow an expression of different views and sharing of experiences. For instance, one teacher noted: "It is a human issue; we all have experiences to bring to the table – my students are older and have a lot to say; I have studied religions, sociology, and philosophy which all provide different approaches or perspectives." Similarly, a school psychologist commented: "I don't pretend to have all the answers; I focus on the subjective experience and try to be honest and age appropriate." Overall, school psychologists were most likely to feel comfortable talking about death, whereas teachers were more likely to state they felt uncomfortable. Furthermore, half of the participants said that they felt only partially satisfied with the explanation they provided about death, and this was true for both teachers and school psychologists. For many, their discomfort and lack of satisfaction about discussing death with children was attributed to feeling unqualified and unprepared. This was a recurring theme for many of our participants.

Similar to past reports (Lowton & Higgenson, 2003; Mahon et al., 1999), less than half of the respondents felt qualified to discuss death with children. There was again a difference based on professional experience (see Figure 5.2). Students (both in education and psychology) were less likely to feel qualified than teachers and school psychologists. Some noted that they felt only partially qualified depending on the circumstances. For instance: "I don't really feel qualified to speak to a child about a close relative who has passed away, but I do feel comfortable with explaining death to a child who hasn't experienced such a loss yet or who has lost a pet or distant acquaintance."

Students often expressed a desire to receive more training and supervision on this issue. One school psychology graduate student stated that although she felt positively about the importance of discussing death with children, she "would like to have this experience while under supervision of someone

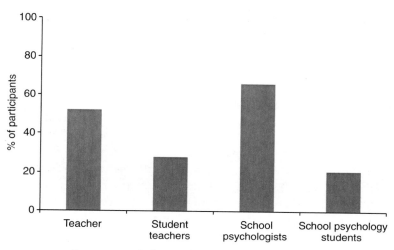

FIGURE 5.2. Percentage of educational professionals who said they felt qualified to discuss death with children.

more qualified." Teachers who had had some specific training on talking to children about death did indicate that they felt more confident and credited their confidence to their training: "I have taken a class about death and feel better prepared because of it. Many people are not comfortable talking about it, but I learned a lot about what to say to someone dealing with death from my course." In our study, the teachers who had training indicated that they had taken extra professional courses or seminars on the topic. However, many teachers said that they did not feel qualified to deal with death in educational settings and felt they had never received adequate training to deal with such issues.

Interestingly, of those participants who said that they had not talked to children about death, most indicated it was because a death had not yet occurred. Thus, many were waiting for a death to occur rather than seeing it as part of their curriculum or talking about it in advance. Most who did not talk about death also felt unqualified as well as uncomfortable discussing death. However, some expressed feelings of regret for missed opportunities:

> I once worked in a high school where many children knew a girl who committed suicide. I wasn't their primary teacher but I was close with some of them and I always wished that I could have gone back and asked the teacher if I could have spoken to them about the situation as a group.

One teacher expressed regret at not talking to a class about the death of another teacher who had been ill for sometime, saying, "had I spoken to them about death before the death occurred they might have been slightly better prepared." In another instance, a school psychologist stated in the case of a child who was ill with cancer: "It might have been beneficial to speak to the child's classmates as a group. This would have helped them understand what the child was going through as well as deal with their potential concerns and fears." Others expressed less certainty about whether they should have discussed death with children. For instance, one teacher reflected on the deaths in the media that were widely discussed after the terrorist attacks on the Twin Towers in New York: "When 9/11 occurred, I think it would have been helpful. I'm still not sure though."

Overall, the participants in our study felt some ambiguity toward discussing death with children. Although they recognized the importance of discussing death in education, many felt some uneasiness or lack of confidence in engaging in such discussions. Given our societal qualms about talking about death, such attitudes are not surprising. The topic of death challenges us to think not only about the end of life, but also about more fundamental questions such as what death means and what happens after death.

## WHAT COMES AFTER DEATH?

When talking about death with children, questions about what happens after death naturally arise. How to address discussions regarding afterlife beliefs has led to a heated debate about the appropriateness of a biological versus religious framework (Schleifer & Talwar, 2009). The place of religion when talking about death is an important question to consider. Although it is possible to discuss death without reference to religion, adults do need to be prepared to answer questions about what happens in the afterlife and, indeed, whether or not there is an afterlife. In our survey, several participants who had talked to children about death found that children had questions about what happened after death or about religious beliefs. Considering that the majority of adults in our society hold some spiritual or religious beliefs concerning the afterlife, it is natural for many to refer to their own spiritual beliefs in their discussions about death and the afterlife.

Some have suggested that religious explanations may impede children's understanding of death (Cotton & Range, 1990). However, this may be partly because of adults' tendency to use confusing euphemisms to explain death (Butler & Lagoni, 1996). Research by Harris and colleagues

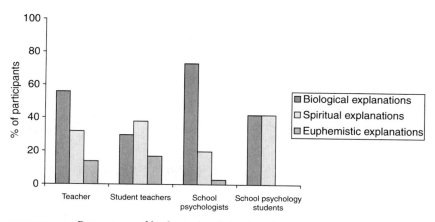

FIGURE 5.3. Percentage of biological, spiritual, and euphemistic explanations of death given to children.

suggests that children's biological conceptions of death develop early and their religious conceptions of death are constructed upon this biological foundation without interference. Like adults, children's biological and religious understanding of death can coexist (Harris & Astuti, 2006; Harris & Gimenez, 2005). Indeed, including religious beliefs can help to give more meaning to the physical explanation of death (Cruchet, 2009). For example, a parent could explain the death of a grandparent both in terms of biological processes and religious beliefs: "Grandpa died because he was very very sick. He died because his body stopped working, his heart stopped beating. We believe that the spirit of the person who dies goes to heaven. We believe Grandpa's spirit is now in heaven." Thus, an adult can truthfully explain what they believe happens after death as part of a larger conversation that also provides a biological explanation of death. A biological explanation provides children with an understanding that death is final and irreversible, whereas a spiritual explanation allows them to consider the meaning of the death and their relationship with the loved one who has died. In our survey, the majority reported using biological explanations of death (e.g., their body has stopped working, their heart has stopped) when talking to children. However, almost half also provided spiritual explanations (e.g., their soul is in heaven; see Figure 5.3).

When children have experienced a loss, it is important that adults explain death in concrete and unambiguous terms (Shapiro, 1994; Webb, 1993). Using euphemisms such as "passed away," "sleeping," or "gone for a rest" can confuse a child. Schleifer (2009) gives a humorous example of a child's confusion about what has happened to her dead grandmother. The parents had told the child that "Grandma, has gone up there now," obliquely referring to a belief that Grandma was now in heaven. Later they were to overhear the child explaining to her friend that "Grandma is up on the roof now." On the whole, few participants in our survey reported using euphemistic terms to discuss death (e.g., "he has gone to sleep forever" or "it's time for her to rest"), and those that did were either teachers or student teachers. Both school psychologists and graduate school psychology students avoided using such terms (see Figure 5.3).

Like the larger society, which holds spiritual beliefs about death as well as a biological concept of death, teachers reflect this duality in their attitudes toward discussing death. In our survey, many educators felt that both biological and spiritual explanations were appropriate. This is similar to other reports of teachers' explanations of death. For instance, Mahon and colleagues (1999) reported that although some teachers believed death is a religious issue that did not belong in schools at all, this did not reflect the views of the majority. Other teachers felt that if they could not talk about religion when discussing death with children, their discussion would be limited. Teachers from religious schools believed it was easier to provide death education, because they could integrate religious considerations into any discussion (Mahon et al., 1999). However, for teachers in secular schools, they are only able to discuss biological explanations of death within the classroom context. The place of biological and spiritual explanations in the classroom is an ongoing debate that is partly informed by cultural, historical, and societal views about the role of education and the place for religious instruction (see Talwar & Schleifer, 2009). Nevertheless, given the wide prevalence of religious beliefs about the afterlife, teachers should be prepared for children to bring up such topics in one-on-one discussions regardless of what is taught in the classroom.

In culturally diverse environments, children may come from backgrounds where there are a range of beliefs and explanations about death. We found that a number of participants expressed the need to be "more informed in dealing with different values or religious views." Participants in our study recognized that understanding this diversity was an important element for helping children talk about death in a supportive manner. Having group discussions about different beliefs and practices surrounding death can be an educational opportunity for children to learn about different cultures and religions.

Many teachers recognize the importance of being able to address children's religious/spiritual conceptions of death and the questions that may arise from these beliefs. In our study, many of the participants stated that when they had discussed death with children, they had provided explanations about death that were grounded in spiritual beliefs about an afterlife in addition to biological explanations. Interestingly, those that indicated strong spiritual or religious beliefs were more likely to say that they felt prepared and comfortable when discussing death. However, they were no less likely to give biological explanations of death than those without spiritual or religious beliefs. Given the prevalence of beliefs about the afterlife, it may be that a frank discussion about death in a supportive and clear manner that includes both biological and spiritually based considerations may help children construct for themselves their own beliefs about the distinction between the fate of the body and the fate of the spirit.

### DEATH EDUCATION IN THE CLASSROOM

In school settings, it has been suggested that the topic of death be included in the school curriculum to facilitate social development and prevent future psychological problems (Deaton & Berkan, 1995). The term "death education" is used to refer to a specific curriculum about death that is either separate or integrated into the class. Its purpose is to inform children about death and related experiences, and to develop healthy attitudes toward death and loss by identifying values that affect feelings and grief. Busch and Kimble (2001) noted that such education should ideally take place prior to children's experiences of death, because it gives them knowledge that may help them to process and deal with another's death. For instance, there is some evidence that children of parents who had terminal cancer were better able to cope with their parents' death when they were able to discuss the death prior to the actual loss (Siegal et al., 1990). However, discussing death does not have to be a topic that is saved for when someone dies. Death education is a proactive intervention and response to children's educational and psychological needs.

Often, however, schools wait until a tragedy strikes and then react. In such cases, interventions are needed to deal with students' feelings and grief. In some cases where resources exist, counselors may be brought into schools to support children who have suffered a loss (Lowton & Higgenson, 2003). Many schools adopt crisis intervention models to address such situations (Aspinall, 1996). These strategies deal with the immediate emotional aftermath of such tragedies. However, death education as part of the everyday curriculum can provide an opportunity for discussion of death without the emotional upset and grief that is present when an actual death has occurred.

For example, one teacher stated, "As a science teacher, I had the opportunity to discuss it [death] during biology class. Talking about death, separated from emotion, before a death has occurred can prepare children to better deal with the inevitable events related to death in their own lives."

The absence of death education in schools may be due in part to practical considerations such as the lack of time in an already crowded curriculum and the lack of qualified personnel to discuss death. With constrained resources and so many demands on time, death education does not place high on the priority list (Aspinall, 1996). Furthermore, training in death education is not typically included in initial teacher training. Given the many misconceptions about children's ability to understand death, teacher training could benefit from developmental information about children's understanding of death and how to provide children accurate and developmentally appropriate information about death (Shapiro, 1994; Webb, 1993). Within schools and in teacher training programs, the question remains: Where in the curriculum should death education be included? Most participants in our survey suggested it belonged in health or biology class.

A few teachers noted that they incorporated it into their regular curriculum and felt that it was a natural fit. Some suggested it could be included within a range of topics. For instance, one teacher noted that "opportunities exist in all courses, whether it be a discussion about diseases or disease prevention, an examination of music lyrics, or different religious practices for funerals/memorials, etc., or reading the newspaper obituaries and writing our own 'humorous' obituary." Another teacher expressed how it can be incorporated naturally when the topic arises from the class materials being used:

> I taught [about death] in literature and Media Studies. The topic cannot be avoided. Such discussions often came out of the material under study. It is important, however, to add that all of these occasions were not equal in profundity. Those about the experience of real grief were on a very different emotional plane from those arising out of the "preposterous violence" of American Media.

Others were less specific about where they thought discussions of death should occur in the curriculum, but indicated that it was an important topic to address as a group in the classroom: "I believe that most children, especially of a young age, might have misconceptions about death based on what they hear in stories and see in movies. A group discussion could help dispel any misconceptions and clarify the realities about death." As noted by the teachers in our survey, there are a number of ways that death education can be incorporated into the curriculum. The arts can be used to allow children to express themselves through dance, drama, drawing, puppets, or the creation of a mural or memory box of an individual who has died. Death can be included informally in classroom discussions when it naturally arises out of the topic of study such as a story (e.g., *Charlotte's Web* or *Harry Potter*) or a historical or current event. Death education can also be included in a cross-cultural or religious studies class comparing funeral rites and religious customs.

Furthermore, it can be included more formally in classes such as science or health classes. Children can be encouraged to make observations of the seasons and the growing cycle. Younger children can grow plants or care for class pets. Students can be taken on nature walks where they identify living and dead things. The goal is to emphasize the normalcy of death within the life cycle and reduce the stigma surrounding the topic of death.

However, deaths such as that of a teenager due to drunk driving or a suicide may be difficult to understand within in the terms of a "normal life cycle." In such cases, interventions that allow students to grapple with their feelings and understand such deaths will be necessary. Discussion of these types deaths (when they are more abstract or after a suitable delay in time if such tragedies have occurred) may become part of a health class on risky behaviors such as dangerous driving and drug abuse. Addressing such topics and such deaths in school is important especially with adolescents who may experience feelings of guilt (e.g., feeling they caused a friend's suicide), distress, and anger (e.g., feeling both sad and angry about a friend who died while driving drunk). Such discussions can also be preventative in helping adolescents realize the consequences of risky behaviors and the impact such behaviors have on their own and others' lives. For younger children, some recommend using less emotionally significant deaths such as the death of a pet as points of departure for discussions about death (Wass, Millet, & Thorton, 1990).

However, when children do experience the death of someone close to them, it is no longer an abstract concept, and they will need to reconcile their feelings about the loss of the person with their understanding of what happens biologically to the body. Children who have suffered the loss of a loved one may also need longer-term interventions and may need to talk outside of the regular classroom activities. Anniversaries of the death of a loved one or other events such as birthdays or holidays (e.g., Christmas, Father's Day) may also bring new feelings of grief to the surface. Children may feel better if they can commemorate the memory of the loved one (e.g., planting a tree) or mark these special anniversaries in some way.

When a child has suffered a loss, intervention and treatment needs to be coordinated among all those involved with the child (Aspinall, 1996). In such cases school psychologists may be called on to provide assistance to the child, the family, and the school.

Another important factor for children is their family's ability to cope with death. A family who minimizes emotional expression, lacks knowledge about children's understanding of death, or avoids talking about death may not adequately respond to the child's feelings and fears. The school psychologist can play an active role in working with families who experience intense grief in a way that is supportive and collaborative with the family while also being child-centered (Aspinall, 1996). In working with families, Shapiro (1994) identified several key areas to address. First, children need to be helped to manage the intensity of their feelings. Second, families need help in stabilizing the family (due to the increased stress) and in developing support networks through the extended family and community. Finally, those working with children and families must be sensitive to cultural issues: rituals, beliefs about death, and the roles of different family members.

Death education and interventions can be an opportunity for teachers and school psychologists to collaborate. Teachers can develop practical applications, and school psychologists can provide theoretical and empirical knowledge about children's understanding of and reactions to death. School psychologists can work with teachers to help them understand how they can provide a supportive environment in the classroom as well as provide opportunities for students to discuss their loss privately in one-on-one sessions. Such interventions can also benefit from coordination with family, school, and community resources. Finally, it is essential that staff explore their own perceptions about death, including their unique personal and cultural influences (Aspinall, 1996). We have to come to terms with our own mortality to deal with others' grief.

## CONCLUSION

It is clear from our survey that educational professionals are aware of the importance of discussing death with children. Yet they do not feel fully equipped to do so. Almost all participants indicated that the biggest challenge to educating children about death was a lack of professional training and a lack of confidence. Some also indicated that dealing with their own feelings of discomfort about the topic was a challenge. Only a few suggested that discussing death should be dealt with "case by case" and should not necessarily be part of classroom time.

Part of the reason death education and intervention may not have been widely embraced in professional training programs, schools, and classrooms may be the lingering taboo surrounding the topic of death and the discomfort it creates. Talking about death requires us to address our own feeling and beliefs about death both individually and collectively. Death is a topic that is easy to ignore or postpone. However, children will still have questions about death, experience feelings of loss and grief, and have fears about death. Not talking about death and avoiding the topic may magnify children's fears and confusion. Educating children about death will help them understand it, reduce their fears, and help them cope with the loss of a loved one. However, first we need to surmount our own fears and taboos about death and educate ourselves about how to openly, without trepidation, discuss the topic of death.

## ACKNOWLEDGMENTS

I would like to thank Sarah Jane Renaud and Michael Schleifer for their collaboration and help on the research that inspired this chapter. I would also like to thank the teachers, school psychologists, and students who gave generously of their time. A special thanks to Paul Harris for his comments and suggestions.

## REFERENCES

Aspinall, S. (1996). Educating children to cope with death: A preventive model. *Psychology in the Schools, 33,* 341–349.

Bering, J. (2006). The folk psychology of souls. *Behavioral and Brain Sciences, 29,* 453–462.

Bering, J. & Bjorklund, D. (2004). The natural emergence of reasoning about the afterlife as a developmental regularity. *Developmental Psychology, 40,* 217–233.

Busch, T. & Kimble, C. (2001). Grieving children: Are we meeting the challenge? *Paediatric Nursing, 27,* 414–418.

Butler, C. & Lagoni, L. (1996). Children and pet loss. In C. Corr & D. Corr (Eds.) *Handbook of childhood death and bereavement* (pp. 179–200). New York, NY: Springer.

Corr, C.A., Nabe, C.M., & Corr, D.M. (2003). *Death and dying, life and living (4th ed.).* Belmont, CA: Wadsworth.

Cotton, C.R., & Range, L.M. (1990). Children's death concepts: relationship to cognitive functioning, age, experience with death, fear of death, and hopelessness. *Journal of Clinical Child & Adolescent Psychology, 19,* 123–127.

Cruchet, D. (2009). Leçons apprises des experts : les enfants en deuil. In M. Schleifer & V. Talwar (Eds.), *La Science et la Religion en education: Comment Reponde aux Questions des enfants* (pp. 59–68). Montreal, QC: Presses de l'Université du Québec.

Cullinan, A.L. (1990). Teachers' death anxiety, ability to cope with death, and perceived ability to aid bereaved students. *Death Studies, 14*, 147–160.

Deaton, R., & Berkan, W. (1995). *Planning and managing death issues in the schools.* Westport, CT: Greenwood Press.

Estes, D. (2006). Evidence for early dualism and a more direct path to afterlife beliefs. *Behavioral and Brain Sciences, 29*, 470–470.

Gaynard, L., Goldberger, J., & Laidley, L. (1991). The use of stuffed, body-outline dolls with hospitalized children and adolescents. *Children's Health Care, 20*, 216–224.

Golman, L. (1994). *Life and loss: A guide to help grieving children.* Washington, D.C.: Taylor & Francis.

Grollman, E. (1990). *Talking about death.* Boston, MA: Beacon Press.

Harris, P.L., & Astuti, R. (2006). Learning that there is life after death. *Behavioral and Brain Sciences, 29*, 475–476.

Harris, P.L. & Giménez, M. (2005). Children's acceptance of conflicting testimony: The case of death. *Journal of Cognition and Culture, 5*, 143–164.

Hogan, N., & DeSantis, L. (1996). Adolescent sibling bereavement: Toward a new theory. In C. Corr & D.B. Balk (Eds.). *Handbook of adolescent death and bereavement.* (pp. 173–195). New York, NY: Springer.

Holland, J. (2008). How schools can support children who experience loss and death. *British Journal of Guidance & Counselling, 36*, 411–424.

(2001). *Understanding children's experiences of parental bereavement.* London, UK: Jessica Kingsley.

Hurd, R. (1999). Adults view their childhood experiences. *Death Studies, 23*, 17–41.

Kenyon, B. (2001). Current research in children's conceptions of death: a critical review. *OMEGA – Journal of Death and Dying, 43*, 69–91.

Lowton, K., & Higgenson, I. (2003). Managing bereavement in the classroom: A conspiracy of silence? *Death Studies, 2*, 717–741.

Mahon, M., Goldberg, R., & Washington, S. (1999). Discussing death in the classroom: Beliefs and experiences of educators and education students. *OMEGA – Journal of Death and Dying, 39*, 99–121.

McCarthy, R.J. & Jessop, J. (2005). *Young people, bereavement and loss: Disruptive transitions?* London, UK: NCB.

McGovern, M., & Barry, M. (2000). Death education: Knowledge, attitudes, and perspectives of Irish parents and teachers. *Death Studies, 24*, 325–333.

Papadatou, D., Metallinou, O., Hatzichristou, C., & Pavlidi, L. (2002). Supporting the bereaved child: Teachers' perceptions and experiences in Greece. *Mortality, 7*, 324–339.

Piaget, J. (1929). *The Child's Conception of the World.* New York, NY: Harcourt, Brace and Co.

Reid, J. (2002). School management and eco-systemic support for bereaved children and their classroom. *Psychology in the Schools, 36*, 219–229.

Renaud, S-J. Talwar, V. & Schleifer, M. (May, 2010). Talking to children about death. Canadian Society for Studies in Education Conference, Montreal, QC.

Rosenthal, N.J. (1981). Attitudes toward death education and grief counseling. *Counselor Education and Supervision, 20*, 202–210.

Schleifer, M., & Talwar, V. (2009). *La Science et la Religion en education: Comment Repondre aux Questions des enfants.* Montreal, QC: Presses de l'Université du Québec.

Schonfeld, D.J. (1989). Crisis intervention for bereavement support. A model of intervention in the children's school. *Clinical Pediatrics, 28,* 27–33.

Sharp, K.C., Candy-Gibbs, S., Barlow-Elliot, L., & Petrun, C.J. (1985). Children's judgement and reasoning about aliveness: Effects of object, age, and cultural/social background. *Merrill-Palmer Quarterly, 31,* 47–65.

Shapiro, E. (1994). *Grief as a family process.* New York, NY: The Guildford Press.

Schoen, A., Burgoyne, M., & Schoen, S. (2004). Are the developmental needs of children in America adequately addressed in the grieving process? *Journal of Instructional Psychology, 31,* 143–150.

Siegel, K., Mesagno, F., & Christ, G. (1990). A prevention program for bereaved children. *American Journal of Orthopsychiatry, 60,* 168–175.

Slaughter, V., & Lyons, M. (2003). Learning about life and death in early childhood. *Cognitive Psychology, 46,* 1–30.

Speece, M., & Brent, S. (1984). Children's understanding of death: A review of three components of a death concept. *Child Development, 55,* 1671–1686.

(1996). The development of children's understanding of death. In C. Corr & D. Corr (Eds.), *Handbook of childhood death and bereavement* (pp. 29–50). New York, NY: Springer., 29–50.

Takeuchi, H., Hiroe, T., Kanai, T., Morinobu, S., Kitamura, T., Takahashi, K., et al. (2003). Childhood parental separation experiences and depressive symptomatology in acute major depression. *Psychiatry & Clinical Neurosciences, 57,* 215.

Talwar, V. (2009). Faut-il mentir à votre enfant au sujet de la mort du poisson rouge? In M. Schleifer & V. Talwar (Eds.), *La Science et la Religion en education: Comment Repondre aux Questions des enfants* (pp. 33–42). Montreal, QC: Presses de l'Université du Québec.

Vianello, R., & Lucamente, M. (1998). Children's understanding of death according to parents and pediatricians. *The Journal of Genetic Psychology, 149,* 305.

Wass, H., Millet, M.D., & Thorton, G. (1990). Death education and grief/suicide intervention in the public schools. *Death Studies, 14,* 253–268.

Webb, N. (1993). *Helping bereaved children.* New York, NY: The Guildford Press.

Wolfelt, A. (1996). *Healing the bereaved child: Grief gardening, growth through grief and other touchstones for caregivers*: Fort Collins: CO: Companion Press.

# 6

## Responsible Believing

MIRIAM MCCORMICK

In most of our decisions as parents or educators concerning how we should talk to children about difficult subjects, the question turns to what degree we should withhold the truth, how much information we should provide, or what details are appropriate. We, as adults, know the answer to the child's question, and the difficulty arises in figuring out what to convey and how. Questions about death and the afterlife are not like this. We – and by "we," I mean especially educated adults of the Western world – are often as confused about what we should believe about these matters as are our children. It seems that an initial step in our thinking about how to engage with children on this topic is to become clearer about how we ought to think about it. I will discuss this matter by engaging with the question of which norms ought to govern the formation and maintenance of our beliefs in general. We can then see how these norms would apply to beliefs about anything supernatural. What we ought to believe does not settle the question of how we should talk to children about our beliefs; we do not always want our children's beliefs to match our own. There may be particular reasons we want our children to believe things we do not (like Santa Claus brings them presents) or not believe things we do (like their noncustodial parent is a jerk); but I will concentrate on how one is a responsible believer in general, which will provide insight into how we can educate children to be responsible believers.

In my first section, I discuss what it can mean to be responsible for beliefs given that one does not exercise control over beliefs the way one does over action. In section two, I turn to the question of whether it is possible to both believe without evidence and still believe responsibly. Most contemporary philosophers would deny the possibility of this conjunction, because most hold that an evidential norm governs belief, namely that one should only believe on sufficient evidence. It may seem that we often restrict the term "belief" to a less confident attitude. That is, when we have compelling evidence for a proposition, we would say we *know* it rather than merely believe it. Most philosophers think of knowledge as a particular kind of belief, one that is at least both true and justified. However, in evaluating beliefs, we can assess whether one has good reasons for holding a particular belief even if it falls short of knowledge.

This evidentialist perspective allows two possible answers to what one should believe about what occurs after death or about the reason for seemingly bizarre or significant life events. The first is that we should suspend judgment about such matters because the evidence is silent – and when we have no evidence or the evidence is neutral, the proper evidentialist attitude is to refrain from forming a belief. The other possible response is to hold that the evidence favors the belief that there is nothing that occurs after death and there is no reason why events occur beyond what can be explained scientifically or causally.

I argue that this evidentialist framework is impoverished and has led to a narrow and overly intellectual picture of the concept of belief. Arguments for evidentialism can show that evidential norms do a good job of providing us with general rules for belief maintenance, but once we understand the reason for why they ought to be followed in general, we see that these norms do not always hold. If beliefs are thought of as having a purpose, the purpose must be of a practical kind. Our beliefs serve the purpose of providing coherence, meaning making, prediction, and navigation, both individually and collectively. It is thus possible for these practical norms to override evidential ones. Once non-evidential norms are admitted, I argue some "supernatural" beliefs are permissible and can be responsibly believed. In my final section, I suggest some ways in which this conclusion impacts decisions about how to talk to children about death.

## RESPONSIBILITY AND CONTROL

The notion of responsibility in the realm of believing is commonly invoked in ordinary practice. We express disapproval and approval for each other's beliefs; we ask in an incredulous tone, "How can you believe that?" or exclaim, "What a ridiculous thing to believe!" Such admonishments seem to reveal that we think the person in question has formed the belief irresponsibly, and it seems we hold him responsible for forming this belief. This notion of responsibility is not simply one that is pointing out the causal genesis of the belief. Holding someone responsible for his beliefs is not like holding the wind responsible for knocking over the tent. That we praise and blame each other for the beliefs we hold seems to indicate, rather, that we view the beliefs one forms to be the consequence of one's agency. Yet attributions of responsibility and other deontological judgments in the doxastic (belief) realm are puzzling, for much of what we believe is beyond our control; we cannot decide to believe the way we can decide to act. It seems that such lack of control should excuse us from responsibility and judgment.

We can formulate our puzzle by considering the following argument:

### The Voluntarism Argument

1. If attributions of responsibility for beliefs are appropriate, then people have voluntary control over their beliefs.
2. People do not have voluntary control over their beliefs.
3. Attributions of responsibility about beliefs are not appropriate.

Yet our practices seem to assume such attributions are appropriate. We would disapprove of someone who believes that whales are fishes or that her neighbor littered the sidewalk when she did not. We think a typically well-informed American ought to believe that the Earth revolves around the Sun and would be critical of someone who believes that the Sun revolves around the Earth. Yet it seems quite clear that one with such a belief could not just decide to change it in the direct way he could simply decide to change his shirt. Nor did he originally decide to acquire the belief the way one could decide to acquire a new pair of shoes.

Three responses to this puzzle are possible. The first response denies the second premise, arguing that, at times, we can effectively decide to believe; this view has come to be called doxastic voluntarism. On one reading of Descartes's fourth meditation, he articulates a very robust form of such voluntarism. He says that our will is completely free to affirm or deny what is presented to the intellect: "The will consists solely in the fact that when something is proposed to us by our intellect either to affirm or deny, to pursue or to shun, we are moved in such a way that we sense that we are determined to it by no external force" (Descartes, 1993, pp. 38–89). For Descartes, we are as free to choose our beliefs as we are our actions, and this is his explanation of both doxastic and moral error; it makes as much sense to blame me for my beliefs as it does my actions, which come from the same faculty. Thus, I can consider the proposition "The Sun revolves around the Earth," and then decide whether to assent to it or not. According to Descartes, I ought to restrain my will and only assent to those propositions that are "clearly and distinctly represented to it [the will] by the understanding." I am thus clearly responsible for not restraining my will when I let myself believe those propositions that I "conceive more confusedly and obscurely." Although contemporary doxastic voluntarists are more moderate, they still hold that, at times, what one believes can result directly from a decision to believe.

A second response to the puzzle argues that although we lack control over our beliefs, we can nonetheless be held responsible for them, thus denying the first premise. This is currently the most common response. Those who argue that we lack meaningful control in the doxastic realm must say what doxastic responsibility does require. If I cannot exercise control over my beliefs, what justifies holding me responsible? The answers given to this question say that when we admonish people for holding certain beliefs, we are really admonishing them for their defective characters or for their failure to cultivate certain virtues. So it is not the holding of the belief, for example, that the Sun revolves around the Earth that is blameworthy. Rather, there is something defective in the person who holds such a belief. Perhaps it is a character flaw that prevents him from being properly attentive or from weighing evidence properly.

Finally, one can respond by accepting the argument as sound, and so deny that we are responsible for beliefs and argue that our common practices of attributions of responsibility are misguided; we are mistaken if we think, for example, someone should be praised or blamed for a belief he holds. Just as I cannot help feeling wet when rain falls on me or hot when the sun is strong, my believing that it is raining or the sun is strong is not something that is "up to me"; it is a state I find myself in when the world impinges on me in certain ways. On such a view, belief is a passive phenomenon and it must be able to do its job. David Hume is often invoked as the exemplar of such a view.[1] Although I ultimately think this is a mistaken characterization of Hume's view, some of what he says about belief supports this passive reading.

If our practice of attributing responsibility for beliefs is appropriate, I think a sense needs to be articulated in which we do have a kind of control

[1] For example, David Owens (2000) characterizes Hume's position in the following way: "In denying the existence of epistemic agency, doxastic responsibility and intellectual freedom, Hume means to reject the idea that belief is subject to reason. He allows that beliefs are governed by the sort of biological norms that apply to the process of breathing, or the workings of the human heart but no one thinks us responsible for non-compliance with such norms." (2) There are many passages in Hume's works where it is evident he does blame people for having or failing to have certain beliefs. How such admonishments are consistent with his theory of belief is a topic discussed extensively by Hume scholars. I discuss these issues in "Why Should We Be Wise?"(McCormick, 2005a) Hume Studies, Vol. 31, no 1, April 2005, pp. 3–19.

over our beliefs. In developing this notion of doxastic control, I draw from John Fischer's discussions of "guidance control." A central feature of this kind of control is the idea of "ownership." Those aspects of our lives for which we take responsibility are the ones we own. I will argue that we can own our beliefs and that we expect each other to do so. Beliefs are products of our agency, something we have an active role in shaping and maintaining. Although we cannot believe at will, neither are we passive in the beliefs we form and maintain. We take responsibility for our beliefs, and taking responsibility includes taking control of them. We are blamed when we lose this grasp, when we do not exercise our reflective competence that helps us believe the way we ought to believe.

It may seem, then, that I am siding with the voluntarists and so denying the second premise of the Voluntarism Argument. Yet I do not think a belief can arise directly from a decision to believe. Many of those who oppose doxastic voluntarism admit that we have a kind of indirect control over beliefs, but they do not think our attributions of responsibility are tied in any way to this kind of control. The kind of control for which I will argue is not the indirect kind that these theorists concede; it is not simply derived from other states over which we do have control. It may be, in the end, that the kind of control I claim we have over beliefs is robust enough to count me among the moderate doxastic voluntarists. It may be that it lacks sufficient directness for those who advocate doxastic voluntarism. It matters little into which category the account is placed. What I want to defend is (i) that attributions of responsibility and other deontological judgments about beliefs are appropriate, and (ii) these attributions and judgments presuppose that we have control in the doxastic realm.

One of the reasons it may seem that we lack control over our beliefs is that so many of them are unavoidable and irresistible. If it is impossible for me to avoid holding a particular belief, how can I be said to have any control over my holding it? For doesn't being in control entail that I could have done otherwise or could have chosen differently? Many theorists have been concerned with formulating a concept of control (and responsibility) that does not entail that one could have done otherwise. For if causal determinism is true (or if God has created one and only one perfect world plan), there may be a sense in which we can never act other than we do. However, it seems we would not want our notions of responsibility and all the practices that go along with them to be rendered meaningless if it turned out that we did live in a deterministic universe. John Fischer calls the kind of control that does not entail alternative possibilities "guidance control." To illustrate the kind of thing he has in mind, imagine that you are driving a car that is a "driver instruction" automobile with dual controls. As long as you are driving in a relatively safe manner, the instructor lets you control the car, and so when you, at the correct time, turn to the right, it is you who is guiding the car to the right. If you had shown signs of confusion and were about to mistakenly turn to the left, however, the instructor would have stepped in and steered it to the right. Thus you could have gone in no other direction but to the right. So although you have guidance control over the car, you lack what Fischer calls "regulative control" – the instructor has that.

In their book, Fischer and Mark Ravizza provide detailed elaboration of this concept of guidance control and argue that it is sufficient for moral responsibility. They are adamant that responsibility requires control, just not the kind of "regulative control" that requires alternative possibilities. An agent exhibits guidance control of an action "insofar as the mechanism which actually issues in his action is his own, reasons-responsive mechanism" (Fischer and Ravizza, 1998, p. 39). Some theorists have argued that only reasons-responsiveness is needed, but if all that were required for responsibility is that the mechanism issuing in the action (or belief) is reasons-responsive, then even if you were directly manipulated (say, had scientists kidnapped you and implanted such a reasons-responsive mechanism), you would still be responsible.

For the mechanism that actually issues in certain behavior to be one's own, one must take responsibility for it. Taking responsibility is understood historically. As one comes to view oneself as an agent, as having an effect on the world as a consequence of one's intentions and decisions, one comes to view oneself as a fair target for the reactive attitudes such as punishment or praise. By viewing oneself as an appropriate target for the consequence of a particular mechanism (say, ordinary practical reasoning), one thereby takes responsibility for it and the behavior resulting from it. Once one takes responsibility for a particular mechanism, then this ownership extends to future operations of the mechanism. It is a process that occurs over time, in which we develop a concept of ourselves as engaged in a kind of conversation. When we are addressed and treated as responsible agents through such attitudes as praising and blaming, we begin to form an internal view of ourselves as responsible and develop our own way of assessing and reacting to others. Fischer and Ravizza describe the process like this: "The goal of achieving a correlation between external and internal attitudes supports the practices that we use to train individuals who are not yet full members of the moral community and to encourage them to develop the internal view that we are extending to them" (Fischer & Ravizza, 1998, p. 212). Thus, taking responsibility need not be any conscious act; rather, the way we react to others and feel about ourselves reveals whether we have taken responsibility for the mechanism in question.

Can this notion of a mechanism be intelligibly applied to the doxastic realm? Fischer and Ravizza are clear that all they mean by "mechanism" is the process that leads to the relevant upshot. This upshot is some kind of behavior, and by "behavior" they mean to include actions and omissions. They also consider that the upshot may be a trait of character or, as we shall see, perhaps an emotional reaction. It seems plausible that one such upshot can be a belief. Examples they give of mechanisms or processes are deliberation, practical reason, brain-stimulation, irresistible (physically based) urges, hypnosis, addiction, and intentions. Given how broadly mechanisms are construed, it seems perfectly legitimate to talk about the mechanisms that result in beliefs. Some of the processes that result in beliefs are inquiry, evidence gathering, attending, reasoning, memory, and perception. We can now ask if any of these mechanisms are such that we can take responsibility for them. Can we own them as a consequence of our agency the way we can the mechanisms that lead to actions? I think we can see that this is possible if we think about our capacity to feel guilty about having certain beliefs. So imagine that I believe, on inadequate evidence, that my brother stole some money from me. I discover my error, perhaps by finding the money or finding the real thief. Even if I never acted on it in any way, I can still feel guilty for having formed this belief at all. Those who deny that responsibility entails control will say my guilt is not really about holding this belief, and it certainly is not about a failure of control, but rather it is my feeling bad about not being a good person in general. Yet if I really viewed myself as lacking control over this belief, would I feel the same kind of guilt for having it? Say I discovered that I had undergone some kind of psychic manipulation such that the mechanism responsible for issuing in beliefs about my brother was one that was controlled (via some remote control) by some evil scientist. I may still feel some shame and view myself as somehow defective, but part of the reason I feel guilty has to do with this belief being a result of my agency. I have taken responsibility for the mechanism issuing in evidentially based beliefs. When the mechanism is faulty it is my fault, and I can be said to have lost some control over this mechanism given that I am failing to guide my beliefs appropriately.

That some notion of control is in play when assigning blame to beliefs is reinforced if we consider when and why we mitigate such blame. If you *cannot* make your higher-order judgments effective about how you ought to believe, there is a sense in which your belief is no longer your own; you are divided and overpowered. In such a case I would blame you less if you really are compelled to believe in a way that deviates from how you ought to. You are not as open to blame as someone who can believe the way he ought but who fails to put in the care and effort required to do so.[2] Let us now look at a number of different cases of defective believing and see where we are apt to assign responsibility and where we are not. It seems that the more control we have over the belief-issuing processes, the more likely we are to attribute responsibility for it. This kind of control seems to come in degrees, and the more control we have, the less it seems we are apt to mitigate responsibility.

Many of our beliefs result from perception. Perceptual beliefs also seem to be the ones that are most obviously not under one's regulative control. However, if we think again about what it means to take responsibility and accept that this is properly seen as a developmental process, it seems that even this most apparently passive mechanism is one over which we do have some degree of guidance control. Imagine that someone is insistent that he sees a unicorn galloping toward him, and based on the usual trustworthiness of his senses, believes there is a unicorn galloping toward him. If, however, this person is aware that he just took powerful hallucinogenic drugs and still believes there is a unicorn galloping toward him, it seems appropriate for us to criticize him. For if I point out to you reasons for thinking that your normally well-functioning mechanism has gone awry, you should revise your assessment of the resulting upshot. Further, you see yourself as appropriately chastised for being overly confident or hasty in the proper functioning of this mechanism. Imagine a case of misperception that is not a result of an external agent (like a hallucinogenic drug). Sam believes his girlfriend was kissing Jack in the car, and he believes this because he saw her doing so. It turns out she was, in fact, not kissing Jack, and somehow his perception was faulty and misled him into forming a faulty belief. If through pleading and insistence, Sam's girlfriend convinces him that she did not kiss Jack, how should Sam view the belief he formed? It seems appropriate that he should feel some shame about it, and again, he should be criticized for forming and maintaining it.

Of course, it is not possible for us to constantly monitor our perceptual faculties to ensure that they are operating free of biases or neuroses that may be leading us astray. Yet there is some presumption that we should be ready to do some monitoring to ensure that this mechanism for which we have taken responsibility is operating correctly. If I find this mechanism is regularly leading me astray, it seems that there is something wrong with me.

[2] I offer a model of a loss of doxastic control in "Compelled Belief" (McCormick, 2005b).

It would not seem appropriate for me to insist that "these beliefs result from perception over which I lack control and so it is not my fault that I keep forming false beliefs." If your perceptual faculties really are "taken over," say, by some severe psychosis, a point does come where we would excuse you from responsibility. However, this again underscores the difference of our assessment in the nonpathological case in which we think assessments of responsibility are appropriate, and so some degree of control is possible.

Another common belief-issuing mechanism is memory, and again, like perception, this seems to be a process over which I exercise relatively little control. If I have a very vivid memory of an occurrence, it seems almost impossible for me to fail to believe that the thing occurred. However, as in the case of perception, thinking about when and how this mechanism goes awry can help show that the appropriateness of attributions of responsibility are tied to our having some guidance control over this process. Unfortunately, I think we have all been in the following situation: Imagine you are conversing with a friend, and you start talking about a conference you were both at the previous summer. You begin recalling together who else was at the conference. You say, "Oh and John was there – I remember liking his talk." Your friend insists that John was not there, and you are emphatic that you remember him being there. If the next day, your friend shows you the program and convinces you that you misremembered, it seems you will feel very sheepish about your firm belief that John was there, and a certain degree of blameworthiness seems appropriate for you having this belief. One may think it is not the believing that is blameworthy, but rather your having certain character traits like dogmatism or overconfidence that we blame you for. Even if I rarely find myself emphatically persisting in my belief and so do not have this character trait, it seems I am blameworthy in this instance.

Contrast this case again with a pathological one. If someone has Alzheimer's disease and so has a severely defective memory mechanism, there comes a point in which we excuse him from responsibility in his memory-induced beliefs; at the point in which he loses ownership of the process, he becomes incapable of correction and of keeping his beliefs in line with his and others' judgments. As such diseases are often gradual, we can find that, at first, we do continue to react in ways that reveal we hold the agent responsible for his beliefs. We will say with frustration, "Don't you remember? You left the keys on your desk." As the disease progresses, however, such admonishments seem less and less appropriate. Just as lack of control over one's faculties excuses one from being admonished for how one acts, similarly it excuses one from being admonished for how one believes. Again, it is not a question of whether I could have believed otherwise about John's presence at the conference. Rather, this is a belief that I have ownership over in that I have the capacity to keep it in line with how I think I ought to believe.

Attributions of responsibility are the most obviously warranted in cases where beliefs result from deliberation or inquiry, and these are processes over which we clearly have guidance control. These mechanisms are responsible for issuing in actions as well as beliefs. One of the examples that Fischer and Ravizza consider is taking responsibility for "acting from the mechanism of practical reason." They refer to these actions as "reflective actions." Beliefs that come about as a result of reflection are clearly ones for which we have taken responsibility in Fischer and Ravizza's sense.

How, then, would this account of doxastic guidance control address the initial puzzle of doxastic responsibility? Consider again the example of the person who thinks the Sun revolves around the Earth. The most prevalent view argues that our criticism of one's holding this belief is in no one way tied to whether having the belief or not is in one's control. I have argued that such criticism and other manifestations of attributions of responsibility are tied to our expectations that one can do better. We expect a well-informed American to be sensitive to the amount of evidence that supports the heliocentric view and expect that his belief will conform to this evidence. This expectation comes, at least in part, from the fact that he has seen himself as a fair target for being chastised in this way, that he takes responsibility for what he believes, and sees his beliefs as issuing from himself as an agent. These are all the necessary components of guidance control. If one does not exhibit this kind of control, it would be inappropriate to criticize him or otherwise hold him responsible.

## THE LIMITS OF EVIDENTIALISM

The examples I have given of faulty beliefs seem to support the view that believing responsibly entails believing on sufficient evidence. If in the investigation of grounds for believing, one discovers that one lacks evidence or epistemic reasons for one's belief, it seems the responsible believer will give up that belief. This is the dominant view among contemporary philosophers: They say that evidential norms govern beliefs; I should follow my evidence and only believe when the evidence is sufficient. Closely tied to this view is that following evidence will tend to provide me with true beliefs, and that beliefs aim at truth.

I think it is important to acknowledge that truth and knowledge are sub-goals; they are instrumental, not intrinsic goods, and so the possibility is left open that they can be trumped by other norms or goals. If the purpose of belief is to help us achieve our goals, flourish, and be excellent human beings, it is possible that some beliefs can do this independently of their truth value or of their being evidentially based.

In fleshing out his evidentialist thesis, Richard Feldman says that if one adopts any attitude toward a proposition, "that person ought to believe it if his current evidence supports it, disbelieve it if his current evidence is against it, and suspend judgment about it if his evidence is neutral (or close to neutral)" (Feldman, 2000, p. 683). It is the last part of this claim I wish to question. There may be times when there is no evidence (and so is neutral), but that it can still be permissible or even a good thing to believe something. There is some evidence from cognitive psychology that suggests that not only have we humans evolved to be able to decode and interpret meaning from our fellow creatures, but that our brains have also adapted to see meaning in life events. To see both other people and life events as meaningful is a distinctive human capacity and one that those with certain cognitive disorders (like autism) lack. In a sense, it is a developmental accomplishment to be superstitious. This meaning making could translate into a theistic or religious perspective, but it need not. Even those people whose illusions have been disrupted by science still have a lot of trouble letting go of this naturally adapted interpretive power.

Jesse Bering calls this capacity to see significance in life events having an existential theory of mind (EtoM). He says, "it is my impression that we would be hard pressed to discover an individual of normal cognitive functioning who has never exercised his or her EToM." He asks us to imagine the following:

> You are on a crowded bus, lost in the newspaper before you, when suddenly you are caught in a dizzy fury of screams, blackness and crushing metal. Your bus has crashed and flipped over a steep embankment. You crawl out of the window, dust yourself off, and realize that you are the sole survivor out of dozens of other passengers. If a week from now, or a year or decade later, you find yourself asking, "Why me?" then quite simply you have an intact EToM. Even if you brush such questions aside because you see them as rather foolish, you still betray your EToM insofar as you can entertain this type of question in the current context. (Bering, 2002, p. 1)

One could see this as evolutionary design of self-deception, but if we are adapted to believe in meaning, it seems this adaptation serves a purpose.

Maybe it is an outdated purpose and one we should try to get rid of, like "natural" male aggression when faced with rivals. Feldman, and others, would clearly see these beliefs as irrational (and irresponsible) because they violate evidentialist injunctions. However, if we remember the reason for following evidentialist norms (because they will help us maximize epistemic value) and if this value is instrumental (it is valuable because it helps us flourish and contributes to our overall good), then these kinds of meaning-making beliefs may be another way of serving this greater good.

We want our beliefs to conform to our view of the world, to help us succeed in the world, to make us happier. Yet once the practical side is acknowledged it becomes clear that even though evidential norms generally govern belief formation, there are times when it may be rational to believe despite a lack of evidence. The problem with this acknowledgment is that we want a way of distinguishing the "warranted" non-evidentially based beliefs from those that are not warranted.

I think there is an important difference between believing against your evidence and believing when you have no evidence or the evidence is neutral. The difference can be illustrated by reflecting on the nineteenth-century debate between W.K. Clifford and William James. Here is Clifford's flourishing defense of evidentialism:

> It is wrong always, everywhere, and for any one, to believe anything on insufficient evidence ... Belief, that sacred faculty which prompts the decisions of our will, and knits into harmonious working all the compacted energies of our being, is ours not for ourselves, but for humanity ... Every hard-worked wife of an artisan may transmit to her children beliefs which shall knit society together, or rend it in pieces. No simplicity of mind, no obscurity of station, can escape the universal duty of questioning all that we believe. (Clifford, 1987, p. 24)

In the case of believing against evidence, I think Clifford is right; believing in this way is harmful and opposed to collective good. However, James is right in the second context, the context in which we have no evidence or it is equally balanced. In James's, "The Will to Believe," he responds directly to Clifford's strong evidentialist stance. He agrees that in many contexts, evidential considerations will settle the matter, but on questions that cannot be decided by the evidence, he says the following:

> Our passional nature not only lawfully may, but must, decide an option between propositions, whenever it is a genuine option that cannot by its nature be decided on intellectual grounds; for to say, under such circumstances, "Do not decide, but leave the question open," is itself a passional

decision, – just like deciding yes or no, – and is attended with the same risk of losing the truth. (James, 1956)

If our "passional" nature has developed to form beliefs about there being significance or meaning in life events, even when there is no evidence, this may give further support for James's view.

In helping to further flesh out this distinction between non-evidentially based beliefs that are pernicious and those that are not, it is helpful to think of true belief as a common good, that the value of true beliefs is comparable to the value of clean water.[3] It may be the case that a particular body of water is of no value to me, and so if I pollute it I will not suffer; but we still think it is wrong because the water has value and should be respected, regardless of whether it is useful to me; clean water plays such an indispensable role in our well-being, we have an obligation – to others – not to pollute in this way, but rather to treat clean water with due respect. Similarly, not every true belief is of value to me; it may even be that one can be harmful. It is because, in general, having true beliefs and knowledge is helpful for an individual and useful for society, that they are valuable. Yet it may also be good and useful for society for people to see meaning in life. Non-evidentially based beliefs that detract from the common good are different from ones that contribute.

I will consider two objections to this distinction. It seems that some obviously false beliefs, or ones that go against all evidence, can be very useful. Imagine that a plane crashes in the middle of winter high in the Rocky Mountains and some people survive. It seems that, even if all evidence points to the likeliness of their imminent demise, it would be good for the survivors to believe against their evidence that they can live. There are abundant examples of people ignoring the evidence of the doctors who tell them they only have a few months to live and such ignoring, perhaps, allows them to live longer. In these cases, even though one can gain personally by believing against the evidence, and we would excuse these believers, they are still cases of pernicious believing. It is important that, in general, we do not believe in this way; the value of attending – of not ignoring – evidence is of more importance overall than the individual value of believing against the evidence in particular cases. The situation is analogous to the value of truth telling. Telling a lie in a particular case can be very valuable and excusable, but this does not undermine the general moral rule that lying is wrong. I think in the cases where there is no evidence, or where there is neutral or barely any evidence, there is nothing pernicious about believing in a way that contributes to your well-being (and perhaps overall

---

[3] I have taken this analogy from Stephen Grimm (Grimm, 2009).

common good). A caveat needs to be added here. Beliefs that lead directly to harmful acts may not be permissible, but this is not because they violate evidentialism; rather, it is because they are so closely tied to immoral action. I will return to this question later.

Second, one may think in the Bering-type cases, where one sees life events as significant, or in questions about what happens after death, that the evidence is not silent. One may think that the principle of simplicity shows that the straightforward causal explanation of why you didn't get killed in the bus wreck is the one supported by the evidence, and so it would be pernicious to believe that there was anything significant in your survival. Bering imagines three cases of mothers – an autistic mother, a religious mother, and a nonreligious mother with normal cognitive functioning – and we are told that each of them just sadly lost her infant as a result of a disease. He says, "We might expect the following responses (or something similar) after asking them why the death occurred ... the autistic mother would speculate that cancerous lesions had gotten a stronghold on her baby's immunosuppressive system; the religious mother would tell us that it was the will of God; and the nonreligious mother would tell us that her baby died so that she can help other bereaved mothers" (Bering, 2002, p. 20).

Someone defending the view that the evidence is not silent on these questions of why things happen would have to say that the autistic person's answer is the one that exhibits the "correct" belief. Yet there is something disturbing in this response, some kind of lack of humanity. James would say that this is a case where our passions have a role to play in what we believe. The problem with the autistic mother is that she has no access to those passions, or emotions, that help answer the question of why her baby died. For her the "why" question cannot be anything but "what was the cause?" Rather than see the noncausal "why" question as meaningless, we could see it as a question which cannot be answered based on the evidence. One could then answer by saying, "I don't know why," but it does seem that one has a certain degree of freedom with respect to what one believes about it. Rather than try to force beliefs of this kind into an evidentialist framework, I think it is better to expose this framework as impoverished – admit that we have no evidence about why our infants die or what happens after death, but still see our beliefs in these matters – whatever they are – as permissible. I say "whatever they are," but a caveat is needed here. Beliefs that lead directly to harmful acts may not be permissible, but this is not because they violate evidentialism. Rather, it is because they are so closely tied to immoral action. I will return to this issue of how much flexibility is acceptable in these matters in my final section.

When I say these non-evidentially based beliefs are valuable, I do not mean merely epistemically valuable. Some will agree that they are prudentially or morally valuable, but that they are incorrect from an epistemic or doxastic perspective. For example, Feldman argues that the "ought" regarding belief is an epistemic ought that is distinct from the oughts of morality or of prudence. He has argued that if these oughts conflict, there is no way to adjudicate between them, no meaningful question about what I ought to believe, all things considered: "We've disambiguated 'ought' and we can't put the various senses back together again" (Feldman, 2000, p. 694). I think this separation of evaluative domains is problematic. There may indeed be a source of normativity that provides force to our practical, moral, and epistemic judgments. Feldman wonders what value would be associated with this "just plain ought." This is a good and difficult question, but not necessarily one that is meaningless or unanswerable. Maybe we just plain ought to do what most contributes to human excellence. It may be hard to adjudicate between different dimensions of excellence, but it could be a meaningful adjudication nonetheless.

The source of normativity that gives truth and knowledge value is the same source that gives value to acting according to common good. When we say one ought to act a certain way and when we say one ought to believe a certain way, the source of these "oughts" is not entirely distinct. It seems there is an ought associated with all our activities as agents, whether these result in beliefs or in actions; beliefs are products of our agency, something we have an active role in shaping and maintaining. Although we cannot believe at will, neither are we passive in the beliefs we form and maintain. We take responsibility for our beliefs, and taking responsibility includes taking control of them. We are blamed when we lose this grasp, when we do not exercise our reflective competence that helps us believe the way we ought to believe. Doxastic, moral, and prudential faults are all faults of agency.

### EDUCATING CHILDREN TO BELIEVE RESPONSIBLY

If how one ought to believe is importantly connected to how one ought to act, then teaching our children to believe responsibly is just one part of their broader moral education. Here there can be disagreement over the best way to teach children to treat others well, to be kind and honest, and so forth, and I do not here have the space to fully defend one perspective on this topic. It seems to me, drawing on my experience as both a mother and teacher of moral philosophy, that it is best to articulate a clear set of rules but to insist on reflection concerning these rules – to realize that for even the seemingly most fixed rules, a time can arise when they can be legitimately violated. We know this from "ticking time bomb" thought experiments. Raise the stakes high enough – to saving the entire universe – and it becomes unclear whether torture is not morally acceptable. Teaching children to be reflective, attentive, to avoid hasty judgments will all tend toward supporting evidential norms for belief. Yet when it comes to questions about death or "supernatural" phenomena, they will have some flexibility in how they believe. How much flexibility? Is any belief permissible when the evidence is silent? Here I return to the caveat I mentioned earlier concerning beliefs that are very closely tied to harmful actions. When we blame someone for having a racist belief, although part of this judgment is owing to the epistemic vices displayed in forming the belief, part of the blame stems from knowledge of how closely tied such beliefs are to treating others unjustly. Similarly, some beliefs about the afterlife are closely tied to questionable moral practices. If your belief about the afterlife entails that I will suffer eternal damnation, this will impact the way you think about me and treat me. Or perhaps even more worrisome are beliefs about the afterlife that seem to condone suicide for a God-serving cause. It seems likely that the strong evidentialist dictum that supports suspending judgment when the evidence is silent is motivated by the worry that permitting freedom here will permit beliefs of this kind. Yet beliefs about a greater power or in something transcendent can also bring one to care more about others, to recognize a connection among all humans and all nature, and to view the world in a more positive and beautiful light than if one chose to suspend judgment. Furthermore, as James pointed out, when there is no evidence even suspension is a choice. It seems that as parents and educators we can teach our children that it is in these moments, the rare ones when one is faced with some freedom of what to believe, that one has to think carefully about what kind of person one wants to be and recognize that the beliefs we adopt both express and shape who we are.

A further worry about accepting that evidential norms do not always prevail is that it may seem to legitimize some policies that we would not want to condone. An example of such a practice is the teaching of intelligent design as part of a standard school curriculum.

As I hope is clear from this discussion, evidential norms can only be overridden in rare contexts – contexts in which evidence is either silent on the issue or where the evidence is completely balanced. Neither of these is the case when it comes to belief about the truth of evolution. To disbelieve evolution requires active suppressing or ignoring of the evidence. These constitute epistemic vices that are unacceptable. One could recognize that some beliefs are resilient and persist even while the epistemic grounds are suspect. However, to teach others to hold views that require a kind of shutting out of overwhelming empirical data is not a sound practice.

Yet it is also important to recognize that in every domain, there will be some presuppositions that are and must remain unquestioned. For science to be so successful in its predictive power and practical success, it must rely on certain assumptions. In ordinary life, I must accept certain truths without grounds or evidence just to be able to navigate my way in what (I assume to be) the world. The beauty of philosophical thinking and philosophy courses is they offer us a chance to examine and question these presuppositions. We can ask why one sort of thing counts as evidence and another does not. We can quite seriously doubt the external world hypothesis and wonder whether there is an objective world beyond my private thoughts. We can even examine why the creation story of Genesis has been seen as a real alternative explanation of the universe by some people. Yet to give it equal attention and legitimacy as a naturalistic explanation would be akin to, in the very earliest stages of the teaching of basic science, introducing the evil-demon hypothesis as an equally plausible explanation of what causes our sense-perceptions. No question should be deemed unacceptable and no topic entirely closed for discussion. Yet the overwhelming success of certain presuppositions – including the presupposition that evidential norms guide belief – permits us to rely on them most of the time. It should not be forgotten, however, that their value is ultimately practical.

## REFERENCES

Bering, J. (2002). The existential theory of mind. *Review of General Psychology, 6,* 1, 3–24.

Clifford, W.K. (1987). The ethics of belief. In G.D. McCarthy (Ed.), *The ethics of belief debate*. Atlanta, GA: Scholars Press.

Descartes, R. (1993) *Meditations on first philosophy*, David Cress, tr, 3rd ed. Cambridge, England: Hackett Publishing Company.

Feldman, Richard. (2000). Ethics of belief. *Philosophy and Phenomenological Research, LX,* 3, 667–695.

Fischer, J., & Ravizza, M. (1998). *Responsibility and control: A theory of moral responsibility*. Cambridge, England: Cambridge University Press.

Grimm, S. (2009). Epistemic normativity. In A. Millar, A. Haddock, & D. Pritchard (Eds.), *Epistemic value*. Oxford, England: Oxford University Press.

James, W. (1956/1898). *The will to believe and other essays in popular philosophy*. New York, NY: Dover.

Owens, D. (2000). *Reason without freedom: The problem of epistemic normativity*. London, England: Routledge.

# 7

## Thoughts and Feelings: Children and
## William James Have It Right!

MICHAEL SCHLEIFER

The "Thought" which we have relied upon in our account is not the brain, closely as it seems connected with it.
William James, Principles of Psychology, p. 346

I do not *fully* understand how we come to our unshakeable belief that thinking exists as a special kind of immaterial process alongside of the material processes of the world.
William James, Principles of Psychology, p. 570

As we have seen (see Chapters 1 and 2 by Harris and Astuti in this volume), children readily accept both the supernatural and the biological conceptions of death. This is because children are not "materialists." Their experiences have led them to their own "theory" of mind that is incompatible with the idea that physical matter is the only or fundamental reality. Children believe that mental events exist, are real, and are different from physical or material ones. In this chapter, I shall argue that children have it right.

One hundred years ago, psychologist-philosopher William James (1842–1910) defended the same nonmaterialist view as is held by children. As we have seen (Chapter 6 in this volume), James maintained that it was reasonable to accept beliefs (including religious ones) even where the evidence was not sufficient. James also provided "evidence and argument" (Myers, 1981, p. xxii) for the nonmaterialist position.

James was centrally involved in the religion-science disputes of the nineteenth century. One hundred years after his death (2010) we are in the midst of our own version of that debate. Although we live in an age of computers, robots, the Internet, e-mail, lasers, and MRIs (none of which James saw in his lifetime), his perspective on science and religion is, I want to maintain, remarkably modern.

In the first section, I will summarize children's nonmaterialist view. Section 2 gives William James's point of view, which is consistent with the intuitions of young children. I then turn in the third section to the "new atheists," who articulate the centrality of the materialist thesis to their perspective. Section 4 takes up a point made primarily by one of the prominent new atheists, philosopher Daniel Dennett. Dennett claims that James's perspective is too individualistic to be called "religious" in a sense relevant to the atheists. Section 4 will examine James's beliefs, which many, despite Dennett, might still call religious. The final section looks at the world of modern science. I will argue that the latest theories and discoveries, particularly in cosmology and quantum physics, are quite compatible with a nonmaterialist perspective like that of children and James. Furthermore, religion and science are not as dramatically opposed as Dennett contends. Dennett claims that religion is particularly dangerous for children as contrasted with science and other subjects. I will argue that indoctrination and brainwashing are possible in science as well as religion and should be avoided in both domains.

## CHILDREN ARE NOT MATERIALISTS

Children accept that there are real things that they experience that are not accessible to everyone. From early on, dreams, thoughts, memories, and mental images occur as private events, and they know that others cannot see, touch, smell, hear, or taste them. They learn about pains that only they feel, and children as young as three can fake these pains, perhaps to get the attention of their parents. Philosopher Michael Antony shares the following with us:

> At age three, my daughter appeared to understand the idea that dreams involve "pictures in her head," and seemed able to sing her favourite song "in her head" and report when she had finished. Also at age three, she went through a brief stage of lying about having hurt herself (for sympathy, hugs, etc.) when noticing her baby sister receiving attention. (Antony, 2006, p. 170)

This kind of parental report resonates with all of us, because we know that it is typical of most young children. We do not, however, have to limit ourselves to this kind of observation. Psychological research has supported what, as parents and clinicians, we already knew. For example, my colleague Victoria Talwar has shown that children as young as three can tell a lie to spare another's feelings. When asked to take a photograph of the experimenter who has an ugly spot on her nose, they say she looks fine. Later they state that she was really ugly (Talwar & Lee, 2002). It is only possible for three-year-old children to tell a lie effectively if they have grasped that their thoughts are private and only available to them. In the same way, Antony's three-year-old daughter can fake her pain because she believed that her sensations were accessible only to herself. David Estes (2006) has summarized some of the empirical evidence:

> Research shows that by 3 years of age children already recognize the defining criteria that distinguish the internal-mental from the external-physical world. They know that mental entities (thoughts, memories, dreams, mental images) are not real in the way that physical entities are, and that they have no permanent existence apart from the mind in which they occur, are inherently private rather than public, and cannot be seen, touched, used, or shared with others in the way that corresponding physical objects can. (Estes, 2006, p. 163)

Estes goes on to emphasize that the psychological research shows not only that preschoolers' knowledge is implicit in their behavior and can be inferred from their responses in different experimental conditions, but also demonstrates that preschoolers have explicit knowledge of how mental and physical phenomena differ, as demonstrated by their capacity to articulate this understanding with convincing verbal justifications for their responses. Estes's review of the literature concerns three-year-olds. There is evidence that even two-year-olds talk about pain and basic emotions (sadness, fear, joy, and anger), showing that they distinguish between the subjective-experiential rather than the situational-external aspects (Wellman, Harris, Banerjee, & Sinclair, 1995, p. 146).

Wittgenstein (1969) taught us how we achieve certainty about the world of physical objects. It is not just the naming of the objects, but the interaction and experience with them that lead to understanding. This is how he puts it:

> We teach a child, "that is your hand" ... that is how a child learns the innumerable language-games that are concerned with his hand. (p. 283)
>
> Children do not learn that books exist, that armchairs exist, etc., etc. – they learn to fetch books, sit in armchairs, etc., etc (p. 476). (see Stroll, 2002)

Just as children learn the basic truths about the physical world, in a similar way they learn about the nonphysical world. Using Wittgenstein's terminology, we can say that at very young ages children also pick up the language-game of the notion of a "dream." We tell children that they were "only dreaming," and they understand that the images, thoughts, and feelings (perhaps very intense) were theirs, and theirs alone. The dream was "real" but not in the same way as a hand is real or an armchair is real. This point is well made by philosopher Curt Ducasse (1961):

> Which things are "material"? The answer to this question is obviously that the things called "material" are the rocks, air, water, plants, animal bodies, and so on, about us; that is, comprehensively, the substances, processes, events, relations, characteristics, etc., *that are perceptually public or can be made so.* ... No doubt it is possible that, originally and fundamentally, these things are the ones denominated "material" or "physical;" i.e., that they are the ones *denoted – pointed at –* by these names. (p. 1)

Which occurrences are denominated "mental"? Again, here is Ducasse (1961):

> The answer to this question is that, originally and fundamentally, the events, processes, etc. denoted by the terms "psychical" or "mental" are *the inherently private ones each person can, in himself and only in himself, attend to in the direct manner which –* whether felicitously or not – *is called Introspection.* (p. 3)

"Mental" or "psychical" events are thus, fundamentally, the immediate experiences, familiar at first hand to children, of which the various species are called "thoughts," "ideas," "desires," "emotions," "cravings," "moods," "sensations," "mental images," "volitions," and so on.

Physical events in our body, it may be thought, are also "private," but, following Ducasse, we can say that looking at them is *difficult,* even more so for the person whose body is concerned than for other persons. An example of what Ducasse has in mind is the beating of the heart. A doctor or a surgeon could observe the heart pumping in the body of another person, which would not be accessible to the person himself. The person, of course, can *feel* the beating or pumping of his own heart.

The privacy of mental events is, as Ducasse says, "inherent and ultimate." I quote Ducasse (1960) one last time:

> Psychical events *themselves* are never *public* and never can be made so. That, for example, *I now remember* having dreamed of a Siamese cat last night is something I can *publish* by means of perceptually public words, spoken or written. Other persons are thus *informed of it.* But to be informed *that I remember* having so dreamed is one thing, and *to remember* having so dreamed is altogether another thing, and one *inherently private.* (p. 86)

Some psychologists (e.g., Bering, 2006; Bloom, 2006) maintain that children have it wrong. They try to show that children's "dualism" leads them to an "illusory" view of the afterlife and psychological immortality. They invoke a series of cognitive biases and attribution errors to explain children's "illusions." Other psychologists have noted, however, that children may not be in error at all. Estes (2006), for example:

> Leaving aside the perennial question of whether there might really be an afterlife of some unknown variety ... perhaps the path from the young child's dualism to a belief in an afterlife for immortal souls might be fairly direct and need no evolutionary solution. As we have seen, very young children already have the distinction between mental and physical phenomena solidly in hand, and thus recognize the existence and nature of immaterial objects. (p. 470)

I believe that Estes, in his criticism of Bering and Bloom, has it right. For further objections to Bering's and Bloom's claims about "common sense dualism" regarding three-, four-, and five-year-old children, see Harris (Chapter 2, in this volume). As noted, there are studies showing children as young as two talking about pain and basic emotions. (e.g. Wellman et al., 1995). In this chapter I have also been discussing younger children, from birth to two years of age. Every infant, for example, experiences pain long before he or she can speak. The adult will then supply the word "pain" or some child-like equivalent such as "ouch" or "boo-boo" to accompany the experience. Whatever words the child eventually uses, the experience itself remains real.

Like children, we adults are often common sense dualists in a practical, pre-philosophical way. We may be concerned about how to prevent our friends worrying themselves into physical illness, how to cure a paralysis that has no apparent physical cause, or what is the relationship between a vitamin deficiency or underactive thyroid gland and intellectual performance (Reeves, 1958). Thus, we have occasional puzzles and queries about the relations of the physical and the mental, but we do not ordinarily concern ourselves with the conundrum that Descartes pondered, namely how causation is possible between substances that seem of such different status. As philosophers, of course, we will ultimately have to take a stand on the mind-body and mind-brain problem.

## WILLIAM JAMES, MATERIALISM, AND THE MIND: SUPPORTING THE CHILDREN

It is probable that for years to come we shall have to infer what happens in the brain either from our feelings or from motor effects that we observe. The organ will be for us a sort of vat in which feelings and motions somehow go on stewing together, and in which innumerable things happen of which we catch but the statistical result. Why, under these circumstances, we should be asked to forswear the language of our childhood I cannot well imagine, especially as it is perfectly compatible with the language of physiology. My conclusion is that to urge the automaton-theory upon us, as it is now urged, on purely a priori and quasi-metaphysical grounds, is an *unwarrantable impertinence in the present state of psychology*. Yet there are much more positive reasons than this why we ought to continue to talk in psychology as if consciousness had causal efficacy. The *particulars of the distribution of consciousness*, so far as we know them, *point to its being efficacious*. (James, 1950/1890, pp. 137–138)

To comprehend completely the consequences of the dogma so confidently enunciated, one should unflinchingly apply it to the most complicated examples. If we knew thoroughly the nervous system of Shakespeare, and as thoroughly all his environing conditions, we should be able to show why at a certain period of his life his hand came to trace on certain sheets of paper those crabbed little black marks that we for shortness' sake call the manuscript of *Hamlet*. We should understand the rationale of every erasure and alteration therein, and we should understand all this without in the slightest degree acknowledging the existence of the thoughts in Shakespeare's mind. (James, 1950/1890, p. 132)

In 1878, James agreed to write a psychology textbook for the American publisher Henry Holt, but it took him twelve years to produce the manuscript, and when he did, he described it to Holt as "a loathsome, distended, tumefied, bloated, dropsical mass" (James, 1926, p. 326). Nevertheless, this two volume work of psychology, physiology, and philosophy has proved to be James's masterpiece. In 1890, when *The Principles of Psychology* was finally published, James devoted two chapters (V and VI) to the analysis and critique of contemporary mind-brain views. Chapter V attacks the "automaton" theory of Thomas Huxley and others (the quotes earlier are taken from this chapter). Chapter VI attacks the "mind-stuff" theory, the notion accepted by many psychologists that our mental states are compounds made up of smaller states. Both chapters present extensive discussions of reasons for and against the views under analysis. The reader, proceeding through the systematic dismantling of each of these views, expects James, at any moment, to produce his own brilliant synthesis. Instead, however, James's "solution" is to opt for a provisional and pragmatic empirical parallelism of the sort to which many psychologists still subscribe:

In Chapter X, accordingly, we must return to its consideration again, and *ask ourselves whether, after all, the ascertainment of a blank unmediated correspondence, term for term, of the succession of states of consciousness with the succession of total brain-processes, be not the simplest psycho-physic formula, and the last word of a psychology which contents itself with verifiable laws, and seeks only to be clear, and to avoid unsafe hypotheses.* Such a mere admission of the empirical parallelism will there appear the wisest course. By keeping to it, our psychology will remain positivistic and non-metaphysical. (James, 1950/1890, p. 182)

This is James the psychologist speaking. Materialism and brain-mind one-to-one correspondence will be assumed as a working hypothesis. Psychology will remain "non-metaphysical," although James will provide us with many healthy doses of metaphysics throughout the *Principles of Psychology*. As philosopher, it is very clear (Barzun, 1983; Myers, 1981; Richardson, 2007) that James rejected Huxley's materialist/mechanist argument, as he also rejected mind-brain correspondence or identity:

I confess, therefore, that to posit a soul influenced in some mysterious way by the brain-states and responding to them by conscious affections of its own, seems to me the line of least logical resistance.... Nature in her unfathomable designs has mixed us of clay and flame, of brain and mind, that the two things hang indubitably together and determine each other's being, but how or why, no mortal may ever know. (James, 1950/1890, pp. 181–182)

In the deservedly famous chapter IX on "The Stream of Thought," James takes himself to be offering a richer account of experience than those of traditional empiricists such as Hume. He believes relations, vague fringes, and tendencies are experienced directly (a view he would later defend as part of his "radical empiricism"). James finds consciousness to be a stream rather than a succession of "ideas." Its waters blend, and our individual consciousness – or, as he prefers to call it sometimes, our "sciousness" – is "steeped and dyed" in the waters of sciousness or thought that surround it. Our psychic life has rhythm: It is a series of transitions and resting places, of "flights and perchings." We rest when we remember the name we have been searching for; and we are off again when we hear a noise that might be the baby waking from her nap. The following long quotation from this chapter clearly places James in solidarity with children, accepting that one's subjective mental experience is inherently private:

When Paul and Peter wake up in the same bed, and recognize that they have been asleep, each one of them mentally reaches back and makes connection with but *one* of the two streams of thought which were broken by the sleeping hours. As the current of an electrode buried in the ground unerringly finds its way to its own similarly buried mate, across no matter how much intervening earth; so Peter's present instantly finds out Peter's past, and never by mistake knits itself on to that of Paul. Paul's thought in turn is as little liable to go astray. The past thought of Peter is appropriated by the present Peter alone. He may have a *knowledge*, and a correct one too, of what Paul's last drowsy states of mind were as he sank into sleep, but it is an entirely different sort of knowledge from that which he has of his own last states. He *remembers* his own states, whilst he only *conceives* Paul's. Remembrance is like direct feeling; its object is suffused with a warmth and intimacy to which no object of mere conception ever attains. This quality of warmth and intimacy and immediacy is what Peter's *present* thought also possesses for itself. So sure as this present is me, is mine, it says, so sure is anything else that comes with the same warmth and intimacy and immediacy, me and mine. What the qualities called warmth and intimacy may in themselves be will have to be matter for future consideration. But whatever past feelings appear with those qualities must be admitted to receive the greeting of the present mental state, to be owned by it, and accepted as belonging together with it in a common self. This community of self is what the time-gap cannot break in twain, and is why a present thought, although not ignorant of the time-gap, can still regard itself as continuous with certain chosen portions of the past ...

Consciousness, then, does not appear to itself chopped up in bits. Such words as "chain" or "train" do not describe it fitly as it presents itself in the first instance. It is nothing jointed; it flows. A "river" or a "stream" are the metaphors by which it is most naturally described. *In talking of it hereafter, let us call it the stream of thought, of consciousness, or of subjective life* (James, 1950/1890, pp. 238–239).

James ends the chapter on "The Stream of Thought" with the importance of interest and attention:

The last peculiarity of consciousness to which attention is to be drawn in this first rough description of its stream is that *it is always interested more in one part of its object than in another, and welcomes and rejects, or chooses, all the while it thinks* (p. 284).... Looking back, then, over this review, we see that the mind is at every stage a theatre of simultaneous possibilities. Consciousness consists in the comparison of these with each other, the selection of some, and the suppression of the rest by the reinforcing and inhibiting agency of attention. The highest and most elaborated mental products are filtered from the data chosen by the faculty next beneath, out of the mass offered by the faculty below that, which mass in turn was sifted from a still larger amount of yet simpler material, and so on. The mind, in short, works on the data it receives very much as a sculptor works on his block of stone. (James, 1950/1890, p. 288)

From sensations to recognition of things, and all the way to our ethical decisions, the key for James is what interests us and the things to which we attend. In case we need guidance, James offers us more clues, telling us to check out chapter XI on "Attention" and chapter XXVI on "Will."

Turning to the chapter on "Attention," here is James in his own words:

When we reflect that the turnings of our attention form the nucleus of our inner self; when we see (as in the chapter on the Will we shall see) that volition is nothing but attention; when we believe that our autonomy in the midst of nature depends on our not being pure effect, but a cause.... We must admit that the question whether attention involves such a principle of spiritual activity or not is metaphysical as well as psychological, and is well worthy of all the pains we can bestow on its solution. It is in fact the pivotal question of metaphysics, the very hinge on which our picture of the world shall swing from materialism, fatalism, monism, towards spiritualism, freedom, pluralism, – or else the other way.... It goes back to the automaton-theory. If feeling is an inert accompaniment, then of course the brain-cell can be played upon only by other brain-cells, and the attention which we give at any time to any subject, whether in the form of sensory adaptation or of "preperception," is the fatally predetermined *effect* of exclusively material laws. If, on the other hand, the feeling which coexists with the brain-cells' activity reacts dynamically upon that activity, furthering or checking it, then the attention is in part, at least, a *cause*.... When we come to the chapter on the Will, we shall see that the whole drama of the voluntary life hinges on the amount of attention, slightly more or slightly less, which rival motor ideas may receive. But the whole feeling of reality, the whole sting and excitement of our voluntary life, depends on our sense that in it things are *really being decided* from one moment to another, and that it is not the dull rattling off of a chain that was forged innumerable ages ago. This appearance, which makes life and history tingle with such a tragic zest, *may* not be an illusion. As we grant to the advocate of the mechanical theory that it may be one, so he must grant to us that it may *not*. And the result is two conceptions of possibility face to face with no facts definitely enough known to stand as arbiter between them. (James, 1950/1890, pp. 447–454)

In his chapter on "Will," the burden of proof, as in the chapters on the stream of thought and attention, is on those who would try to defend materialism/mechanism. James opposes the theory of his contemporary Wilhelm Wundt that there is one special feeling – a "feeling of innervation" – present in all intentional action. In his survey of a range of cases, James finds that some actions involve an act of resolve or of outgoing nervous energy, but others do not. For example:

> I sit at the table after dinner and find myself from time to time taking nuts or raisins out of the dish and eating them. My dinner properly is over, and in the heat of the conversation I am hardly aware of what I do; but the perception of the fruit, and the fleeting notion that I may eat it, seem fatally to bring the act about. There is certainly no express fiat here. (James, 1950/1890, p. 522)

James argues that the essential phenomenon of will is effort of attention. James applies his insight to everyday examples that we can all relate to such as getting out of bed on a cold morning. We understand what James means when he says, "the fiat demands great volitional effort though the muscular exertion be insignificant" (p. 524). More dramatically, he applies his idea to examples where muscular effort involves a special volitional effort:

> Exhausted with fatigue and wet, the sailor on a wreck throws himself down to rest. But hardly are his limbs fairly relaxed, when the order "To the pumps!" sounds in his ears. Shall he, can he, obey it? Is it not better just to let his aching body lie, and let the ship go down, if she will? So he lies on, 'til, with a desperate heave of the will, at last he staggers to his legs, and to his task again. (James, 1950/1890, p. 564)

Finally, James relates his concept to fundamental, moral decisions:

> Every reader must have felt some fiery passion's grasp. What constitutes the difficulty for a man labouring under an unwise passion of acting as if the passion were unwise? Certainly there is no physical difficulty. It is as easy physically to avoid a fight as to begin one, to pocket one's money as to squander it on one's cupidities, to walk away as from, as towards a coquette's door. The difficulty is mental; it is that of getting the idea of the wise action to stay before our mind at all.... How many excuses does the drunkard find when each new temptation comes? ... The effort by which he succeeds in keeping the right *name* unwaveringly present to his mind proves to be his saving moral act.... Everywhere then the function of the effort is the same; to keep affirming and adopting a thought which, if left to itself would slip away. (James, 1950/1890, p. 565)

These remarks of James not only resonate with our everyday experiences, but they have proved useful in clinical psychology and psychotherapy.

One recent example is the work of Schwartz (2002) on treating obsessive compulsive disorders (OCD). Directly inspired by this chapter of James, this therapist has shown that mental force can be more useful than behaviorist methods in helping many patients. It is of interest that the routine makes use of Relabeling, Reattributing, Refocusing, and Revaluing, all suggested by James's notion about correctly "naming" (see quote earlier). The other James concept used by Schwartz and many other psychologists is that of attention. To use the OCD example once again: "In OCD, the brain circuit representing 'wash your hands' for instance, fires over and over. Therapy introduces the idea that the OCD patient might go to the garden instead of to the sink. Attention can change the odds on which thought wins" (Schwartz, 2002, p. 362). Before leaving James, there are two points of clarification to be made. It is clear that James, like children, rejected materialism. He was a "dualist" in the sense that he accepted that mind was different from brain/body and was equally real. Apparent counterexamples are his famous analysis of emotions (James, 1950/1890, chapter XXV) which seems to be stubbornly materialist. The second difficulty arises from his work toward the end of his life where James called himself a "monist." Let me briefly address each of these issues.

James's chapter on emotions in *Principles of Psychology* sets out the theory – also enunciated by the Danish physiologist Carl Lange – that emotion follows, rather than causes, its bodily expression:

> Common-sense says, we lose our fortune, are sorry and weep; we meet a bear, are frightened and run; we are insulted by a rival, are angry and strike. The hypothesis here to be defended says that this order of sequence is incorrect ... that we feel sorry because we cry, angry because we strike, afraid because we tremble ... (James, 1950/1890, p. 450)

The significance of this view, according to James, is that our emotions are tied in with our bodily expressions. He asks what would grief be "without its tears, its sobs, its suffocation of the heart, its pang in the breast-bone?" Not an emotion, James answers, for a "purely disembodied human emotion is a nonentity" (James, 1950/1890, p. 452). It sounds like James is here a materialist, even though, as we have seen, he argued against materialism throughout the *Principles*. How can this apparent contradiction be resolved?

Gerald Myers, in his introduction to his 1981 Harvard University Press re-edition of the *Principles of Psychology*, makes the intriguing suggestion that the chapter on emotions is meant by James as a challenge to show that materialism is wrong. There is another more straightforward explanation, provided by a clue offered by James himself in his article on the emotions in the journal *Mind* (James, 1884). What James there states is that his analysis applies to emotions that have distinct bodily expressions:

> I should say first of all that the only emotions I propose expressly to consider here are those that have a distinct bodily expression. That there are feelings of pleasure and displeasure, of interest and excitement, bound up with mental operations, but having no obvious bodily expression for their consequence, would, I suppose, be held true by most readers. Certain arrangements of sounds, of lines, of colours, are agreeable, and others the reverse, without the degree of the feeling being sufficient to quicken the pulse or breathing, or to prompt to movements of either the body or the face. (James, 1884, p. 1)

An important distinction must be made between basic emotions such as fear, anger, sadness, joy, surprise, and disgust, which research has shown to have universally recognized bodily expressions. More complex emotions, however, such as frustration, disappointment, envy, or pride do not have typical bodily or facial expressions. For these, and many other emotions, we need the information, as Nussbaum (2001) and others have argued, about the situation, how we see it, why it is important, and how it relates to our values. We agree with Nussbaum that the crucial ingredient for emotions is judgment and cognitive appraisal rather than any specific bodily expression. As Nussbaum asserts, the notion of disembodied emotions is not ruled out conceptually. James, I think, would agree.

Turning to the second discrepancy: How can James be a dualist, as I maintain he clearly was, if he called himself a monist at the end of his life? (Richardson, 2006, pp. 450–461) The discrepancy is resolved by pointing out that James's insistence on the reality and causal efficacy of mind remained intact. In that sense, he remained a dualist; mind and matter were both equally real. In what sense, then, was he a monist? He was never a materialist like Thomas Huxley nor an idealist like Berkeley and Bradley. What kind of a monist was he?

In *The Principles*, he had already begun to flirt with the idea of a "pure" description of the stream of thought that does not presuppose it to be either mental or material, a pursuit that anticipates his later radical empiricism. James calls this "neutral monism." A posthumous collection (James, 1943/1912) includes James's groundbreaking essays on "pure experience," originally written in 1904–1905. James's fundamental idea is that mind and matter are both aspects of, or structures formed from, a more fundamental stuff – pure experience – that (despite being called experience) is neither mental nor physical. Pure experience, James explained, is "the immediate flux of life which furnishes the material to our later reflection with its conceptual categories ... a *that* which is not yet any definite *what*, tho' ready to be all sorts of whats..." (James, 1943/1912, p. 46). These "whats" may be minds and bodies or people and material objects. This depends, however, not on a fundamental ontological difference among these pure experiences, but on the *relations* into which they enter. Certain sequences of pure experiences constitute physical objects, and others constitute persons; but one pure experience (say the perception of a chair) may be part both of the sequence constituting the chair and of the sequence constituting a person. Indeed, one pure experience might be part of two distinct minds, as James explains in chapter IV, entitled "How Two Minds Know One Thing." James was still working on objections to his pure experience doctrine, when he died in 1910. Bertrand Russell thought this was James's best contribution to philosophy (Richardson, 2006, p. 461).

THE NEW ATHEISTS

Just as Bering (2006) and Bloom (2006) try to correct children's "illusions," the new atheists are out to show how to help adults rid themselves of their corresponding "delusions" (Dawkins, 2006; Dennett, 2006; Hitchens, 2007). These disparaging terms were chosen by Bering and Dawkins to convey the message that children's opposition to materialism is irrational and in error; those of us who agree with the children suffer from a similar lack of rationality.

What is at stake here is the very kernel of the atheists' contention. Richard Dawkins (2006) makes this clear: "Mind is a manifestation of matter and cannot exist apart from matter" (p. 179). He tells us that the core belief of atheists is: "There is only one kind of stuff in the universe and it is physical" (p. 13).

The importance of this materialism for Dawkins is to bolster the perspective that denies not only God but any kind of afterlife. For if all "immaterial" things are impossible, then any form of thoughts and feelings without body or brain are, by definition, also impossible. Dawkins, a biologist, relies heavily on philosopher Daniel Dennett, another of the new atheists. Because Dennett's materialism extends to robots, Dawkins has amended his materialism to include Dennett's stance: "Mind is material, in a brain, *or perhaps a computer*" (Dawkins, 2006, p. 174, my emphasis).

Dennett (1994) contends that robots will have consciousness if sufficiently complex. It is worthwhile citing him on this:

> The best reason for believing that robots might some day become conscious is that we human beings are conscious, and we are a sort of robot ourselves. That is, we are extraordinarily complex, self-controlling, self-sustaining physical mechanisms, designed over the eons by natural selection, and operating according to the same well-understood principles that govern all the other physical processes in living things: digestive and metabolic processes, self-repair and reproductive processes, for instance. It may be wildly over-ambitious to suppose that human artificers can repeat Nature's triumph, with variations in material, form, and design process, but this is not a deep objection. It is not as if a conscious machine contradicted any fundamental laws of nature, the way a perpetual motion machine does. Still, many skeptics believe – or in any event want to believe – that it will never be done. *I wouldn't wager against them, but my reasons for skepticism are mundane, economic reasons, not theoretical reasons.* (Dennett, 1994, p. 1)

The popular portrayal of Dennett's view can be seen in the film *Bicentennial Man*, starring Robin Williams as the complex robot, who can speak and love as a human can. I am ready to bet that we will never see a robot like that. My reasons, are not merely practical (lack of time and resources); they are also theoretical. These arguments are beyond the scope of this chapter. I will simply make two very brief points: (1) If the experience of a young child is crucial to learning language, then this would explain why artificial intelligence programmers have been notoriously unsuccessful in getting computers to simulate linguistic competence. (2) No computer can be programmed to win against top-level bridge players, and I am ready to wager this will always be the case. (Schleifer, 1992) Unlike chess, the game of bridge requires a large dose of judgment and communication between partners. It is no accident that after fifty years of trying, artificial intelligence has been unsuccessful in regard to this game.

As we have seen in Section 2, William James (1950/1890) argued against Thomas Huxley's nineteenth-century version of Dennett's materialist/mechanist view. One hundred years later, his arguments still count against the philosophical position that sees minds and brains as identical or in one-to-one correspondence. Dennett's perspective is far from achieving philosophical unanimity, even among his fellow materialists (see for example, Searle, 1980, 1984, 1992, 1998). In the twenty-first century, we are still grappling with the mystery of consciousness. Even those who are convinced materialists (e.g., Pinker, 1997) and who agree with Dennett on the identity of mind and brain, admit that consciousness remains far from understood.

Of course, we are not obligated to accept the brain-mind identity thesis, and James has provided many good reasons for not doing so. One alternative is to accept that mind is real and can be causally efficacious, interacting with brain processes. Recently, Noë (2009) reminds us that the prevailing neuroscientific view – the way neuroscientists tend to think about consciousness – is that it must be something that happens in the human brain, just as digestion takes place in the stomach. Noë disagrees with this view. For Noë, our consciousness depends not only on what is appearing in our brain, but also on our history and our current position and interaction with the wider world. Toward the end of his book, Noë speaks of the "Foundation Argument," which holds that because we can induce consciousness experiences by electrodes implanted in the brains of monkeys or people, the brain causes consciousness. These impulses, he observes, are only fleeting events, not the whole of consciousness. We affect consciousness by interplay with our loved ones, driving a car, making a speech, or talking with others at the office. The brain, for Noë, may be necessary for mind (for human beings) but it is not sufficient.

In the current debate between atheists and believers, each side is involved in a battle for conversion with the tone becoming shrill and somewhat abrasive. Richard Dawkins (2006) admits that he wants to convert his readers to atheism as much as any evangelist tries to do for religion. One amusing sideline of the competition between atheists and believers involves recruitment for their "team." Both sides, for example, claim physicists Albert Einstein and Steven Hawking (Dawkins 2006), with citations bolstering their case. Although the religious side can cite Einstein and Hawking (1988, 2005) talking about God, Dawkins retorts that this God is not a personal, supernatural God.

William James would not have joined either team. He refused to accept organized religion and yet acknowledged the possibility of a "power not ourselves." James got into trouble with scientific colleagues as well as with the religious establishment. The religious group did not like the fact that James's views were compatible with polytheism or even reincarnation. For James, there was no guarantee of *personal* immortality, even if there is some kind of afterlife. Not to mention, of course, that he sarcastically suggested to his audience of scientists that their atheism was perhaps a result of a malfunction of their liver.

Richard Dawkins, although he neither mentions nor cites James in his book, would not be pleased with him, because for Dawkins, polytheism is as bad as theism, and arguably even worse because many Gods are invoked rather than one. Dawkins, one could guess, would have dismissed James for having flirted with psychical research on ESP; he might dismiss James as "nuts," using a similar ploy to his dismissal of psychoanalyst Carl Jung and physicist Paul Davies. Whether James was crazy or not, as we have to stress, has no logical bearing on whether his views are true or well argued. It is important to emphasize that James, Einstein, and Hawking are certainly not "wishy-washy" agnostics; they were strong-minded, autonomous thinkers, as were the two original agnostics, Thomas Huxley and Charles Darwin (it was Huxley who coined the term). Having doubts is perfectly compatible with thinking for oneself. The error of too much certainty is made by Dawkins as surely as it is by religious extremists.

Carl Sagan, although an avowed atheist and materialist (Sagan, 1996), also had a great affinity for James. Sagan, like James, retained the idea of a power beyond us and an open mind about parapsychological phenomena as well as the ultimate questions about the origins and description of the universe. Sagan defended science against those who attacked it in the name of religion, and he opposed religion when it was intolerant or because many had justified slavery in its name (Sagan, 1996). He maintained that the God of most common religions was too small for this small blue dot that is earth. William James would approve.

## WAS JAMES RELIGIOUS? IS ANYBODY?

I have presented the nonmaterialistic views of children (Section 1) and shown that the great thinker William James defended a similar perspective (Section 2). Acceptance of the immaterial as real and causally efficacious is a direct challenge to the core beliefs of the new atheists (Section 3). Daniel Dennett has tried to show, however, that James is completely irrelevant to the atheists' concerns. This is because, for Dennett, James is not truly "religious." Dennett offers two arguments for this exclusion of James. The first (Dennett, 2006, p. 9) is to deny that James was religious at all because his religion was private and did not involve a church or a social network. Dennett prefers to call James "spiritual." Others (e.g., Taylor, 2002) agree that James had too individualistic a view of religion, but do not deny that he was religious. The second argument Dennett invokes to deny that James was really religious is summarized in the following quote: "The core phenomena of religion invoke gods who are effective agents in real time and who play a central role in the way the participants think about what they ought to do" (Dennett, 2006, p. 9).

The second part of Dennett's criteria for using the word religion that was just cited would eliminate William James and also every philosopher who has thought about ethics. It would make Charles Taylor (2007), a professed Catholic, nonreligious. Taylor would never accept Dennett's idea that the gods "tell us what we ought to do." In the present section, I will look at what James said about religion, in *Varieties of Religious Experience* and *Human Immortality*. The record will make clear that Dennett's recommended definition of religion is quite narrow, and we can continue to consider James as relevant to the defense of children's views, as well as relevant to countering some claims of the new atheists.

The first thing worth noting is that Ralph Barton Perry (1937), Jacques Barzun (1983), and Robert Richardson (2006), three biographers of William James, all agreed that James was "deeply religious and a man of faith." His letters and diary attest to this. At the age of twenty-five, he was deeply depressed and recovered from mental and physical illness with an extraordinary act of will. The seeds of his personal religious experience can be traced, according to his father and his biographers, to these events.

James's interest in religion also arose in large part because of personal tragedies. These included the death of his eighteen-month-old child Hermann as well as the illness and untimely death of his good friends Minnie Temple, Richard Hodgson, Charles Elliott Norton, and his sister Alice. According to Dennett's narrow definition of religion, one must believe in prayer as talking to a specific God who really does listen and forgive. James apparently attended Harvard chapel regularly, and perhaps he prayed; but if he did, it was almost certainly not to a specific monotheistic God. Many people pray, in the sense of "wishing very hard" or "feeling gratitude," particularly in times of illness for themselves or loved ones. The prayers are not necessarily to a specific God; they may be to a nebulous group of listeners, to one's lucky stars, or just to plain old luck. We pray when we feel there are things we cannot control (see James, 1994/1902, for his views on prayer).

James argued for the possibility of some form of immortality (James, 1956/1898). Whether this was a personal immortality or something different was not the primary issue. "One may conceive the mental world beyond the veil in as individualistic a form as one pleases" (James, 1956/1898, p. 30). The important part was James's demonstration that immortality and the afterlife were reasonable possibilities, even if we know there is no brain function after death.

For James, the crux is to see the brain as a "permissive" organ, not as a "productive" one. The brain is not like the tea kettle producing steam. The brain is rather like the trigger of a crossbow that has a releasing or permissive function; it removes the obstacle that holds the string and lets the bow flow back to its original shape. Another example offered by James is the keys of an organ that have a permissive function. The organ keys do not produce the air, but allow some columns of air to escape by opening successive pipes and by letting the wind in the air chest escape in different ways. If thought is a function of the brain (like a tea kettle), then no afterlife or immortality is possible. If, however, we include the permissive idea (the brain is like a set of organ keys or a cross bow trigger), immortality of some kind becomes possible!

In *The Varieties of Religious Experience*, James (1994/1902) studied the part of human nature that is, or is related to, religious experience. His interest was not in religious institutions, rituals, or even, for the most part, religious ideas, but in "the feelings, acts, and experiences of individual men in their solitude, so far as they apprehend themselves to stand in relation to whatever they may consider the divine" (James, 1994/1902, p. 31).

James sets out a central distinction of the book in early chapters on "The Religion of Healthy-Mindedness" and "The Sick Soul." The healthy-minded religious person – Walt Whitman is one of James's main examples – has a deep sense of "the goodness of life" (James, 1994/1902) and a soul of "sky-blue tint" (James, 1994/1902). Healthy-mindedness can be involuntary and just natural to someone, but often comes in more willful forms. For "The Sick Soul," in contrast, "radical evil gets its innings" (James, 1994/1902):

> No matter how secure one may feel, the sick soul finds that unsuspect-edly from the bottom of every fountain of pleasure, as the old poet said, something bitter rises up: a touch of nausea, a falling dead of the delight, a whiff of melancholy.... These states are not simply unpleasant sensa-tions, for they bring a feeling of coming from a deeper region and often have an appalling convincingness. (James, 1994/1902, p. 136)

James's main examples are Leo Tolstoy's "My Confession," John Bunyan's autobiography, and a report of terrifying "dread" – allegedly from a French correspondent but actually from James himself. Some sick souls never get well, whereas others recover or even triumph: these are the "twice-born." In chapters on "The Divided Self, and the Process of Its Unification" and on "Conversion," James discusses St. Augustine, Henry Alline, Bunyan, Tolstoy, and a range of popular evangelists, focusing on what he calls "the state of assurance they achieve" (James, 1994/1902, p. 247). Central to this state is "the loss of all the worry, the sense that all is ultimately well with one, the peace, the harmony, the *willingness to be*, even though the outer conditions should remain the same" (James, 1994/1902, p. 248).

*Varieties'* classic chapter on "Mysticism" offers "four marks which, when an experience has them, may justify us in calling it mystical" (James, 1994/1902, p. 380). The first is ineffability: "It defies expression ... its quality must be directly experienced; it cannot be imparted or transferred to others." Second is a "noetic quality": Mystical states present themselves as states of knowledge. Third, mystical states are transient. Fourth, subjects are passive with respect to them: They cannot control their coming and going. James ends the chapter by asking if these states are "windows through which the mind looks out upon a more extensive and inclusive world?" (James, 1994/1902, p. 428)

In "Conclusions," James finds that religious experience is on the whole useful, even "amongst the most important biological functions of mankind," but he concedes that this does not make it true. Nevertheless, James articulates his own belief – which he does not claim to prove – that religious experiences connect us with a greater reality, not accessible in our normal cognitive relations to the world: "The further limits of our being plunge, it seems to me, into an altogether other dimension of existence from the sensible and merely 'understandable' world" (James, 1994/1902, p. 560). The following quote is quite explicit, reflecting James's acceptance of something transcendental: "Religious experience ... unequivocally testifies ... that we can experience union with *something* larger than ourselves and in that union find our greatest peace" (James, 1994/1902, p. 570).

### MODERN SCIENCE

Is there anything inherently irrational about accepting the supernatural alongside the biological conception, as children do? Daniel Dennett (2006) thinks so. Dennett challenges parents to stop indoctrinating or brainwashing their children; he calls this psychological abuse. I have argued elsewhere (Schleifer, 2009) that, in agreement with Dennett, indoctrination is dangerous and perverse because it infantilizes the learner, shows a lack of respect for him or her, and does not foster critical thinking in children. Where I differ from Dennett is in his insistence that teaching children about science is so vastly different from teaching them about religion.

It is worthwhile to contrast Dennett and James on science and religion. First Dennett:

> That is the most important difference between the division of labor in religion and science ... the experts do understand the methods they use – not everything about them, but enough to explain to one another and themselves why the amazing accurate results come out of them. It

is only because I am confident that the experts really do understand the
formulas that I can honestly and unabashedly cede the responsibility of
pinning down the propositions (and hence understanding them) to them.
In religion, however, the experts are not exaggerating for effect when
they say they don't understand what they are talking about. (Dennett,
2006, p. 220)

William James did not accept the kind of distinction being made by Dennett
(2006) and echoed by Dawkins (2006), Hitchens (2007), and all of the other
new atheists. Here is James:

I believe that the claims of the sectarian scientist are, to say the least,
premature. The experiences which we have been studying ... plainly
show the universe to be a more many sided affair than any sect, even
the scientific sect allows for. What, in the end, are all our verifications
but experiences that agree with more or less isolated systems of ideas
(conceptual systems) that our minds have framed? ... Science gives to
all of us telegraphy, electric lighting, and diagnosis, and succeeds in
preventing and curing a certain amount of disease. Religion in the shape
of mind/cure gives to some of us serenity, moral poise, and happiness,
and prevents certain forms of disease, as well as science does ... and
why, after all, may not the world be so complex as to consist of many
interpenetrating spheres of reality, which we can thus approach in alter-
nation by using different conceptions and assuming different attitudes,
just as mathematicians handle the same numerical and spatial facts,
by geometry ... by algebra, by the calculus ... and each time come out
right? On this view religion and science, each verified in its own way
from hour to hour and from life to life, would be co-eternal. (James,
1994/1902, p. 137)

Some of the theories and facts that form part of the consensus in science in
the year 2010 seem to be as puzzling, mysterious, and as perplexing as talk
about God. For example, we are given as facts that our universe is about 13.7
billion years old, and that time is relative (the identical twin on the space-
ship accelerating at close to the speed of light may age twenty years, but
when he returns to earth his twin brother will be 400 years older). The most
common theory in cosmology is that the "visible" universe is part of an infinite set of universes or "multiverses" (Davies, 2007; Hawking, 1988, 2005;
Sagan, 2006). Dawkins's contention that talk of God is more complex than
any scientific explanation is here put to the test. I find little to distinguish
between "God" talk and "infinite multiverse" talk in regard to complexity.

Turning from the huge universe to the smallest particles, we find more
complicated facts and theories, particularly in quantum physics. There are

particles like photons and neutrinos, which carry energy and are termed "radiation." These particles do not have rest mass and are therefore not considered matter. Photons are light particles, and travel at the speed of light in a vacuum, slighter slower otherwise. A recent experiment in Switzerland showed that two photons of light nearly seven miles apart responded simultaneously to a stimulus applied to only one of them. The twin-photon experiment was the most spectacular demonstration yet of the mysterious long-range connections that exist between quantum events that in theory can reach instantaneously from one end of the universe to the other. The photons are "entangled" particles that share common origins and properties. They continue to communicate with one another even when very far apart. Einstein sneered at this possibility, calling it "spooky action at a distance." It is today seen as a correlation in the quantum behavior of correlated systems. The correlation is encoded in the systems before the photons are separated. As amazing as all this is, our use of lasers is based on the existence of these same photons. Although, as we have seen, photons are energy and radiation and not matter, they are nevertheless real!

Some scientists (Schwartz, 2002; Stapp, 1993) have argued that James's views on the reality and causal efficacy of the mental in the *Principles of Psychology* are consistent with, and even supported by, the fundamentals of quantum physics. Schwartz, a clinical psychologist, was briefly discussed in Section 2. His work, using a cognitive, "mindfulness" approach to treating patients, is directly attributed to James's insights on attention and the will. Stapp, a physicist himself, argues in his book that James anticipated the basic insights about the importance of the observer one hundred years ahead of his time!

One does not need to use examples from cosmology or quantum physics to make the point about imparting scientific facts to children. For example, at a relatively young age, we tell our children about the planets, about the movement of the earth around the sun and so on. In answer to a child's question about how fast the earth is moving, I must tell him that it is revolving around about one thousand miles an hour on its axis and at about sixty-seven thousand miles an hour in its orbit around the sun. Other sciences have offered us other amazing facts to tell our children about: from biology, the fact that the human heart beats about one hundred thousand times every twenty-four hours; from neurology the fact that the brain consists of more than twenty-five billion cells.

Children readily accept both the supernatural and the biological conceptions of death. This is because children are not materialists. Their experiences have led them to their own theory of mind that is inconsistent with the idea that physical matter is the only or fundamental reality. Children know that mental events exist, are real, and are different from physical or material ones. William James, as we have seen, agreed with the children. There is nothing about modern science that would make these ideas preposterous.

## REFERENCES

Antony, M.V. (2006). Simulation constraints, afterlife beliefs, and common-sense dualism. *Behavioral and Brain Sciences, 29*, 462.
Barzun, J. (1983). *A stroll with William James.* Chicago, IL: University of Chicago Press.
Bering, J.M. (2006).The folk psychology of souls. *Behavioral and Brain Sciences, 29*, 453–498.
Bloom, P. (2004). *Descartes' baby: How the science of child development explains what makes us human.* New York, NY: Basic Books.
Davies, P. (2007). *Cosmic jackpot.* New York, NY: Penguin.
Dawkins, R. (2006). *The God delusion.* Boston, MA: Houghton Mifflin.
Dennett, D.C. (1994). Consciousness in human and robot minds. In L.Ito (Ed.), *Cognition, computation and consciousness.* Oxford, England: Oxford University Press.
(2006). *Breaking the spell.* New York, NY: Penguin.
Ducasse, C. (1960). In Defence of Dualism. In S. Hook (Ed.), *Dimensions of mind.* New York, NY: Collier.
(1961). *A Critical examination of the belief in a life after death.* Charles Thomas.
Estes, D. (2006). Evidence for early dualism and a more direct path to afterlife beliefs. *Behavioral and Brain Sciences, 29*, 470.
Hawking, S. (1988). *A Brief history of time.* London, England: Bantam.
(2005). *A Briefer history of time.* London, England: Bantam.
Hitchens, C. (2007). *The portable atheist.* Philadelphia: Dacapo Press.
James, H. (1926). *The Letters of William James.* (Ed.), Boston, MA: Little, Brown.
James, W. (1884). What is an emotion? *Mind, 9*, 188–205.
(1956/1898). *Human immortality.* New York, NY: Dover Publications.
(1950/1890). *The Principles of psychology.* New York, NY: Dover Publications.
(1994/1902). *The Varieties of religious experience.* New York, NY: The Modern Library.
(1943/1912). *Essays in radical empiricism.* New York, NY: Longman Green and Co.
Myers, G. (1981). *Introduction to principles of psychology.* Cambridge, England: Harvard University Press.
Noe, A. (2009).*Out of our head: Why you are not your brain, and other lessons from the biology of consciousness.* Los Angeles, CA: Farrar, Straus & Giroux.
Nussbaum, M.C. (2001). *Upheavals of thought: The intelligence of emotions.* Cambridge, England: Cambridge University Press.
Perry, R.B. (1935). *The thought and character of William James.* Boston, MA: Little Brown and Co.
Pinker, S. (1997). *How the mind works.* London, England: Allen Lane.

Reeves, J.W. (1958). *Body and mind in Western thought*. London, England: Penguin Books.

Richardson, R. (2006). *William James: In the maelstrom of American modernism*. Boston, MA: Houghton Mifflin.

Sagan, C. (1996). *The Demon haunted world*. New York, NY: Ballantine Books.

(2006). *The varieties of scientific experience*. New York, NY: Penguin.

Schleifer, M. (1992). *La formation du jugement*. Montreal, Quebec, Canada: Loqiques.

(2009). Moral education and indoctrination. In Schleifer, M., & Talwar, V. (Eds.), *Science and religion in education*. Calgary, Alberta, Canada: Temeron Press.

Schwartz, J. (2002). *The mind and the brain*. New York, NY: Harper.

Searle, J.R. (1980). Minds, brains, and programs. *Behavioral and Brain Sciences, 3,* 417–457.

(1984). *Minds, brains, and science*. Cambridge, England: Harvard University Press.

(1992). *The rediscovery of the mind*. MIT Press.

(1998). *The mystery of consciousness*. London, England: Granta Books.

Stapp, H. (1993). *Mind, matter and quantum mechanics*. New York, NY: Springer-Verlag.

Stroll, A. (2002). *Wittgenstein*. Oxford, England: Oneworld Publications.

Talwar, V., & Lee, K. (2002). Emergence of white-lie telling in children between 3 and 7 years of age. *Merrill-Palmer Quarterly, 48,* 160–181.

Taylor, C. (2002). *Varieties of religion today: William James revisited*. Cambridge, England: Harvard University Press.

(2007). *A Secular age*. Cambridge, England: Harvard University Press.

Wellman, H., Harris, P., Banerjee, M. & Sinclair, A. (1995). Early understanding of emotion: evidence from natural language. *Cognition and Emotion, 9,* 117–149.

Wittgenstein, L. (1969). *On certainty*. Oxford, England: Blackwell.

# 8

# How the Law Constructs Its Understanding of Death

RAY MADOFF

We often think of the law as something that operates outside of daily life, only affecting us when we engage in commerce or conduct that constitutes the most egregious transgressions. This is particularly true in a place like the United States, where the legal system is intentionally drawn to preserve personal autonomy. For example, there are few rules regarding personal decisions as how to dress, and individual liberties are protected by a constitutional right of privacy. Nonetheless, in all societies the law plays a vital role in shaping norms, and a study of its rules can provide insight to our most fundamental beliefs about the world. Nowhere is this more true than in the rules governing death. These rules serve as a reflection of both our metaphysical beliefs about the nature of death as well as our values about the proper relationship between the living and the dead – including what, if anything, the dead owe the living and what the living owe the dead. Moreover, the law acts as part of a feedback mechanism. Legal rules are based on people's beliefs about the world, and then the rules themselves provide their own norms, which in turn shape people's beliefs about the world.[1]

Through its rules the law has to come to terms with some of the most difficult questions that life has to offer, including:

- What is the nature of death? Is it a permanent end to human life, or is it possible for people to return from death either through reincarnation or physical resurrection?
- When does death occur?

Portions of this chapter were previously published in my book *Immorality and the Law: The Rising Power of the American Dead* (Yale University Press, 2010) and reproduced here by permission of the publisher. Copyright (c) 2010 by Ray D. Madoff.

[1] For example, one could argue that one reason that Americans value the right to transmit property at death is because there has long been a rule allowing this "freedom of testation."

- Do the dead have an interest in their reputations after death?
- What, if any, financial obligations do the dead have to the living?
- To what extent are the dead able to continue to exert control over the living?

The choices made according to these rules play an important role in shaping children's understanding of death.

This chapter explores what the law reveals about our understanding of death as well as what mechanisms it provides for transcending death. Because the law of death is very much shaped by the culture of which it is a part, the chapter focuses primarily on the law of one country, the United States, but also points out how other countries have made choices that reflect different values and perhaps even different understandings of death.

American law has a split personality when it comes to its understanding of what it means to be dead. On the one hand, with respect to a person's body and reputation, American law takes the position that death marks the permanent end of the person and that individuals have little interest in, and fewer rights to, control of what happens after they are gone. However, with respect to property interests, American law does a dramatic about-face. Here the law provides many opportunities for individuals to posthumously control their property, thereby allowing them to transcend death. The American rules governing the control of property and the lack of protections for reputation stand in sharp contrast to the rules adopted by many other countries and reveal important truths about what the society values for the living.

## THE FINALITY OF DEATH

As a general rule, American law operates under the principal that death marks the end of human life on earth. Thus, the focus of the law is on managing this permanent transition out of life by establishing rules for the disposition of the person's body, the distribution of the person's property, and the care of the person's children.

When it comes to the person's body, the corpse is seen as something distinct from its former inhabitant. One judge described the challenge of creating laws around the corpse as follows:

> A corpse in some respects is the strangest thing on earth. A man who but yesterday breathed and thought and walked among us has passed away. Something has gone. The body is left still and cold, and is all that is visible to mortal eye of the man we knew. Around it cling love and memory.

Beyond it may reach hope. It must be laid away. And the law – that rule
of action which touches all human things – must touch also this thing
of death.[2]

People only have limited authority to control what happens to their bodies
after death. American law uses as its starting place the English common
law doctrine of *corpus nullius in bonis* – the body belongs to no one,[3] and
a person's wishes regarding the disposition of her body or what happens at
her funeral is generally not enforced by the law.[4]

There have been numerous cases in which a spouse and other blood
relatives have disagreed over what should happen to the body of a loved
one. States have responded by enacting statutes – most of which are still in
force today – that list an order of preference for who makes this decision.
The most common order starts with the husband or wife of the deceased
and then goes to adult children, parents, and finally other blood relatives.[5]
However, such statutes do not seem to fully resolve the issues, and there are
still a surprising number of cases in which courts are brought in to decide
who will have the power to control the burial of a body.[6]

---

[2] *Louisville & N.R. Co. v. Wilson*, 51 S.E. 24, 25 (Ga. 1905).

[3] Although many posit that the root of this rule is in the view that the body is sacred,
Professor Lori Andrews suggests another possible interpretation – that under the
common law in England, there was a notion that people's bodies belonged to the crown.
This would be consistent with the feudal law that it was a crime to maim oneself because
this rendered one less able to fight for the king. Andrews, L. (2006). Who owns your
body? A patient's perspective on Washington University v. Catalona. *Journal of Legal &
Medical Ethics, 34*, 400.

[4] Grace Metalious, the author of the blockbuster 1950s novel *Peyton Place*, left specific
instructions about the disposition of her body after death. She instructed in her will that
she wanted "no funeral services [to] be held for me, and that my body be given [to] the
Dartmouth School of Medicine, for the purpose of experimentation in the interest of
medical science." To ensure that her wishes be carried out, she also provided a backup
plan: "If Dartmouth does not accept then to Harvard Medical School." Metalious's family,
however, had other plans. At the time of her death, her husband and children objected
to this provision. Undoubtedly to avoid controversy, the medical schools declined to
accept her body. The family also had other ideas about a funeral and began planning one.
Although the executor of Metalious's estate tried to get a court to stop the funeral on the
grounds that it was against her wishes, the court refused the request and allowed a funeral
service to take place. *Holland v. Metalious*, 198 A.2d 654 (N.H 1964).

[5] Hernández, T. (1999). The property of death. *University of Pittsburgh Law Review,
60*, 971.

[6] The Anna Nicole Smith case is a contemporary example of one of these disputes. *Wynkoop
v. Wynkoop* and *Weld v. Walker* are older cases that present almost identical facts in which
a spouse (the wife in Wynkoop and the husband in Weld) is seeking to move the body
which had been buried by the next of kin. These cases are discussed in 14 *American Law
Review* 57 (1880). Although the facts in the case are virtually identical, the courts come
out differently in the two cases.

Although a number of states have enacted statutes that purport to give more authority to people to control their bodies, close study of these rules reveal that the protections are more apparent then real. The key reason for this is that these statutes are primarily the product of lobbying from the funeral industry, which was concerned with avoiding liability from litigious family members. Thus, the focus of the statutes is to allow funeral directors to rely on instructions left by a decedent, provided they are expressed in a particular form. Although these statutes might provide some protection for people who have survivors interested in carrying out their wishes, they provide no protection where no one steps forward to represent the decedent's wishes. The statutes provide no enforcement mechanism for failure to fulfill the person's stated wishes. Moreover, many statutes that purport to grant rights of control actually limit this control in substantive ways. For example, some hold that the wishes only need to be carried out if they are "reasonable and do not impose an economic or emotional hardship"[7] or are "reasonable under the circumstances" (taking into account a variety of factors, including the size of the estate, cultural or family customs, and the person's religious or spiritual beliefs).[8] The effect of such qualifications is that these statutes provide more of a hope than a promise that a person's wishes regarding his or her body will be carried out.

There is an additional level of uncertainty for any person interested in controlling what happens to his or her body after death: the autopsy. In a full autopsy, internal organs are removed, examined and placed back inside the body (although not necessarily reattached). In addition, in many states when an autopsy is conducted, the coroner is also given the right to remove corneas, pituitary glands, and other organs for transplant without the consent of the decedent or his family.[9] State laws generally give broad authority to conduct a full autopsy in the case of unnatural death or for any public health reason regardless of the wishes of the decedent or his or her family.[10] Individuals may

---

[7] Arizona, Ariz. rev. Stat. Ann. § 36–831.01.

[8] Delaware, 12 Del. Code Ann. tit. 12 § 265.

[9] See discussion on presumed consent statutes.

[10] States have broad discretion to determine when a medical investigation into the death of an individual (including autopsy) should be held. See 18 Am. Jur. 2d Coroners § 7. In most states, a medical examiner may review any death that has occurred under violent or criminal circumstances. Likewise, most states provide that a coroner may investigate any deaths that occur "suddenly" when the decedent appeared to be in good health. *See e.g.* Florida (Fla. Stat. § 406.50); Virginia (Va. Code Ann. § 32.1–283). Finally, states commonly provide for an autopsy in the event the death is considered to have occurred by accident or under any suspicious or unusual circumstances. See Florida's Fla. Stat. § 406.11 and Alaska's Alaska Stat. § 12.65.005.

have personal objections to the performance of an autopsy on their body. In addition, a variety of religious and ethnic groups (including Hmong, Orthodox Jews, Mexican Americans, Muslims, and Navaho) include many believers that a person enters the afterlife with the body in its condition at the time of death or that a body can continue to feel pain for as long as several days after bodily death. Therefore, members of these groups often object to autopsies as a form of proscribed "mutilation of the dead."[11] Whereas some states allow people to register religious objections to autopsy, the vast majority of states do not. Moreover, even in those states that allow religious objections to be made, autopsies can nonetheless be allowed over these objections provided that the state has a strong enough reason for wanting the information that an autopsy can provide.[12] These statutes have been widely accepted as constitutional.[13]

The feasibility of organ transplants as well as the need for organ donors have made their own impact on the rules governing the disposition of a person's body at death. The first successful organ transplant occurred in December 1967, when Dr. Christiaan Barnard, a young South African surgeon, took the healthy heart of a young woman who had been killed in an automobile accident and transplanted it into the body of a man dying of heart disease. Although the transplant recipient died eighteen days later, this operation was a milestone in a new field of life-extending surgery, and resulted in a need to enact new rules governing the treatment of corpses as well as the definition of death itself.

The first problem was that it was not clear who had the power to donate a human body to provide the organs for transplant. Based on the common law legal principle, American law had developed that a corpse is *nullius in bonis*, that is, belongs to no one. This rule may have been adequate at a time when a body was primarily an obligation, something to be handled and disposed of, but it became deeply problematic as the potential value of – and thereby the number of people interested in – dead bodies increased.

To address this problem, shortly after the famous heart transplant, a group of influential U.S. lawyers, judges, and professors got together in 1968 to draft model legislation specifically addressed to the issue of cadaver

[11] Renteln, A. (2001). The rights of the dead: autopsies and corpse mismanagement in mulit-cultural societies. *South Atlantic Quarterly, 100,* 1006–07.
[12] *Snyder v. Holy Cross Hosp.*, 352 A.2d 334 (Md. App. 1976) (a case in which the court allowed an autopsy to determine the cause of death, following the sudden and unexplained death of the father's 18-year-old son, who had been in apparent good health, over the religious objections of the father).
[13] Hall, M.A., Bobinski, M.A., & Orentlicher, D. (2005). *Bioethics and public health law.* New York: Aspen Publishers. p. 365. See also *Reilly v. City of New York*, (E.D.N.Y. 1992) (holding autopsy laws to be clearly constitutional).

organ donation. This model statute, called the Uniform Anatomical Gift Act (UAGA), provided a mechanism for the donation of bodies at death for transplant, and was highly successful in that it was adopted by all fifty states and the District of Columbia within five years of first being proposed.

The 1968 UAGA accomplished several goals. Most important, it provided a clear mechanism through which people could donate organs at death. Prior law had been a mish-mash of rules that considered a variety of factors in determining who could make decisions regarding a person's body after death. Under the UAGA, an individual could state his wishes to donate his body either through a provision in a will or by a witnessed document (usually in the form of an organ donor card issued by a state's department of motor vehicles). The UAGA also provided a mechanism through which family members (in ranked order) could donate part or all of the decedent's body. By creating a statute that was adopted throughout the United States, the UAGA also provided national uniformity for the laws governing organ donation. This was particularly important because a nationwide program increased the ability to find compatible matches between organ donors and organ recipients. Finally, the UAGA established standards for which organs could be donated and which organizations could be recipients of organ donations.[14]

The 1968 UAGA was extremely successful in providing mechanisms for donation and national uniformity. However, it was less successful in terms of procuring sufficient donors to meet the burgeoning demand of potential transplant recipients. Almost twenty years after the enactment of the 1968 UAGA, the problem was described as follows:

An overriding problem common to all organ transplantation programs as well as to the well-established programs in tissue banking (for corneal, skin and bone transplantation) is the serious gap between the need for the organs and tissues and the supply of donors. Despite substantial support for transplantation and a general willingness to donate organs and

---

[14] The UAGA was expansive in this area and provided for the donations of any human body or body part to:

  (1) any hospital, surgeon, or physician, for medical or dental education, research, advancement of medical or dental science, therapy, or transplantation; or
  (2) any accredited medical or dental school, college or university for education, research, advancement of medical or dental science, or therapy; or
  (3) any bank or storage facility, for medical or dental education, research, advancement of medical or dental science, therapy, or transplantation; or
  (4) any specified individual for therapy or transplantation needed by him. 1968 UAGA §3.

tissues after death, the demand far exceeds the supply. At any one time, there are an estimated 8,000 to 10,000 people waiting for a donor organ to become available.[15]

There are a number of reasons for the shortage of organs available for transplantation. Some people do not donate their organs due to the fear that doctors and hospitals will not do everything possible to save the life of an organ donor, electing to let them die in order to harvest their organs. Additionally, organs procured from people who die outside the hospital are often not viable for transplant, because they have been deprived of blood supply for too long.[16] Moreover, there is a general lack of motivation to donate organs as well as a reluctance to face death.[17]

In response to the problem of insufficient organ donations, states incorporated two types of provisions into their statutes (*required request* and *presumed consent*). These provisions both sought to increase the number of available organs while still taking into account the desire of individuals to control what happens to their bodies or the bodies of their loved ones. However, the balance was struck very differently in the two different provisions.

Required request provisions sought to encourage more people to think about organ donation by requiring hospitals to ask people about organ donation upon admission to the hospital and to ask family members for permission to retrieve organs from patients who died.[18] States generally accepted these provisions and they remain in force today.[19] In addition, the federal government put its own imprimatur on the required request approach by making it a condition if hospitals are to receive Medicare and Medicaid reimbursement.[20]

---

[15] 1987 UAGA Prefatory note, quoting "Organ Transplantation: Issues and Recommendations" (April 1986) Task force on Organ Transplantation. The problem has only gotten worse over the last 20 years. As described in the Prefatory Note to the 2006 UAGA: As of January, 2006 there were over 92,000 individuals on the waiting list for organ transplantation, and the list keeps growing. It is estimated that approximately 5,000 individuals join the waiting list each year.... Every hour another person in the United States dies because of the lack of an organ to provide a life saving organ transplant. Revised UAGA (2006) Prefatory Note at <http://www.law.upenn.edu/bll/ulc/uaga/2006final.htm>.

[16] Jane E. Brody, The solvable problem of organ shortages, *N.Y. Times*, Aug. 28, 2007, at F7.

[17] Dunham, C. (2008). "Body property": challenging the ethical barriers in organ transplantation to protect individual autonomy. *Annals of Health Law, 17*, 45.

[18] 1987 UAGA §5.

[19] Jaffe, E. (1990). "She's got Bette Davis['s] eyes": Assessing the nonconsensual removal of cadaver organs under the takings and due process clauses. *Columbia Law Review, 90*, 535.

[20] 42 U.S.C. § 1320b-8 (2002).

Presumed consent provisions also had as their goal the procurement of more organs for donation. Under presumed consent statutes, however, the focus is more directly on society's needs for organs and less on preserving control by individuals or their families. Presumed consent statutes seek to increase the number of organs available for transplant by presumptively eliminating the need for consent in certain situations. These statutes provide that in any case in which a body is subject to autopsy, the coroner is entitled to donate parts of the decedent's body for transplant purposes, unless the coroner has direct knowledge of a refusal or contrary indication by the decedent or the decedent's family.[21] This last provision might seem to provide some protection for the decedent or his or her family in that their objections must be taken into account. However, because the coroner is under no obligation to make any inquiry about the preference of the deceased or her family members, and he is relieved of liability so long as he does not know of any contrary instructions, this arrangement encourages coroners to embrace ignorance rather than to search for true intent.

Presumed consent statutes have been subject to court scrutiny because several families have complained about the removal of corneal tissue for donation to eye banks without the family's consent.[22] Nonetheless, these statutes have generally been upheld on the theory that (1) neither the decedent nor his family member has a property interest in his body, and (2) whatever constitutional right of privacy may exist with respect to the integrity of the body, such right is personal and ends with death.[23] The one case that ruled in favor of the family, *Brotherton v. Cleveland*, failed to find a property right in the decedent's body, but nonetheless held that the decedent's wife had a legitimate claim of entitlement protected under federal law.[24]

Many other countries have presumed consent statutes.[25] However, these statutes differ from U.S. law in two important ways: (1) These statutes

---

[21] 1987 UAGA §4. Some state versions of presumed consent limit its application to certain body parts, such as corneas, pituitary glands and other tissues. Other versions, including the UAGA apply to all organs.

[22] *Brotherton v. Cleveland*, 173 F.3d 552 (6th Cir. 1999); *State v. Powell*, 497 So.2d 1188 (Fla. 1986), *cert. denied*, 481 U.S. 1059 (1987); *Georgia Lions Eye Bank v. Lavant*, 335 S.E.2d 127 (Ga. 1985); *Tillman v. Detroit Receiving Hosp.*, 360 N.W.2d 275 (Mich. Ct. App. 1984).

[23] *Tillman v. Detroit Receiving Hosp.*, 360 N.W 2d 275, 277 (Mich. Ct. App. 1984).

[24] *Brotherton v. Cleveland*, 173 F.3d 552 (6th Cir. 1999).

[25] Presumed consent laws have been implemented in 22 countries including, Austria, Spain, Portugal, Italy, Belgium, France, Luxembourg, Norway, Denmark, Finland, Sweden, Switzerland, Latvia, Czech Republic, Slovak Republic, Hungary, Slovenia, Poland, Greece, Israel, and Singapore. Jacob, M. (2003). On silencing and slicing: presumed consent to post-mortem organ 'donation' in diversified societies. *Tulsa Journal of Comparative & International Law*, 11, 239.

provide mechanisms through which people can opt out of presumed consent, and they know that such wishes will be upheld; and (2) these statutes apply to all individuals – not just those whose deaths are subject to state investigation.

When it comes to the legal treatment of the body, American law is largely shaped by the biological conception of death – one that focuses on the cessation of vital functions being the end of the individual. Nonetheless, as a country that supports religious beliefs, there is another thread of American law that allows people, in some circumstances, to pursue the possibility of a religious afterlife. Thus, many states take into account a person's religious beliefs when it comes to decisions about burial and autopsies. However, when these goals conflict – as in the case of religious objections to autopsies where there is a significant state interest in the results – the law generally takes sides with the notion that death marks the end of all existence.

## THE MOMENT OF DEATH

When does death occur? In biological terms death is not a discrete event, but instead is a gradual process.[26] Thus, even after a person's heart stops beating, other muscle, skin, and bone cells may live on for several days. Nonetheless, because the legal (as well as moral) duties owed to a living person differ significantly from those owed to dead persons, the law has required that we pick a moment in the process and call that the "moment of death." This choice is in some ways arbitrary and has a complicated history.

The debate about what constitutes death began in earnest in 1740 with the writings of the French physician and anatomist Jacques Winslow. Winslow was terrified by the thought of premature burial and sought – unsuccessfully – to discover a definitive surgical test to determine whether death had occurred (considering but ultimately rejecting such tests as pinpricks and incisions). Winslow came by his fear honestly. As a child he had twice been abandoned for dead, only to revive and discover that he had been placed in a coffin.[27]

Building on the work of Winslow, some argued that all signs of death, except for putrefaction (decomposition of the body), were inconclusive and therefore that a corpse should only be dissected, embalmed, or buried after

---

[26] Iserson, K.V. (1994). *Death to Dust: What Happens to Dead Bodies*. Tuscon: Galen Press (p. 13).

[27] Alexander, M. (1980). "The rigid embrace of the narrow house": premature burial & the signs of death. *Hastings Center Report*, 25, 26.

it had begun to decompose because "the laws of Religion and of humanity forbid advancing death even one moment."[28]

However, although putrefaction of the body as a standard for death protected people against premature burial, the standard created significant problems of its own. First of all, at a time when most people died at home, waiting for a body to decay was not simply an inconvenience but also a health risk to the family and neighbors of the deceased. Second, the putrefaction standard also posed a problem for anatomists (a growing group in the eighteenth and nineteenth centuries), who needed to study cadavers before they had been changed by decay.[29]

Fortunately for neighbors and anatomists, medical tools were developed that enabled medical professionals to adopt a new standard for death: the cessation of the beating heart and the breathing of the lungs. This "cardiopulmonary criteria" became widely adopted by the medical profession and in turn allowed the definition of death to be viewed as a technical problem that could be solved by the application of medical expertise.[30] This resulted in the development of the almost universal law that "a person is dead when a physician says so."[31]

Although for a brief period, there seemed to be some certainty to the situation – an agreed upon standard (cessation of heart) and a mode of determining whether the standard had occurred – such certainty was not to last. The reason was the continuing development of medical technology that raised new issues as to the appropriateness of the cardiopulmonary standard of death.

The first of these was the development of the mechanical ventilator that made it possible to support a person's heart and lung function even after brain function had ceased. A person's heartbeat could now continue even when the patient had no discernible brain activity and respiration was mechanically sustained. This put hospitals in the difficult position of maintaining care for individuals who seemed to be more dead than alive.[32] It also raised an additional problem that under a cardiopulmonary definition of death, the removal of a mechanical ventilator from a person with no brain activity technically constituted murder. This resulted in some peculiar legal

[28] Id.
[29] Id.
[30] Id., at 31.
[31] Iserson, *supra* note 27, at p. 19 quoting fn 26. See also 22nd World Medical Assembly in Sydney Austrailia in 1968.
[32] Lizza, J.P. (2006). *Persons, Humanity, and the Definition of Death*. Baltimore: Johns Hopkins University. (p. 7).

cases, including one case in which a defendant charged with murder argued that the doctors who removed the life support, and not him, caused the death of the victim.[33]

The possibility for organ transplants raised another problem for using the cardiopulmonary definition of death. That is, after the heart stops pumping, organs quickly begin to decay and soon are no longer suitable for transplant. Therefore, the cardiopulmonary definition of death impeded the availability of organs for transplant.

A highly influential report by an ad hoc committee at Harvard Medical School came to the rescue by proposing a new definition of death: cessation of brain function. This definition made a certain degree of sense in a society that associates personal identity with the brain. Happily, it also served the goals of organ transplants by providing that organs could be harvested from a body after the brain had ceased functioning, even if the person was still breathing and still had a heart rate (due to mechanical ventilation). Shortly after this report appeared, all fifty states had adopted some version of the brain death standard either by statute or via case law.

The most widely adopted statute, the Uniform Definition of Death Act, provides that a person can be declared dead when he has sustained either: (1) irreversible cessation of circulatory and respiratory functions or (2) irreversible cessation of all functions of the entire brain.[34] This statute has been adopted in forty-three states. States that have not adopted the Uniform Definition of Death Act have either adopted their own statutes or developed case law allowing the use of brain death as a standard for death. Brain death has been adopted as a standard throughout much of the rest of the world as well.

One of the last countries to adopt the brain-death standard was Japan, which didn't fully adopt the standard until 2009. Much has been written to explain Japan's outlier status on this issue, but one factor that seems relevant is the differing view in Japan of what it means to be a person. In the West, personhood is often equated with an individual's brain or consciousness (building on Descartes's famous "I think therefore I am"). However, under the Japanese view, the "person" is not equated with individual consciousness, nor is the person located in the brain. Rather, personhood is diffused throughout the mind and body and is a condition that is

---

[33] *State v. Schaffer*, 574 P. 2d 205 (1977); see also *People v. Eulo*, 472 N.E.2d 286 (N.Y. 1984).

[34] This is the standard set out in the Uniform Determination of Death Act. As of 2009, this statute has been adopted in some form in forty states. This standard is different from a permanent vegetative state in that the brains of a person in a PVS still functions, albeit at a very rudimentary state.

fundamentally social rather than individualistic.[35] Given this differing view, it is not surprising that brain death was not as readily accepted in Japan as a standard of death.

Despite this near-universal adoption of the brain-death standard, this is not likely to be the end of the issue. There are several reasons. First, a person who is brain dead does not necessarily appear dead to outsiders. To many people, it is disconcerting to call a person who is warm and has a heartbeat "dead." Moreover, many religions have their own official views of when death occurs, and these standards are sometimes at odds with the brain-death standard. Finally, as technology develops, it is able to detect more and more subtle levels of brain activity, calling into doubt the ability to measure brain death with any accuracy.

As a result of these issues, disagreements can arise regarding whether a person is in fact dead. This conflict played out in a 2007 case involving Cho Fook Cheng, a seventy-two-year-old grandfather who suffered a heart attack the day after Thanksgiving. He was brought to the hospital and placed on a ventilator. Soon thereafter, the doctors declared Cheng dead based on the brain-death standard and sought to have him removed from life support. The family, however, practiced a Taiwanese form of Buddhism in which a person is not considered dead until his heart stops beating. The case was heading for a court showdown, but was rendered moot when Cheng's heart stopped on its own.[36] Yet based on the plain meaning of the governing statutes as well as case law from other jurisdictions, it seems likely that the hospital would have been within its legal rights to remove life support. Once a person is declared dead under the governing authority, the family is not entitled to demand life-support measures.[37]

In response to such difficulties, some scholars have suggested that the moment of death be at least partially a function of individual choice. New Jersey has enacted a statute that does this by allowing a patient's religious belief to be taken into account in determining whether death has occurred. New Jersey's law is similar to the law of other jurisdictions in providing for doctors to apply either the cardiopulmonary or brain-death standard, but it goes on to provide that the brain-death standard is not to be used if the physician authorized to declare death has reason to believe that the brain-death

[35] Lizza, *supra* note 87, at 160.

[36] Megan Tench, After Buddhist dies, legal battle continues: Kin, hospital split on when death occurs, *Boston Globe*, December 3, 2006, 1A; Megan Tench, End-of-life lawsuit outliving its subject: Kin to appeal dismissal ruling, *Boston Globe*, December 6, 2006, 3B.

[37] See Hall et al., *supra* note 14, at p. 336; *In re Welfare of Bowman*, 617 P.2d 731, 738 (Wash. 1980); *In re Long Island Jewish Medical Center*, 641 N.Y.S.2d 989 (Sup. Ct. 1996).

standard would violate the person's religious beliefs. In such a case, only the cardiopulmonary standard is to be used.[38]

These issues have caused some American scholars to argue that each individual should be allowed to choose which standard of death he or she wants to use. Indeed, one scholar has argued that the ability to choose one's definition of death is mandated by the Constitution's protection of the free exercise of religion.[39] Notwithstanding the various religious protections, there is general agreement that death is defined as the cessation of vital biological organs.

## DO THE DEAD HAVE AN INTEREST IN THEIR REPUTATIONS AFTER DEATH?

Whereas Americans have only limited rights to control what happens to their bodies after death, their rights are even more scarce when it comes to protecting reputations. Whereas reputations are protected by the doctrines of defamation and privacy during life, these protections largely disappear at death.

The law of defamation (which is the umbrella term for the legal claims of libel and slander) protects living people's reputations against false and derogatory comments.[40] Defamation generally protects individuals against the publication of false statements that harm their reputation. The only limitation on claims for defamation during life is that if the person making the claim is a public official, then she must prove that the person publishing the falsehood did so either knowingly or recklessly.[41] A person who has been defamed is entitled to recover for all harms caused by injury to her reputation.

After death the picture is a very different one. Here the law does a radical about-face and provides virtually no protection against defamation. The reason most commonly given for this rule is that a dead person is beyond harm or benefit. As one court described it: "Once a person is dead, there is no extant reputation to injure or for the law to protect."[42] This principle

---

[38] N.J.S.A. 26:6A-5.

[39] Stacy, T. (1992). Death, privacy, and the free exercise of religion. *Cornell Law Review*, 77, 490.

[40] Dan Dobbs, D. (2000). *The Law of Torts.* St Paul: West Group. (p. 1117). Whereas both libel and slander apply to false communications, libel applies to written communications and slander applies to oral communications.

[41] *New York Times Co. v. Sullivan*, 376 U.S. 254 (1964).

[42] *Gugliuzza v. K.C.M.C., Inc.*, 606 So.2d 790, 791 (La.1992).

was illustrated in a recent case when a husband and wife were murdered by one of their six children. As if the story was not lurid enough, the television station reporting the story added the following tidbit: "In an odd twist to this story, sources close to the investigation say that David Johnson, Sr. and his wife Ruby were also twins, brother and sister." This rather remarkable story of twin siblings marrying each other and giving birth to six children was completely false, and the television station was promptly informed of this. Nonetheless, the station continued to report the story and refused to issue a retraction. The other children of the murder victims brought a defamation suit against the television station on behalf of their deceased parents. However, the court ruled that there could be no claim brought on behalf of the parents because their reputation no longer existed after death, and therefore it couldn't be harmed.[43]

What about family members or other loved ones – surely they suffer when falsehoods are published about those they love who are no longer living? Surprisingly, the law is clear that family members also cannot sue for defamation of their loved ones (whether alive or dead). Thus, in the aforementioned case, the court ruled that not only was there no claim on behalf of the parents, but there was also no claim on behalf of the children because the harm was personal to the parents.[44]

The lack of legal protections for interests of the dead encourages the spreading of highly sensational material, because this tends to be most profitable for publishers. However, because the public is generally not aware of the lack of protection for the dead, they may assume that the publishers have the same incentives for veracity that they do when publishing information about living people. The prevalence of this kind of journalism can therefore have negative social consequences because it permits inaccuracies and untruths to flourish.

Periodically state legislatures have taken up proposals that would allow defamation claims to survive death, but these proposals have been largely unsuccessful. Thus, the New York legislature considered adopting a statute that would have created a new cause of action for defamation of the dead and would have allowed family members to bring a defamation claim within five years of a person's death. Although it was considered in a variety of forms over multiple years, the legislation never passed.[45] To date, the only state

[43] *Johnson v. KTBS, Inc.*, 899 So. 2d 329 (La. Ct. App. 2004).
[44] *Johnson v. KTBS, Inc.*, 899 So. 2d 329 (La. Ct. App. 2004).
[45] Mandel, R. & Hobbs, R. (1991). The right to a reputation after death. *Communications and the Law, 13*, 29–31.

to enact any protections against defamation of the dead is Rhode Island. However, the Rhode Island protections are extremely limited – applying only to defamatory remarks made in an obituary within three months of a person's death.

People's reputations during life are also protected by the right of privacy. However, like the law of defamation, the right of privacy does not extend its protection – either directly or through family members – to people who are no longer living.

The right of privacy owes its inception to an 1890 law review article written by Samuel Warren and Louis Brandeis (later Supreme Court Justice).[46] In that article Warren and Brandeis urged courts to recognize the development of a common law right to privacy. This right "to be let alone"[47] was designed to secure an individual's ability to protect his solitude by controlling the public use of his name or likeness.[48] According to the authors, the need for recognition of this right stemmed from changes in technology and business methods that made this additional protection necessary: "Instantaneous photographs and newspaper enterprise have invaded the sacred precincts of private and domestic life; and numerous mechanical devices threaten to make good the prediction that what is whispered in the closet shall be proclaimed from the house-tops."[49] The

---

[46] Warren, S. & Brandeis, L. (1890). The right to privacy, *Harvard Law Review*, 4, 193. Although the article was written as if it were describing a preexisting phenomenon, the article is widely regarded as having given birth to the right of privacy. See Slough, M.C. (1969). *Privacy, Freedom and Responsibility*. Springfield, Ill.: Charles C. Thomas. (pp. 27–42).

[47] Warren & Brandeis, *supra* note 47, at 193.

[48] Singer, B. (1992). The right of publicity: Star vehicle or shooting star? *Cardozo Arts & Entertainment Law Journal*, 10, 6. It is reported that Brandeis and Warren first became interested in the problem of privacy and decided to write their article as a direct result of the Boston newspapers' practices of reporting on the affairs of Warren and his wife in lurid detail. Nimmer, M. (1954). The right of publicity, *Law & Contemporary Problems*, 19, 206.

[49] Warren & Brandeis, *supra* note 47 at 195. The significant technological change involved the advancements in photography. As the authors later explain: "While, for instance, the state of the photographic art was such that one's picture could seldom be taken without his consciously 'sitting' for the purpose, the law of contract or of trust might afford the prudent man sufficient safeguards against the improper circulation of his portrait; but since the latest advances in photographic art have rendered it possible to take pictures surreptitiously, the doctrines of contract and of trust are inadequate to support the required protection and the law of tort must be resorted to. The right of property in its widest sense, including all possession, including all rights and privileges, and hence embracing the right to an inviolate personality, affords alone that broad basis upon which the protection which the individual demands can be rested." Ibid., 211.

right to privacy was thus fashioned as a right to maintain human dignity in an increasingly undignified world.[50]

The right to privacy first enunciated by Warren and Brandeis was subsequently explicitly recognized in every state, either by common law or statute.[51] However, in practice it has provided far less protection than early proponents had hoped, because it has been curtailed by the constitutional protections afforded free speech, particularly by the press. Within this protection, anything that is deemed "newsworthy" (tending to cover anything that a newspaper is interested in publishing) is not protected by the right of privacy.[52] Although more limited than originally envisioned, the right of privacy still affords some protections for individuals against disclosure of their personal information.

However limited the protections of privacy are during life, they are completely absent after death. It is a settled principle of American law that the right of privacy (like the claim for defamation) does not continue after death. Thus, one leading treatise describes the rights of the dead in this area as follows: "The law allows scholars, pop history writers and gossip magazines to roar away about the dead: they are beyond caring. If offspring and relatives are upset, their remedy is to respond with the truth."[53] The reason for this failure to protect reputational interests of the dead is both theoretical and practical. The theory of privacy law is that it protects against feelings of embarrassment. American law takes the position that because a dead person cannot be embarrassed, she cannot suffer the harm protected by defamation or invasion of privacy. The failure to protect reputational interests

[50] "The press is overstepping in every direction the obvious bounds of propriety and of decency. Gossip is no longer the resource of the idle and the vicious, but has become a trade which is pursued with industry as well as effrontery. To satisfy a prurient taste the detail of sexual relations are spread broadcast in the columns of the daily papers. To occupy the indolent, column upon column is filled with idle gossip which can only be procured upon intrusion into the domestic circle. The intensity and complexity of life, attendant upon advancing civilization, have rendered necessary some retreat from the world, and man, under the refining influence of culture, has become more sensitive to the publicity, so that solitude and privacy have become more essential to the individual; but modern enterprise and invention have, through invasions upon his privacy, subjected him to mental pain and distress, far greater than could be inflicted by mere bodily injury." Ibid., 196.

[51] Selz, T.D., et al. (2nd ed., 1996). *Entertainment Law: Legal Concepts and Business Practices.* St. Paul, MN: Thompson-West (p. 21, fn 17).

[52] Whitman, J. (2004). Two western cultures of privacy: dignity versus liberty. *Yale Law Journal*, 113, 1209. James Whitman explores how, starting with the famous Sidis case of 1940, American law began to favor the interests of the press over almost any claim to privacy.

[53] Thomas, J. & McCarthy, J.T. (2nd ed., 2007), *The Rights of Publicity and Privacy*. St. Paul, MN: Thomson-West (p. 383).

also effectively avoids a more practical problem: If a right of privacy was found to exist for dead people, how could the claim be asserted? American law lacks a mechanism through which a dead person's reputational interest can be exercised. A dead person's wishes with respect to his property are protected through the legal system of probate, which appoints a representative of the decedent's wishes for the limited period of time necessary to distribute the estate. However, if there was posthumous legal protection for reputation, there would need to be a mechanism through which that person's interest could be represented for so long as the right existed. Because there is no such mechanism under current American law, it makes practical sense that this interest is not protected.

The reasoning behind the refusal of American law to extend protection to reputations of the dead is often couched in terms of logic: After death there is no reputation to be harmed nor for the law to protect. In this way, harm to reputation is treated like pain and suffering – something that obviously does not apply to the dead. However, the simplicity of this statement belies the complexity of the issue of posthumous harm, and in particular the question of whether a person can be harmed by assaults on her reputation after death. This question has puzzled philosophers for centuries.[54] Therefore, it should come as no surprise that different societies have taken different positions with respect to this issue. Whereas American law provides virtually no protections for reputations of the dead, European law has taken a very different approach. In general, continental Europe provides extensive protections for an individual's reputation, even after death. A comparison of Italian law with American law illustrates several critical differences.

The first area where Italian law stands in stark contrast with American law is in terms of enforcement. One issue that is inherent in any system that seeks to protect interests of the dead is what mechanism is available for enforcement. One of the limitations of American law is that there is no individual or entity charged with representing the privacy interests of deceased individuals. For distribution of property, American law has an elaborate system of executors, trustees, and other individuals charged with representing the decedent's wishes. For property committed to charitable purpose, the state attorney general is charged with representing the

---

[54] One philosopher described the problem of posthumous harm as one of the most puzzling: "Plausible and well considered arguments can be presented to support positive or negative answers to these questions. And yet ... either response to each of these questions may appear, for clear and evident reasons, to be strange and outlandish; in a word, these questions seem to be such that no answer can put us fully at ease." Partridge, E. (1981). Posthumous interests and posthumous respect. *Ethics*, 91, 243.

decedent's interests. Yet when it comes to reputational interests, there is no individual or governmental entity charged with protecting the deceased individual's reputation under American law. However, Italian law addresses this problem by establishing a governmental agency whose purpose is to protect individuals' privacy. This agency is known as the Authority for the Protection of Privacy (Garante per la protezione dei dati personali).

The agency protecting privacy interests has issued a number of rulings that give the flavor of the extent of the Italian protections of the dead. A classic example of a case protected under Italian law involved a man named Franco Scoglio who died during the filming of a television show. The Authority for the Protection of Privacy issued a press release that stated that the television images could not be displayed because it would be a violation of Scoglio's right to privacy. He had a right to have the moment of his death not displayed before the public.[55]

The privacy protections under Italian law are not limited to individuals who generally live outside the public eye. Thus, when Saddam Hussein was executed in December 2006, the Privacy Authority issued a press release to the media directing them to be careful of how they showed the events. They were ordered to be careful to protect the dignity of the person.[56]

Finally, *Chi* magazine purchased the worldwide exclusive right to publish pictures of Lady Diana that were taken at the moment after her fatal accident when the emergency medical technicians had just arrived at the scene of the accident. They also acquired the findings of the autopsy that was performed on her body. The court ruled ex officio that it was a violation of Princess Diana's personal dignity to disclose any of this information, and that such disclosure was not justified under any need for free information to the public. It also ruled that any further dissemination of this information would be forbidden and that anyone violating the order could be subject to criminal sanctions, including a prison sentence of up to two years.[57]

Italian law is particularly protective of the interests of minors. When a teenage boy committed suicide in Italy, a newspaper published pictures of the boy's house as well as the text of an essay that he had written on the day of his suicide.

---

[55] Communicata stampa-04 ottobre 2005 *Il Garantesu Franco Scoglio no alle immagini della morte Roma,* 4 ottobre 2005.

[56] Communicata stampa- 30 dicembre 2006, *Immagina morte Saddam: dichiarazone di Francesco Pizzetti, Persidante dell'Autorita Garante per la privacy, Roma, 30 dicembre 2006.* Provvedimento del 15 luglio 2006 [Formal decision, ex officio, greater force than press release].

[57] Provvedeimento [Formal decision ex officio, greater force than a Press Release] del 15 luglio 2006. Roma, 15 luglio 2006.

The boy's father asked that the newspaper stop publication of these things and also sought damages for past publication. The agency ruled that the privacy of minors after death is subject to special consideration. It ordered that damages be awarded and also that the magazine had to stop publishing pictures of the house as well as excerpts from the boy's essay. The agency also issued that there should be an investigation into how the reporter got the essay.[58]

This case stands in sharp contrast to a similar case from the United States involving a teen suicide. In the American case, police officers took photographs of the sixteen-year-old as he lay in his coffin and subsequently displayed the photographs at a public gathering. There, the officers made statements that the boy's involvement in gang-related activities had caused his death. The boy's mother sued for invasion of privacy. The court, in rejecting her claim, ruled that there was no cause of action for invasion of privacy on behalf of the boy, because he was dead, and no cause of action on behalf of the mother, because any claim of right to privacy was personal to the son.[59]

Italy is not alone in providing this type of postmortem protection for a person's reputation. The "right of personality" has been recognized in the German constitution since 1954. This section guarantees protection of every person's human dignity and right to free development of personality.[60] The protection of human dignity has been found to continue, even after death, by the German Constitutional Court in a famous case referred to as the *Mephisto* case. The *Mephisto* case involved a novel written by Klaus Mann (son of Thomas Mann) in 1936 after he was forced to leave Germany. One of the fictional characters in his novel was based on the life of German actor and theatre director Gustav Gründgens, who had cooperated with the Nazis in order to advance his artistic career. When the novel was about to be published in West Germany in 1963, both Mann and Gründgens were dead. Nonetheless, Gründgens's adoptive son (and sole heir) successfully sued the publisher to prevent it from publishing the novel on the grounds that it would violate the honor, reputation, and memory of Gründgens. In siding with Gründgens son, the court ruled that an individual's death does not put an end to the obligation of a country to protect that individual against violation of his or her human dignity. The court also ruled that there was no set time period

[58] Provvedimento del 11 ottobre 2006. Il Garante Per Law Protezione Dei Dati Personali.
[59] *Riley v. St. Louis County of Missouri*, 153 F.3d 627 (1997). Even if the officer's statements about the boy were intentionally false, there would still be no cause of action because of the notion that the dead cannot be defamed.
[60] BHG NJW 2000, 2195, 2197 discussed in Bottner, G. (2001). Protection of the honour of deceased persons a comparison between the German and the Australian legal situations. *Bond Law Review, 31(1)*, 109. Found at <http://www.austlii.edu.au/au/journals/BondLRev/2001/5.html> (15 Oct. 2008).

for this right of dignity and it could survive longer than thirty years after the person's death. The *Mephisto* decision had limited practical effect as the book had already been published in East Germany and was readily available to the West. Although *Mephisto* was eventually published in West Germany in 1980 (by a different publisher), the case highlights some of the costs of having the right of privacy survive death. In particular, the ability to write biography, history, and even fiction can be limited by this type of protection.

What explains this different treatment of privacy such that American law sees no violation where Italian and German law does? Legal scholar James Whitman has noted that although European countries and the United States all provide protections for privacy, the notions of what constitutes a violation of privacy are very different. American law is primarily concerned with privacy as a mode of protecting individual liberty, particularly from governmental intrusion, whereas European law views privacy as a way to protect human dignity, particularly from being degraded by the press. In this way, European law is far better at capturing the concerns originally set out by Warren and Brandeis in their seminal article that gave birth to American privacy law.

European privacy law stems from the extensive set of rules available to the aristocratic classes in the nineteenth century to allow them to protect their reputations. The effect of the greater equalization that occurred over the twentieth century was that protections for reputational interests, previously applicable only to the aristocratic class, became available to everyone. Professor Whitman refers to this phenomenon as "equaling down." He describes this phenomenon as follows:

> After many generations of experience, Europeans have come to value a certain kind of personhood: a kind of personhood founded in the commitment to a society in which every person, of every social station, has the right to put on a respectable public face; a society in which privacy rights are not just for royalty, but for *everybody*.[61]

Ironically, it may have been the early attempts to erase class distinctions in the United States that has resulted today in so few protections for the reputations of the average person.

## WHAT FINANCIAL OBLIGATIONS, IF ANY, DO THE DEAD HAVE TO THE LIVING?

If you ask an American about the legal rights of dead people, you will most likely get an answer having to do with people's rights to control who

[61] Whitman, *supra* note 53, at 1211.

gets their property after they die. This right to control the disposition of property at death is central to the American psyche. Although people are often vague in their understanding about many aspects of the law, one thing that is often clear in their minds is the right to write a will that controls who will – and who will not – get their property after they die.

The treatment of the dead under American law with respect to property interests stands in sharp contrast to the treatment of the dead with respect to their bodies and reputations. When it comes to bodies and reputations, the law generally takes the position that the dead person is permanently gone, with no continuing interest in what happens in the world of the living. However, when it comes to property interests, American law grants significant deference to the wishes of the dead.

The effect of this ability to control property after death, and the power it conveys to the property owner, is a theme that has been frequently explored in the American arts. Whether it is Tennessee Williams's *Cat on a Hot Tin Roof* or Rodney Dangerfield's *Easy Money*, Americans easily recognize the image of would-be heirs currying favor with the future dead in order to secure an inheritance. In this way, it is well understood that property owners can control much more than just their property; through their right to control the disposition of property at death, they can control the behavior of others during their lives. After all, is there any doubt that many May-December unions – marriages between older men and much younger wives and vice versa – would likely not occur if "December" did not have the power to transmit wealth to "May" at the end of the day?[62]

The right to control the disposition of property at death is often seen as part and parcel of the very notion of private property. It is hard for most Americans to imagine a system of private property that doesn't include this right to control what happens to it after death. The Supreme Court itself intimated as much when it called the right to transmit property at death "one of the most essential sticks in the bundle of rights that are commonly characterized as property."[63]

Although this connection between property ownership and the right to control it after death may seem inseparable to Americans, this is not the case in other parts of the world. There are many countries with strong systems of private property that nonetheless draw a distinction between lifetime and

---

[62] Although some of these advantages can also be obtained through life-time gifts, the natural desire to hold onto power and property as long as possible (as well as the specter of King Lear) makes lifetime gifts far less desirable than transfers at death – when the owner's separation from his property is unavoidable.

[63] *Hodel v. Irving*, 481 U.S. 704, 716 (1987).

posthumous control. Indeed, most other legal systems impose significant restrictions on people's ability to control property after death. Although they may not be aware of it, Americans have greater rights to control their property after death than anyone else in the world. As one scholar has described it: "As American inheritance law embarks on a new millennium, the scope offered for freedom of testation remains as broad as it has ever been, and it is now indeed a scope without parallel elsewhere in the Western world."[64]

The law of the United States provides that people are generally free to give their property at death to whomever they choose, even at the expense of children or other blood relatives. Although states generally provide some protections against disinheritance for surviving spouses (through community property or elective share rights), the United States stands virtually alone in providing no protections against disinheritance for adult children. Moreover, in forty-nine out of the fifty states (the exception being Louisiana), Americans are also given broad latitude to disinherit their minor and dependent children, even if the effect of this disinheritance is that the children become wards of the state.

Part of the explanation for this system stems from the fact that the United States (with the exception of Louisiana) is a common law country. Common law countries are those whose laws are based on the common law of England. The common law has as its starting point that property is owned by individuals (traditionally men) and that families have very little claim to the husband/father's property. Most English-speaking countries (United States, Australia, New Zealand, and Canada, with the exception of Quebec) are common law countries, although as we will see, most common law countries (other than the United States) have modified their laws to provide greater protections for families.

In contrast to the United States and other common law countries, many other countries – including most of continental Europe – are civil law countries. Civil law countries view property as something that is owned by a family unit as opposed to an individual.[65] As a result, individuals are limited in their ability to control the disposition of their property at death. Civil law countries have statutes that require that a significant portion of the person's estate be given to family members. These statutes, called forced succession statutes, are found in civil codes throughout continental Europe,

---

[64] Hirsch, A. (2007). American history of inheritance law. FSU College of Law Working Paper, Public Law Research paper No. 258.

[65] Watkin, T.G. (1999). *An historical introduction to modern civil law.* Hampshire, UK: Ashgate. (pp. 192–218).

South America, and in Japan. They generally provide protection against disinheritance for the decedent's spouse, children, and grandchildren. Some statutes also provide protection for the decedent's parents and more distant blood relatives as well. These protections designate a set share for family of between 50 and 80 percent of the decedent's estate, leaving the decedent with freedom to control as little as 20 percent of his estate.[66]

Thus, in civil and common law countries throughout the world, children are protected against disinheritance by their parent either by being provided a fixed share of the parent's estate (through forced succession statutes) or by being given the right to make an equitable claim against the decedent's estate (through family maintenance statutes). However, in the United States, a disinherited child is largely left without recourse.

The ability to disinherit minor children is particularly surprising in light of the fact that virtually every state imposes an obligation on parents to support their minor children during life.[67] It is also ironic in that although parents can disinherit their minor and dependent children, these children cannot generally disinherit their parents due to the fact that they do not have the capacity to make a will. Moreover, in a majority of American jurisdictions, a parent who fails to support his child during life can nonetheless inherit from the child in the event of the child's death.[68]

Although disinheritance of minor children is usually not a problem for the child who lives with both parents, it can be a significant problem for children with a noncustodial parent. This is particularly likely to be a problem when the noncustodial parent has remarried and formed a new family. One scholar has described the situation as follows:

> Increasing numbers of instances are likely to occur such as those in which the noncustodial father bequeathed $1 of his $400,000 estate to an infant daughter from a former marriage;[69] or bequeathed $1 to his infant

[66] Reimann, M. & Zimmermann, R. (2007). *The Oxford handbook of comparative Law*. New York: Oxford University Press. (p. 1085). Hayton, D.J. (1991). *European succession laws*. London: Chancery Law Publishing.

[67] See Brashier, R. (1996). Protecting the child from disinheritance: Must Louisiana stand alone? *Louisiana Law Review, 57*, 5 & fn. 23.

[68] There are generally two situations in which fathers inherit significant assets from their children. The first is when a child has no assets during life, but on death his estate has value as a result of a wrongful death claim. The second situation is when a child accumulates substantial earnings or receives a large personal injury or wrongful death award during the child's lifetime (typically for a parent's death). Monopoli, P. (1994). Deadbeat dads: Should support and inheritance be linked? *University of Miami Law Review, 49*, 257.

[69] *Hornung v. Estate of Lagerquist*, 473 P.2d 541, 543 (Mont. 1970) (indicating, however, that the support obligation extended beyond parent's death).

daughter a few weeks after divorcing the child's mother;[70] or devised everything to his current wife after acknowledging his infant child from an earlier marriage;[71] or left $10 of a $64,000 estate to his infant daughter being reared by his ex-wife.[72]

Children of divorce are not the only ones who are likely to be disinherited – nonmarital children are also susceptible to this fate. Nonmarital children have reached epidemic proportions, as almost 40 percent of all children born in the United States are born out of wedlock. When a paternity action is brought against the putative father of a nonmarital child, he will often dispute the claim. If the claim is proven and support is ordered, the father may view the child merely as an unwanted source of debt. However, unlike other creditors, who cannot be written off or "disinherited" by a will, the disinheritance of his child is perfectly permissible.[73]

In recent years, a few cases have upheld probate court decisions to impose child support obligations against the estate of a deceased parent.[74] These cases, however, do not impose a general obligation on deceased parents to provide for their children, they merely allow probate courts to make such a determination. Moreover, most courts have taken the position that these obligations cannot be imposed without explicit statutory authority from the legislature.[75] To date, only Louisiana imposes a direct obligation on parents to provide for their minor and dependent children upon death.

The American rule allowing disinheritance of children has been criticized by many scholars. Some have suggested that states should adopt a forced heirship (similar to the rules that exist in civil law countries), or that states should adopt a discretionary rule similar to that adopted in England and other common law countries, or that the support obligation for minor children be extended to include the obligation to support children at death.[76] Yet these suggestions have largely fallen on deaf ears. To date, no new jurisdiction has added statutory protections against disinheritance for children, and the one state that provides such protections, Louisiana, has recently cut back on the protections provided for its children.

---

[70] *Hill v. Matthews*, 416 P.2d 144, 144 (N.M. 1966).

[71] *In re Estate of Brown*, 597 P.2d 23 (Idaho 1979).

[72] *Herring v. Moore*, 561 S.W.2d 95, 96–97 (Ky. Ct. App. 1977). As cited in Brashier, *supra* note 11, at 11.

[73] Brashier, *supra* note 68, at 11.

[74] See, *L.M. v. R.L.R.*, 451 Mass. 682 (2008).

[75] *Benson ex rel. Patterson v. Patterson*, 830 A.2d 966 (Pa. 2003).

[76] Brashier, *supra* note 68.

## TO WHAT EXTENT ARE THE DEAD ABLE TO CONTINUE TO EXERT CONTROL OVER THE LIVING BY IMPOSING CONDITIONS ON THE RECEIPT OF PROPERTY?

During life, people can use their wealth to induce behavior. They can give money to someone for quitting smoking, for marrying a particular person, for breaking off an engagement, or even divorcing their spouse. Provided the desired behavior is not illegal (like paying someone to murder your spouse or paying for sex), these agreements are recognized and enforced.[77] What about after the person has died? To what extent will the law allow people to continue to exert control in this way?

In considering this question it is important to remind ourselves that the law often treats the dead differently from the living – particularly when it comes to enforcing their wishes about a world they no longer inhabit. We do not let individuals who are no longer living leave votes to be cast in elections occurring after the person's death because (1) we believe that the dead cannot make good decisions about situations that they cannot fully know about, and (2) the dead don't suffer the consequences of bad decisions. Yet when it comes to controlling property, the law treats the dead very much like it treats the living.

American law has been very liberal in terms of allowing individuals to posthumously control the behavior of others through the use of conditional trusts. The theory that courts have consistently espoused in enforcing these provisions is that because no one has the right to demand an inheritance, the person giving the property can generally impose whatever conditions she chooses. In upholding these provisions courts have regularly noted that because the children could have been disinherited entirely, they cannot complain about having conditions imposed on their bequests. As one court described it: "It must be borne in mind in all such instances that the legacies and devises were acts of bounty merely. The testator was free to withhold them altogether, or to subject them to conditions, whether sensible or futile. The gift is to be taken as made or not at all."[78] The only limitations that courts put on these conditions is that they cannot be "illegal" or "against public policy."

---

[77] In one case well known by every law student, an uncle promised his nephew $5,000 if he would refrain from drinking, using tobacco, swearing, and playing cards until his twenty-first birthday. The court found that it was a valid contract and the nephew was entitled to receive the $5,000 from his uncle's estate. *Hamer v. Sidway*, 27 N.E. 256 (1891).

[78] *In re Rolosm's Will*, 155 NYS 2d 140, 146–7 (N.Y.Sur. 1956).

The restriction against illegal conditions means that presumably a court would not enforce a provision that said that the beneficiary was obligated to kill the testator's former boss in order to receive his inheritance. Although the rule against illegal conditions is often cited by courts and is a favorite of law professors, it is rarely applied because there are no actual cases on record involving illegal conditions.[79]

Thus, the only relevant restriction on conditional bequests is that a court will not enforce a condition that is "against public policy." Theoretically, this public policy exception could severely restrict conditional bequests because the term is infinitely malleable. However, in practice, this has not proven to be much of a limitation because American courts have generally been loathe to use their authority to restrict these conditions, seeing it as outside their bailiwick. As one court described it:

> [A] testator has the right to grant bequests subject to any lawful conditions he or she may select. Beneficiaries of a testamentary instrument have no right to testamentary bequests except subject to the testator's conditions, and it is generally not the role of the court to rearrange those bequests or conditions in keeping with the court's sense of justice.[80]

One area where people often seek to impose conditions is with regard to marriage. Although the right to marry is constitutionally protected, courts have consistently upheld bequests conditioned on either forbidding the beneficiary from marrying or requiring the beneficiary to marry someone of a particular group on the theory that these provisions do not restrict the beneficiary's right to marriage, they only restrict the beneficiary's right to inherit.[81]

Courts have been particularly understanding of husbands conditioning their wives' inheritance on remaining unmarried after their husband's death. As one court saw it: "It would be extremely difficult to say, why a husband should not be at liberty to leave a homestead to his wife, without being compelled to let her share it with a successor to his bed, and to use it to hatch a brood of strangers to his blood."[82] When it comes to children, testators have

---

[79] Sherman, J. (1999). Posthumous meddling: An instrumental theory of testamentary restraints on conjugal and religious choices, *University of Illinois Law Review, 1999*, 1280 fn.34.

[80] *Tunstall v. Wells*, 50 Cal.Rptr.3d 468, 565 (Cal. Ct. App. 2006).

[81] *Loving v. Virginia*, 388 U.S. 1, 12 (1967).

[82] *Commonwealth v. Stauffer*, 10 Pa. 350 (1849). [Source: Sherman, *supra* note 80.] Although courts also support wives conditioning their husband's bequest on the husband not remarrying, the opportunity for women to impose these conditions is far more limited because women historically control far less property than their husbands and also tend to live longer than their husbands.

been more interested in requiring them to marry someone of a particular religion or background, and courts have generally been supportive of these controls as well. Thus, in one case, in order to inherit his share of his father's estate, the son was required to marry "a Jewish girl of whose both parents were Jewish" within seven years of his father's death.[83] In another case the testator's daughter was required to marry a "man of true Greek blood and descent and of Orthodox religion" before receiving her inheritance.[84]

Sometimes a testator is not just interested in preventing or requiring a new marriage, but is instead interested in ending an existing marriage. The official position of courts is that conditions designed to encourage divorce are against public policy, and accordingly courts have refused to enforce these conditions in several cases.[85] However, this rule is easy to circumvent, because whereas courts will not enforce conditional bequests where the testator intended to encourage divorce, they will enforce such conditions if the testator intended to provide support in the event of divorce. As one court described it:

> A condition to a devise, the tendency of which is to encourage divorce or bring about separation of husband and wife, is against public policy, and void. However, if the dominant motive of the testator is to provide support in the event of such separation or divorce, the condition is valid.[86]

This exception is particularly easy to take advantage of because courts tend to give testators the benefit of the doubt when it comes to determining intent. In one case the testator gave money to his nephew on condition that at the time of the death of the testator, the beneficiary "is not married to his present wife." Although the court noted that conditions intending to encourage divorce or separation were against public policy, the court said that this provision did not violate this rule and enforced the restriction. In doing so, the court explained:

> It is of no consequence that the settlor objected to his nephew's marriage and was unfriendly and hostile to his wife . . . and that several years before

[83] *Shapira v. Union Nat. Bank*, 315 N.E.2d 825 (Ohio Ct. Com. Pl. 1974). [Dukeminier, J., Johanson, S.M., Lindgren, J. & Sitkoff, R.H. (7th ed., 2005). *Wills, Trusts, and Estates.* New York: Aspen Publishers.]
[84] *In re Estate of Keffalas*, 233 A.2d 248 (Pa. 1967). [Source: Sherman, *supra* note 80.]
[85] For example, in the *Keffalas* case requiring the children to marry spouses "of true Greek blood and descent and of Orthodox religion," the court refused to apply the limitation to those children who were already married to other spouses and would therefore have been required to divorce and remarry someone of the appropriate background in order to inherit. Ibid.
[86] *Hall v. Eaton*, 631 N.E.2d 805, 808 (Ill. App. Ct. 1994).

he said to his nephew: "If you get rid of her I will make you richest of the family." The intention of the settlor and the validity of the condition is to be ascertained from the unambiguous language used, which cannot be enlarged or restricted by extrinsic evidence. The wording of the gift holds out no inducement to the nephew to separate from his wife. The condition having been valid, the failure of respondent to bring himself within it deprives him of any share in the trust estate ...[87]

Another surprising area for testators to be able to exert their control is over the beneficiaries' practice of religion. Freedom of religion is one of the cornerstones of our Constitution. Yet courts have consistently upheld bequests that are conditioned on the beneficiary either practicing or refraining from practicing a particular religion. For example, in one case a woman was entitled to receive income from the trust only "so long as she live up to and observes and follows the teachings and faith of the Roman Catholic Church and no longer."[88] Another testator required that the grandchildren would only inherit if they were "members in good standing of the Presbyterian Church."[89] Yet another testator conditioned his son's inheritance on attending "regular meetings of worship of the Emmanuel Church near the village of Cashton, Wisconsin, when not sick in bed or prevented by accident or other unavoidable occurrence."[90]

In a culture that values religion, these conditional bequests may be understood as being based on the theory that encouraging people to be more religious is not against public policy. However, this justification does not explain why courts also regularly allow conditional bequests that require the beneficiary to *refrain* from practicing a particular religion. Thus, in one case the testator's daughter would only receive her inheritance if at the age of thirty-two she proved conclusively to the trustee that "she has *not* embraced, nor become a member of, the Catholic faith nor ever married a man of such faith."[91] In another case the court allowed a trust that required the testator's brother to "withdraw from the priesthood in the Roman Catholic Church" in order to receive his inheritance.

---

[87] *Chamberlian v. Van Horn*, 141 N.E. 111 (Mass. 1923).

[88] *Delaware Trust Co. v. Fitzmaurice*, 31 A.2d 383 (Del. Ch. 1943); aff'd in part and rev'd in part on other grounds sub nom, *Crumlish v. Delaware Trust Co.*, 38 A.2d 463 (Del. Super. Ct. 1944).

[89] *In re Lanning's Estate*, 339 A.2d 520 (Pa. 1975).

[90] *In re Paulson's Will*, 107 N.W. 484 (Wis. 1906). [Source: Sherman, *supra* note 80.]

[91] *U. S. Nat. Bank of Portland v. Snodgrass*, 275 P.2d 860 (Or. 1954). [Source: LeFevre, E. (1956). Validity of provision of will or deed prohibiting, penalizing, or requiring marriage to one of a particular religious faith, *American Law Reports 2d.*, *50*, 740.]

These conditional bequests are not without their critics. Professor Jeffrey Sherman has argued that such "posthumous meddling" should not be allowed because they are against public policy. However, to date, Professor Sherman's arguments have fallen on deaf ears. There is nothing to suggest that either courts or legislatures have any interest in curtailing this type of dead-hand control.[92]

CONCLUSION

Children develop an understanding of death from a multitude of sources, including parents and religious authorities who typically provide the most direct teachings about the nature of death. The law provides its own teachings about the nature of death. Although less explicit, these teachings are arguably all the more powerful due to their pervasive application.

American law sends two powerful messages when it comes to death. First is the notion that biological death, measured by cessation of function of the brain or the heart, marks the end of human life. This is the dominant message of American law as legal rules are primarily focused on providing a transition from presence to absence through the disposition of the body, the distribution of property, and the transfer of care for children. The laws governing a person's body and reputation directly adopt this position of death marking the end of a person's interest in what happens in the world of the living.

However, there is an important counter-theme in the law when it comes to property. Here, although the law still operates on the assumption that the person is gone and is not coming back, American law still grants significant deference to the wishes of the dead regarding the control of property. In this way, death's grip is eased, giving American property owners a form of virtual afterlife. Although it may be tempting to see this as arising from an alternative notion of death, in the end, it may reveal more about American's notion of the power of property.

REFERENCES

Alexander, M. (1980). "The rigid embrace of the narrow house": Premature burial & the signs of death. *Hastings Center Report*, 25, 26.
Dunham, C. (2008). "Body property": Challenging the ethical barriers in organ transplantation to protect individual autonomy. *Annals of Health Law*, 17, 45.

---

[92] Sherman, *supra* note 80.

Hall, M.A., Bobinski, M.A., & Orentlicher, D. (2005). *Bioethics and public health Law.* New York, NY: Aspen Publishers.

Hayton, D.J. (1991). *European succession laws.* London, England: Chancery Law Publishing.

Hernández, T. (1999). The property of death. *University of Pittsburgh Law Review, 60,* 971.

Hirsch, A. (2007). American history of inheritance law. FSU College of Law Working Paper, Public Law Research paper No. 258.

Iserson, K.V. (1994). *Death to dust: What happens to dead bodies.* Tuscon, AZ: Galen Press.

Lizza, J.P. (2006). *Persons, humanity, and the definition of death.* Baltimore, MD: Johns Hopkins University.

Mandel, R. & Hobbs, R. (1991). The right to a reputation after death. *Communications and the Law, 13,* 29–31.

Reimann, M. & Zimmermann, R. (2007). *The Oxford handbook of comparative law.* New York. NY: Oxford University Press

Renteln, A. (2001). The rights of the dead: autopsies and corpse mismanagement in mulitcultural societies. *South Atlantic Quarterly, 100,* 1006–07.

Selz, T.D., et al. (1996). *Entertainment law: Legal concepts and business practices.* St. Paul, MN: Thompson-West.

Sherman, J. (1999). Posthumous meddling: an instrumental theory of testamentary restraints on conjugal and religious choices. *University of Illinois Law Review,* 1280 fn.34.

Stacy, T. (1992). Death, privacy, and the free exercise of religion. *Cornell Law Review, 77,* 490.

Thomas J., & McCarthy, J.T. (2007). *The rights of publicity and privacy.* St. Paul, MN: Thomson-West.

Watkin, T.G. (1999). *A historical introduction to modern civil law.* Hampshire, UK: Ashgate.

# Index